The WORLD ATLAS of
DIVINATION

The WORLD ATLAS of
DIVINATION

THE SYSTEMS·WHERE THEY ORIGINATE
HOW THEY WORK

Consultant Editor JOHN MATTHEWS

BCA
LONDON · NEW YORK · SYDNEY · TORONTO

CONTENTS

This edition published 1992
by BCA by arrangement with
HEADLINE BOOK PUBLISHING PLC

CN 8508

10 9 8 7 6 5 4 3 2 1

AN EDDISON · SADD EDITION
Edited, designed and produced by
Eddison Sadd Editions Limited
St Chad's Court
146B King's Cross Road
London WC1X 9DH

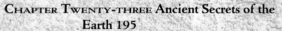

INTRODUCTION

WHAT IS DIVINATION?

Picture the scene. There is a cave, dark save for the leaping shadows cast by a fire burning low in a scraped-out hollow in the earthen floor. A figure clad in skins crouches before the glowing embers, staring into them, seeking to read there events that have yet to happen....

The scene changes. Outside now, under a blue sky filled with hurrying clouds, a figure stares into a pool of still water, watching the shapes of the clouds passing overhead – seeking, once again, to read in the shapes a destiny that has yet to occur....

Now we see someone entering a brightly coloured tent, in which sits a woman with dark eyes and rings in her ears. In front of her on a table is a crystal ball, lit with strange light. As she looks within it, it begins to glow....

From caveman to shaman to Gypsy fortune-teller, people the world over have sought the answer to the question: what does the future hold for me? The ways in which answers have been found have varied hugely, but in almost every instance they have been arrived at through some method of divination.

The Shorter Oxford English Dictionary defines 'divination' as the various methods by which events are interpreted or explained, as prognostication or prediction or intuition; while a 'diviner' is also a soothsayer, a seer or a successful conjecturer. This brings into play all kinds of considerations that do not necessarily leap to mind when one first considers the idea of divination.

For in addressing the answers to questions concerning the future, it is not simply a matter of predicting what will come to pass, but also of divining the truth. There may well be more than one possible future, other choices to be made, and the skilled diviner must be able to point to one of these with authority. Hence both intuition and prophecy are included in the definition of the diviner's art, which is not simply the mastery of a technique or set of correspondences, but more rightly a deeply intuitive sense that puts the diviner in touch with the source of creation and enables him or her to foresee the possible outcome of future events.

We can see this clearly in the two most common types of divinatory technique, into which most of the examples described in this book can be seen to fall. These are the ecstatic and the inductive. The first consists in making a contact with the spirits of the dead or with beings of the inner worlds in order to enquire of them the answer to certain specific questions. To this end the diviner goes into a trance state in which he or she converses with the being or spirit and receives answers, which are then brought back and repeated – sometimes while still in a trance and in terms that are not immediately understandable.

The other method consists in the observance of natural events, such as the direction of the wind, the fall of a leaf, or the throwing of bones, sticks or stones, which are then interpreted according to often extremely ancient precepts. We shall meet with these two broad kinds of divination again and again in this book, from lands as far apart as the subarctic region and Australasia, leading us to a conclusion of the commonality of interest and method used by diviners throughout the world.

THE BEGINNINGS OF DIVINATION

The earliest practitioners of both kinds of divination were undoubtedly the shamans who are discussed in the first chapter of this book. As an embodiment of the earliest known form of spiritual discipline (as yet too basic to be called a religion), one of their tasks was to interpret omens and signs that pointed to the meaning of events that had either already occurred or would occur in the future. On another, slightly different level, they would also have had to divine the causes (and, where possible, the cures) of sickness, which was recognized as an imbalance in the soul as much as the body whenever the problem was anything more than the breaking of a limb or other such physical forms of complaint. We get a glimpse of the kind of equipment such shaman-diviners might have carried in the grave goods discovered at Rockbourne Down in Hampshire. Among other ritual objects were four rectangular bronze tablets, each marked with a star or a lozenge. Similar bone tablets found in a round barrow near Stonehenge suggest that these objects – whose precise use we can only guess at – may once have been part of the native British shaman's equipment.

DIVINATION TODAY

Today, in many parts of the world – notably Africa, Australia, New Zealand, parts of North America and Lapland, and both the Far and Middle East – shamans still pursue their calling, still use the ancient methods of foretelling events to come or the causes of sickness. In what are usually referred to as the more civilized areas of the world (though in fact these are merely less in touch with the natural world and with the primal instincts that once shaped and directed the flow of our lives), these methods of divination have undergone many degrees of change. Thus, on the one hand, some of the oldest forms of prediction, such as the Chinese Book of Changes (the *I Ching*) or the study of palmistry, have become rigorously systematized; while on the other, such an ancient and once world-wide method as astrology has been generalized into the daily horoscopes that appear in newspapers and magazines everywhere.

However, despite the changing tides of fashion which have caused divination to be alternately studied and despised, the folk memory of the peoples of the world has kept its methods alive. In almost every culture there are traces of ancient divinatory methods enshrined in sayings attributed to unknown wise-folk. It is still common for those who have remained in touch with the patterns of the natural world to observe the sky or the weather and to predict what will occur. In Tibet there still exists a state oracle, who is consulted on matters of importance such as the identification of a reincarnated lama; while in modern-day Hong Kong the construction of a major new bank building could not be successfully completed until a resident expert in Feng Shui (a Chinese method of creating harmonious environments) was called upon to give his reading of the chosen site and his suggestions for alterations to the design of the building.

In our own time, we have seen perhaps the greatest explosion of interest in methods of divination since ancient times. Not only have Tarot, astrology and numerology been taken up and practised with skill and authority, but new versions, adapted from ancient records, have been made available to an eager public.

It seems that the old question is still being asked, today perhaps with ever-increasing urgency. As we enter the end of the millennium and the beginning of a new age, we are as eager as ever to know what the future holds for us.

JOHN MATTHEWS
OXFORD, 1992

CHAPTER ONE

SEERS AND HEALERS

The Ancient Tradition of Shamanism

Nevill Drury

Shamanism is the world's earliest and most widespread religious tradition, extending back to the Paleolithic era. Remnants of it are still found as far afield as Siberia, the United States, Mexico, Central and South America, Japan, Tibet, Indonesia, Aboriginal Australia and Nepal.

Anthropologists and archaeologists associate the first dawnings of human spiritual awareness with Neanderthal cave sites in Europe and Central Asia. In a cave at Le Moustier in France the bones of a dead youth were discovered, lain in repose and accompanied by a selection of tools and bones of animals, which suggests a belief that such implements could assist the youth in his future life. Similarly, in a grave in Uzbekistan a circle of Ibex horns had been placed reverently around the body of a dead child.

But it is at other locations like the Franco-Cantabrian cave of Les Trois-Frères that the shamanic bond with Nature can more clearly be seen. Here, cave art dating back some 15,000 years reveals the quite specific figure of a hunter-shaman armed with a bow and disguised as a bison amidst a herd of wild animals. From earliest times, shamans have mimicked birds and animals in their rituals, have revered sacred plants and have developed what we would, in the twentieth century, regard as a 'holistic' relationship with the Cosmos.

Shamanism, though, is more than just imitative magic. It can be regarded as a visionary approach to Nature and the Cosmos, which utilizes altered states of consciousness as a means of contacting the denizens of the spirit world. The shaman – who can be a man or a woman, depending on cultural determinants – is essentially a magical practitioner who, through an act of will, can enter into a state of trance, and who then journeys to the land of the gods or perhaps, closer to home, divines by visionary means the causes of sickness and malaise.

Underlying all forms of shamanism is the notion that the universe is alive with gods and spirits. The shaman's role is to divine the presence of harmful or malicious spirits which are causing individual illness or 'cursing' members of the tribal group. The healer-shaman is thus an intermediary between the natural and metaphysical worlds, meeting the spirits on their own territory.

A classic example of shamanic journeying is found in the following account of shamans in Siberia, one of the areas of the world in which shamanism has been extensively practised up until recent times. The anthropologist A.A. Popov recorded trance journeys among the Nanay people of the Tungus region in the 1920s. Here, in a state of trance, the shaman would descend to the 'lower world' and would meet magical animals – usually an ermine or a mouse – that could act as spirit guides.

During an initiatory visionary journey, the Nanay shaman would be suckled by a cosmic deity known as the Mistress of the Water and

A display of shamanic regalia from the American Northwest. This Tsimshian shaman figure has a carved staff, rattle, crown and necklace.

then, with his animal guides, would be shown a community of spirits responsible for sickness in the world. Later the shaman would 'fly' in spirit form to the top of an enormous tree that would explain to him: 'I am the tree that makes all people capable of living.' The tree spirit would then provide the shaman with a branch with three offshoots that could be used in the construction of three special drums: one for performing shamanic rituals over women in childbirth, the second for treating the sick and the third for aiding those who were dying. In Siberia the drum itself had a special role because it was on the rhythmic drumbeat that the shaman 'rode' into a state of ecstasy. And the idea of shamanism as a 'journey' into the metaphysical world is a feature not only of Nanay cosmology, but of shamanic cultures generally.

It therefore comes as no surprise that among the Jivaro of Eastern Ecuador, for example, the normal everyday world is considered to be false or a 'lie', while the truth about the real nature of things is to be found only by entering the 'supernatural' world. Undertaking this vision quest, clearly, is the role of the shaman.

BECOMING A SHAMAN

Shamanism is a magical vocation. Some shamans adopt their role in society as part of an ancestral lineage, while others are called to the path through dreams or spirit-visions. The Chukchee of Siberia say that future shamans have a certain look in their eyes which indicates that they can see beyond the domain of everyday reality to the realms of spirit which lie beyond. And perhaps because this visionary capacity is restricted to just a few, shamans have often found themselves somewhat on the edge of society – rather like visionary eccentrics. Often introverted and sometimes smitten themselves by disease or misfortune, potential shamans by definition function in parallel mental universes and, as a result, some psychiatrists have compared them to schizophrenics. There is, however, a crucial difference between shamans and schizophrenics. Schizophrenics move in and out of different mental states continually and without control,

thus dwelling in a world of experiential chaos, while shamans have to learn to integrate their visionary capacities and subject them to the individual will. For this reason, the noted scholar of comparative religion, Mircea Eliade, referred to the shaman or medicine man as one 'who has succeeded in curing himself'. With this self-mastery comes the ability to undertake spirit-journeys, to drive away evil spirits and to cure the sick.

Often during the initiatory process of becoming a shaman there are special revelations. The North American Gitksan Indian Isaac Tens began falling into trance states when he was 30 and frequently experienced terrifying visions. On one occasion, animal spirits and snake-like

Luisah Teish (above) is a voodoo priestess of African, Haitian, Native American and French ancestry. A priestess of Oshun, 'Mother of the Spirit', she uses healing trance.

Drums and percussive instruments have traditionally played a central role in shamanism because they provide the rhythms of sound on which the shaman 'rides' into an altered state of consciousness.

A Colombian shaman (left) prepares for a magical ceremony. South America is one of the last regions where shamanism is still practised today.

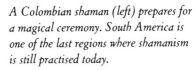

trees seemed to be chasing him, and an owl tried to attack him and lift him up. Later, on a hunting trip, Tens again saw an owl and shot it, but was unable to locate its body. He fell into a trance. His body began to 'boil' and 'quiver' and he found he was singing spontaneously:

A chant was coming out of me without my being able to do anything to stop it. Many things appeared to me presently: huge birds and other animals. They were calling me. I saw a meskyawawderh *(a kind of bird) and a* mesqag-weeuk *(bullhead fish). These were visible only to me, not to the others in my house. Such visions happen when a man is about to become a* halaait; *they occur of their own accord. The songs force themselves out, complete, without any attempt to compose them. But I learned and memorised these songs by repeating them.*

Similarly, the Paviotso shaman Dick Mahwee had his first shamanic visions while dreaming in a cave. Aged around 50, Mahwee was in a state of 'conscious sleep' and had a mystical encounter with a tall, thin Indian holding an eagle tail-feather. The Indian instructed him in ways of curing sickness. Mahwee now enters a trance state to perform shamanic healing:

I smoke before I go into the trance. While I am in the trance no one makes any noise. I go out to see what will happen to the patient. When I see a whirlwind I know that it caused the sickness. If I see the patient walking on grass and flowers it means that he will get well; he will soon be up and walking. When I see the patient among fresh flowers and he picks them it means that he will recover. It the flowers are withered or look as if the frost had killed them, I know that the patient will die. Sometimes in a trance I see the patient walking on the ground. If he leaves footprints I know that he will live, but if there are no tracks, I cannot cure him.

REGALIA AND RITUALS

As noted earlier, the shaman was perceived as a master of ecstasy: the shaman's role was to fly in

the spirit vision to where the gods were, for it was here that the revelations were received. And since the shaman was able to travel from one dimension of reality to another, it was understandable that his rituals and clothing would embody all that was sacred or mythically relevant within the given culture.

Sometimes shamans would decorate their clothing with motifs relating to their magical animal allies, or with relevant symbols from their mythology.

Traditional Japanese shamans wore caps of eagle and owl feathers and their cloaks were adorned with stuffed snakes. Siberian Yakut shamans wore kaftans embellished with a solar disc – thought to be the opening through the earth leading to the Underworld – while Goldi shamans wore coats depicting the Cosmic Tree and magical animals like bears and leopards. Buryats wore costumes laden with iron ornaments, symbolizing the iron bones of immortality, and also used motifs representing the bears, serpents and lizards that they had befriended as their helper spirits.

This bone was used by Batak shamans from Sumatra to read magical chants. It is carved with a spirit figure, magical symbols and pentacles.

Shamans, as we have already noted, imitate birds and animals in their dances. Yakuts could imitate the lapwing, falcon, eagle and cuckoo, while Kirghiz shamans learned not only bird songs but also how to imitate the sounds of their

wings in flight. Zuni Pueblo Indians still summon their Beast Gods in ceremonies involving dancing, rattling and drumming. Wearing ritual masks, they work themselves into a state of frenzy where they feel they are becoming the animals themselves through an act of ritual identification. According to anthropologist Dr Michael Harner, who has observed them, the Zuni dancers are doing much more than simply impersonating animal forms. Transported into an altered state of consciousness by the dancing, drumming, rattling and whirr of bull-roarers, the shaman 'becomes for the time being the actual

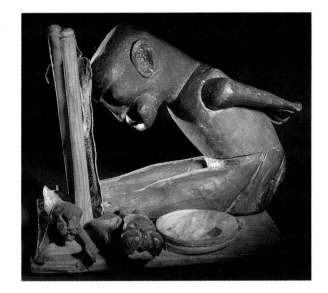

This Eskimo woodcarving represents a shaman in the middle of a seance, with his two animal helper-spirits nearby. His shaman drum is close at hand.

An Eskimo figurine from Point Hope, Alaska. Here we see a shaman engaged in leaving his body in spirit form to fly into the celestial realms. The figurine is fashioned from whale vertebrae, walrus ivory, wood, seal hide and stone.

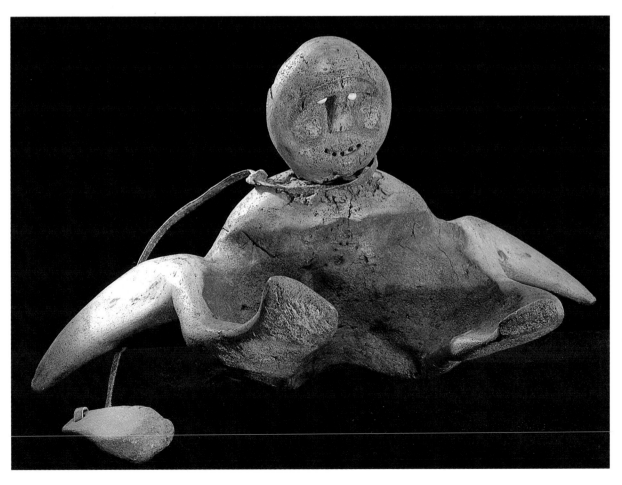

embodiment of the spirit which is believed to reside in the mask'.

As one can see from accounts like this, the drum plays a vital role in shamanic practice: it is literally the 'vehicle' that carries the shaman into the magical world. The rhythmic sound of the drumbeat acts as a focusing device for the shaman, enabling him to enter the trance state in a controlled way. Some shamans also embellish their drums in ways that are symbolically significant. Lapp shamans decorate their drums with motifs like the Cosmic Tree, the Sun, the Moon or a rainbow, while traditional Evenks fashioned their drum rims from sacred larch.

SACRED PLANTS, HELPER SPIRITS AND DIVINATION

In divining the origins of sickness, some healer-shamans have frequent recourse to sacred mind-altering plants and helper spirits, or 'familiars'.

The Mazatec Indians of Mexico, who have female shamans as their healers, make use of sacred psilocybe mushrooms; the shamans use the altered state of consciousness induced by the mushrooms to determine the cause of the sickness or affliction. Among the Mazatecs, both the patient and the shaman take the sacred mushrooms so that the sick person may in due course hear the healing words which issue forth from the spirit world, and thereby share directly in the cure.

When the adventurer and former banker Gordon Wasson visited the Sierra Mazateca in 1955, he made contact with the renowned shaman Maria Sabina. Maria had become well known in the town of Huatla for assisting people who were ill, suffering some sort of loss or theft, or wishing to recover from the effects of an accident. Wasson obtained permission to attend a *velada*, or all-night healing vigil. During the *velada* Maria took thirteen pairs of mushrooms while the other participants took five or six pairs each, the idea being that the mushrooms would eventually 'speak' through the voice of the shaman. The spirits of the sacred mushroom were invoked and, at a very special point during

the evening, divinatory pronouncements were made. As Maria Sabina explained to Gordon Wasson: 'I see the Word fall, come down from above, as though they were little luminous objects falling from heaven. The Word falls on the Holy Table, on my body: with my hand I catch them. Word by Word.'

A similar use of sacred psychedelic plants is found in the divinatory ceremonies of Peruvian shaman Eduardo Calderón. Like Maria Sabina, Calderón blends Christianity and native Indian traditions. Born in 1930, he grew up in a Spanish-speaking, Roman Catholic family, but at the age of 24 began an apprenticeship with a *curandero* who was the uncle of his second wife. This healer made ritual use of the psychedelic San Pedro cactus and also had an altar, or *mesa*, containing various magical 'power objects'. After successfully treating a sick person through his newly learned shamanic techniques, Calderón became a *curandero* in his own right.

According to Calderón, the visionary cactus enables him to contact healing energies in the Cosmos and allows him to interpret the magical influences afflicting his patients. Calderón's *mesa* includes symbolic zones pertaining to the polarities of good and evil, and also has a middle zone where the opposing forces are held in balance. The left zone is ruled by Satan, the right by Jesus Christ, and various artefacts and images of the saints are used in the divinatory ritual.

During a healing session Calderón drinks a San Pedro infusion and in due course this 'activates' the artefacts on the magical altar, enabling him to 'see' the cause of witchcraft or bad luck affecting his patient. Once diagnosed, such evil influences can be ritually exorcized. Well educated as he is, Calderón was able to describe the process to anthropologist Douglas Sharon in terms familiar to the Western mind:

The subconscious is a superior part (of man) ... a kind of bag where the individual has stored all his memories.... By means of the magical plants and the chants and the search for the roots of the problem, the subconscious of the individual is opened like a flower.

A South Korean shaman in trance. In Korea, shamanism predated the arrival of Buddhism, and was introduced from the Altaic and Tungusic regions of Central and Northern Asia.

Dr Michael Harner (below) with his shaman drum. Harner, a former anthropology professor, introduced shamanism to contemporary psychological understanding and has been a major influence in bringing shamanism to the West.

If sacred plants are often a vital ingredient in shamanic healing rituals, so too are magical helper spirits or 'allies'. There are many different terms for these entities – they are variously known as 'familiars', 'guardian spirits', 'dream healers' or 'power animals' - but it is generally agreed by scholars of comparative religion that healer-shamans need spirit guides of one form or another in their divinatory practices. As Michael Harner has written: 'A shaman may be defined as a man or woman who is in direct contact with the spirit world through a trance state and has one or more spirits at his command to carry out his bidding for good or evil.' These allies appear to the shaman in dreams and visions and on some occasions can be purchased or inherited from other shamans or family elders. Allies can be summoned into action through songs and dances and often require ritualistic offerings. Some shamans have even claimed to be married to their spirit guides!

The divinatory functions of helper spirits are diverse. They might be sent by the shaman into the patient's body in order to detect the cause of sickness, or they might be despatched in order to locate missing objects. Healer spirits may also accompany the shaman on the visionary journey to the magical world.

The Yurok Indians of north-western California still practise shamanic healing using spirit guides. Yurok healer Tela Lake describes a shaman as 'a holistic healer who uses the physical and spiritual forces of Nature to effect a cure'. She believes that the soul is the very essence of a human being, and that the body, mind and soul are held together by a force-field of power or spirit. It is this energy field that can be treated by the shaman through spirit divination.

Patients abstain from drugs, sex and alcohol for four days prior to a healing ceremony with Tela Lake: they are then considered 'clean'. After the patient arrives, Tela goes outside to consult with her familiar spirits and then accepts or rejects the patient for the healing ceremony (refusal usually arising only when the patient contravenes the spiritual laws of the Yurok in some way). Immediately before the actual ceremony, all participants are required to bathe and various plants and herbal medicines are used to purify the patient.

As the ceremony begins, the shaman sits in front of her patient, facing east, and invokes her spirits through song and prayer. According to Tela, the spirits will feel welcome if the area is 'clean' and they assist her in identifying the cause of the patient's problems. She says that some spirits can fly backwards in time to seek the origins of disease, while other 'interpreter' spirits can divine information received magically in different languages. Included among Tela's helper spirits are a woodpecker (able to remove pain from the patient's body) and a hummingbird (able to suck out poison). She also summons bear and wolf allies to fight off sickness and a spirit fish to eat away at illness, as the need arises.

The Shoshoni medicine-man, Tudy Roberts, on the other hand, told Professor Ake Hultkrantz in the 1950s that he had spirit helpers of both animal and human appearance. Once he had a dream-vision where he saw three bear spirits, one of which claimed to be immune to bullets and offered one of his ears to the shaman as a protection. Later Roberts found a dead bear, cut off its ear, and began to wear it during the important Sun Dance ceremony, which was performed by the Shoshoni as a thanksgiving to the Supreme Being.

Roberts also had contact with three humanoid spirit beings after performing a Sun Dance and then falling asleep in the foothills of Fort Washakie. These spirits looked like Indians but wore feathers in their hats and had 'very clean clothes'. Roberts

learned that they were lightning spirits and that they would help him in his healing practices. The spirits showed him how to perform shamanic divination using an eagle tail and eagle wing, and he subsequently gained the power to cure diseases like colds, measles and paralysis. However Roberts never sought to cure anybody unless he received instructions from his helper spirits in shamanic dream-vision.

The divinatory practices of shamans like Tela Lake and Tudy Roberts epitomize a point made earlier: that it is in the world of spirit that we gain the most profound perspectives on the true nature of our life, our health and our well-being on the planet.

From the viewpoint of the modern reader, keen to understand this most ancient of all religious and divinatory systems, we can think of shamanism as a means of recognizing the spiritual dimension in Nature and of awakening the magical potentialities within our very being. Shamanism reminds us that we all share a common destiny on the planet, since we are all born of the Earth Mother. If we can begin to attune ourselves to a holistic understanding of both Nature and Cosmos, we will find ourselves entering into a spiritual tradition which is as old as humanity itself.

In shamanism the drum is literally the vehicle for transporting the healer or magician into a state of trance. This shaman's drum is from the Magar tribe of Nepal.

THE
CIRCUMPOLAR
REGION

In the long, cold nights of the Far North, when no one could be certain if the sun would ever rise again once it had set, it became especially important to know what the future held in store. For this reason the divinatory methods described in this section are particularly detailed and precise. They range from the detailed study of animal bones, through the observance of rings or bone fragments gyrating on a beaten drum-skin, to the questioning of dead spirits. We also encounter the presence of animal 'totems' or helpers, both personal and tribal, who gave assistance to the diviners in their search for the hidden reasons behind daily events.

Here again we meet the class of official diviners who are named shamans, whose work consists in maintaining a close and harmonious relationship with the natural world – a thread in the tapestry of divination which reappears again in many of the methods described in this book.

As we saw in Chapter One, the shamans possessed many skills, of which divination was only one. In the subarctic regions, and in the lands which stretched to the south, west and east into modern-day Russia, Siberia and Eurasia, where the nomadic tribes moved with the seasons and whose whole life was geared towards the observance of natural events, the shamans became especially skilled in the reading of hidden, inner meanings in the thousand and one variations of sky, clouds, winds, and animal presence and migration.

They also made direct contact with spirits of the great dead, of shamans who had gone into the other worlds and could thus be consulted on a variety of topics of which they now possessed an even deeper knowledge. Thus the definition of the diviner's art is here already widened. The shamans of the frozen North divined the causes of illness and death among both human patients and the vast reindeer herds, the best places to make camp for the wandering tribes they served, and the future fortunes of new-born children.

The many layers of the inner worlds to which the shaman travelled in search of inner truth were as complex and multi-layered as rock formations. Each level possessed a different significance and was to be visited for a different reason. Yet all were linked by a central pole of meaning, a world-tree that grew through all the worlds. Thus the shaman-diviner travelled in trance or other altered state of consciousness into the inner realms and returned with wisdom and knowledge, which he or she then passed on to the tribe.

We learn that divination is much more than foretelling the future – a fact that will be encountered again and again throughout this book – but that it is rather an intimate part of our lives, touching us at many levels, from the dreams we seek to have interpreted to the decisions we make about where and how we live, and the very objects with which we choose to surround ourselves.

CHAPTER TWO

THE FROZEN NORTH

Divination Among the Peoples of the Arctic and Eurasia

Alan Haymes

Three kinds of divination were once widely practised throughout Eurasia: ecstatic or intuitive divination, whereby the necessary information is obtained by a shaman who acts on behalf of the tribe by mediating with the world of spirits; inductive divination, involving the reading of signs according to preconceived systematic procedures; and interpretative divination, which combines aspects of the other two and would include, for example, the understanding of dreams.

Eurasia covers a vast expanse of the surface of the Earth, with the Ural Mountains accepted as a natural frontier between Europe and Siberia, which stretches all the way to the Bering Sea in the east and down to the borders of China and Mongolia in the south. In places, climatic conditions can be extreme, with winter lasting as long as ten months and temperatures dropping to 70°C below zero. During the brief ten week summer, however, there is a dramatic turn around with temperatures rising to levels of 40°C above freezing.

Over 30 different native peoples are still to be found in Siberia, but their collective number is small, at around the million mark, when compared to the total population of the region which is about 30 million. The traditional occupations of the indigenous peoples loosely displayed a north/south divide, with fishing, hunting and reindeer herding being practised in the north and nomadic pastoralism and agriculture in the south. The closeness to animals in the wild and the often desperate need to hunt for food simultaneously accommodated a strong

respect and reverence for certain animals, most notably the bear. This animal was regarded as being particularly special by many Northern Eurasian peoples because it was believed to have a soul and thus be close to humanity, if not an ancestor in another guise. As a result elaborate bear-hunting rites evolved to reconcile the problem of killing a sacred animal for food: the

THE PEOPLE OF THE NORTH

At least three specific varieties of vegetation are encountered across the vast land mass of Eurasia, including the Tundra of the polar north, the coniferous forests of the Taiga and the scrubland of the Steppes towards the south. The Ural mountain range, which partly dissects the region from north to south and acts as a natural frontier between Europe to the west and Siberia to the east, also lends its name to one of the two main groups of languages that are spoken in the region, that is 'Uralic'. Categorization on linguistic grounds is a useful method of identifying the various indigenous peoples encountered in Eurasia. The other prominent language family is the 'Altaic', which similarly takes its title from a mountain range, the Altai

mountains, which lies to the south where Siberia meets Mongolia. A third, but much smaller linguistic grouping, that of 'Palaeo-Siberian', covers the ancient unrelated languages of four peoples, including the Kets of the River Yenisey district. Most of the 24 million Uralic speakers reside in areas to the west of the Urals, and include the Finns, Estonians, Saami (Lapps) and Hungarians. Those that inhabit the Siberian territories are mainly the Samoyed, Mansi (Voguls) and Khanti (Ostyaks). Siberian speakers of the Altaic languages number about a million and are normally categorized into three groups, examples of which are the Turkic-speaking Sakhas (Yakuts) and Tuvans, the Mongolic-speaking Buryats and the Tungusic-speaking Evenki.

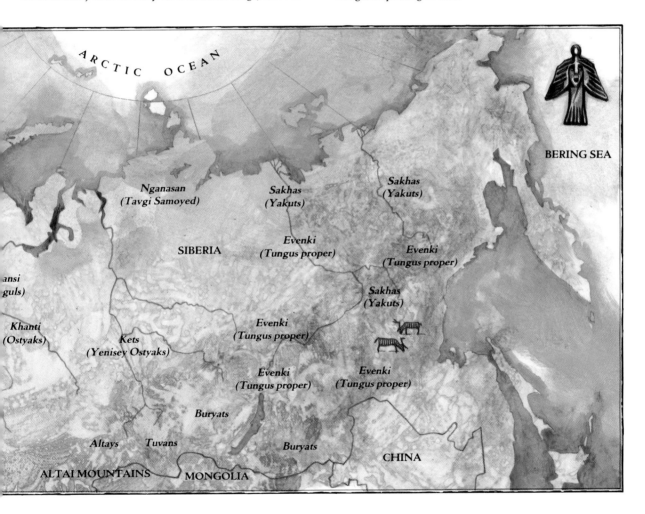

spirit of the bear had to be placated and appeased, perhaps by blaming others, because it was feared that it would take revenge when it realized its physical misfortune. Totemic clan animals also played a significant part in many tribes' identification of themselves within their surroundings, and the influence of ancestral spirits guided many of their day-to-day activities.

ECSTATIC DIVINATION

The bedrock of the spiritual well-being of most of the communities in Siberia was the figure of the shaman, although in many areas the encroaching influences of other religious systems, such as Russian Orthodox Christianity, Islam, and Buddhism, were also felt. The term shaman is indigenous to Siberia and is derived through the Russian from the Tungusic languages, of which the Evenki variants *xaman* and *saman* are prime examples.

Central to the definition of Eurasian shamanism was the leading part played by spirits. It thus follows that ecstatic divination was very much the prerogative of the shaman because it involved soul flight and spirit mediation. Divination of this kind was used to seek the causes of illness, to locate lost possessions, to determine the success of the hunt, to gauge the future prosperity of the community and to obtain from the spirits knowledge of the sacrifices required to ensure successful outcomes. Fundamental to the shaman undertaking this form of divination was the belief that each person has at least two main souls, a body soul and a free soul. The body soul was active during waking consciousness and covered functions such as, breathing, the pulse, emotions and volition. The free soul was active during altered states of consciousness and thus under certain conditions wandered free from the body. These states covered the dream of the sleeper, the coma of the sick and the trance of the shaman. The free soul was often regarded as residing in the head and was crucial to the beliefs in ancestral rebirth; it thus had an element of immortality about it.

The Otherworld to which the free soul of the shaman journeys during an ecstatic trance can be one of two realms, the Upperworld or the Lowerworld. Together with the middle earth of physical manifestation there are thus three worlds for the shaman to be active in. Linking these three worlds is normally a Cosmic Tree or a Cosmic River. In journeying to them, the shaman is in effect returning to the sacred centre of space and the primordial time of the first ancestral shaman. Above the World Tree shines the Pole Star, which as the 'nail of heaven' is the hook upon which the sky realm hangs. The macrocosm of the World Tree with the three worlds is often symbolized in microcosmic form by the *yurta* (a skin tent common to the area) with a central pole pointing up towards the smoke hole.

The Lowerworld tends to be the domain of the dead and is often regarded as the obverse of the land of the living with everything occurring in reverse. Thus it is upside down and backwards, with the dead getting 'younger' every day until they return to the point of their original conception. In addition to the dead, numerous spirits of disease also inhabit the Underworld and it is to these that the shaman travels when divining for the location of a stolen soul of a sick patient. In the Upperworld reside the spirits benevolent to humanity.

Ultimately it is the spirits, very often those of the ancestors, that elect a new shaman, even in those cultures which had hereditary shamanic families. To resist the call of the spirits was to court serious illness and death. In the Evenki tradition the free soul of the elected person was guided by the ancestors down to the Underworld where it was eaten by the great clan mother animal and then reborn as a shamanic soul. In some traditions the souls of future shamans lived as young birds in nests upon the branches of the World Tree, awaiting rebirth in the human plane. Very often the Underworld transformation of the shaman took the form of an attack by the spirits who stripped away flesh and dismembered the skeleton, only for the bones to be reset and the body remade.

In journeys to the Otherworld the shaman's free soul could take on the form of an ancestral tutelary spirit, which was usually that of a deceased shaman, or that of a clan totem animal. To some extent and depending on the culture, the shaman gained empowerment from the Underworld and received wisdom from the Upperworld. Since spirits were generally regarded as being ambivalent towards humanity, the shaman had to protect the community by mastering and controlling them. These spirits

The skins of Saami shaman drums were decorated with important symbols from Saami cosmology and helped the shamans by guiding them on their journeys to other worlds. These drums show, from left to right, the three levels of the cosmos, the upper, middle and lower worlds; the four cardinal directions and the four intermediate directions for use during the eight seasons of the Saami year; and the Sun surrounded by other celestial bodies.

became the shaman's spirit helpers and in turn aided the shaman in his or her work when summoned during rituals and divinations. These spirit helpers also took on various guises, such as the forms of fish, wild animals and birds. When calling upon and in certain cases incarnating the spirits the shaman was always in control and never possessed by them.

Chants were often sung in strange animal or bird-like voices to induce an altered state of consciousness in the shaman, but the sound of the steady beating of a drum was probably the principal method used for falling into an ecstatic trance. In the Altaic-speaking cultures of Siberia the shaman resorted to forms of ecstatic divination in order to find the materials to make a drum. Thus the Tuvan shaman conducted an oracle to locate the special tree which would furnish the wood for the drum frame, whilst the Evenki shaman relied on dreams to find the reindeer which would supply the hide needed for the drum skin. The shaman's drum was rich in symbolism since the wood could represent the shaman's particular World Tree and the skin the shaman's animal soul guardian. Depending on the culture, the shaman often 'rode' his drum as a reindeer or horse to the Otherworld, the drumbeats representing both the heartbeats and the hoof-beats.

The outer surface of the skin of a Saami drum tended to be richly decorated with the images of the indigenous cosmology and thus acted as a map to guide the shaman on his journeys between the worlds. It is likely that the drums were viewed from different angles depending on the time of year, and particular star alignments may have indicated when gateways were open to facilitate the shaman's journey to the Otherworld. Special markings were also to be found inside many drums indicating tribal and clan sigils and sacred symbols known only to the shamans themselves. One other significant feature of the drums were various holes which acted as entrances for the shaman's free soul to travel through during its ecstatic flight.

In performing one of his or her most important functions, that of healer, the shaman often had to use ecstatic divination to locate the whereabouts of a patient's lost soul. Illnesses were deemed to result from two major causes, soul loss and spirit intrusion, with the former occurring during a loss of consciousness, as in a coma, and the latter applying to ailments of a physical nature. The shaman who travelled to the realm of the dead was always in great danger of losing his own soul and thus exercised his spirit helpers to protect him. The spirits of the Underworld inevitably demanded sacrifices to be performed in exchange for anything given up by them. In the *Kalevala*, the national epic of Finland, a character who shows strong shamanistic traits, Lemminkäinen, lost his soul in the

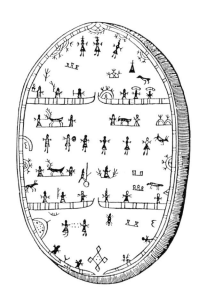
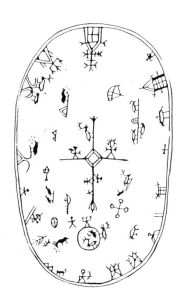

River of the Dead and is dismembered in the process. His mother became aware of his fate when blood oozed from her son's brush, the bristles probably coming from an animal that represented Lemminkäinen's animal soul guardian. Taking on the mantle of a shaman, she eventually located her son's lost soul and journeyed to the Rapids of Death, where, using a rake, she collected up the various parts of his body. With the help of charms and ointments she reassembled Lemminkäinen's body and restored his soul, and thus in effect brought him back to life.

READING THE SIGNS

Whereas ecstatic divination tended to play a central role in the ritual performance of the shaman, inductive methods of divination were very often carried out by the shaman towards the end of the ceremony for the benefit of other members of the community or the community in general. One form of inductive divination is the casting of lots, which involved the cutting of slithers of wood from the branches of an alder tree. This was used by Väinämöinen, a principal character in the *Kalevala*, to locate the whereabouts of the Sun and Moon which had both been hidden by Louhi, the mistress of Pohjola, a magical land to the north.

Elsewhere in the *Kalevala* Louhi ordered her serving maid to throw rowan twigs into the fire so that she could divine from the types of sap that oozed out of the wood the purposes of the approaching Väinämöinen and Ilmarinen. If blood flowed from the twigs then war would follow, if it was water then there would be peace, and if it was honey then a wedding would ensue. In this case it was honey that dripped from the rowan and this prompted Louhi to recommend that her daughter marry Väinämöinen.

A curious method of divination is mentioned in the Estonian *Kalevipoeg*, the national epic of Estonia, involving both the spinning of a brooch on a thread and the simultaneous reading of the flight patterns of an 'alder-beetle'. Flight by the beetle in a southerly direction was deemed fortunate, with the opposite applying if the

A scene from the Kalevala, *in which Lemminkäinen's mother used ecstatic divination to locate her son's soul in the underworld and restore him to life.*

direction was northwards. In this part of the epic, Kalev was lying seriously ill forcing his wife Linda to use divination to ascertain whether assistance could be called upon. She took hold of a brooch and spun it around on a thread, and at the same time sent an alder beetle on a series of four journeys, each of seven days length, to seek aid from, in turn, the Moon, the evening star, the Sun, and the wind. On each occasion the brooch span for seven days, but the whole exercise was to no avail because Kalev died before the beetle returned from its fourth flight. Presumably the brooch would cease to spin if the beetle suffered a mishap during flight, thus resulting in the divination being aborted.

Among many of the Siberian Altaic speakers, the bow was used as a method of divination. This could take the form of looking into a fire along the length of a bow string or by listening to the sound made by the string as the tension was changed. A third way was to balance the bow by holding the bow string in the middle with the thumb and forefinger and then interpret the extent of any swing made by the bow in response to the questions put. The bow was of great symbolic significance in Siberian culture and some have regarded it as a precursor to the shaman's drum when it was used as a one-stringed instrument to induce an altered state.

Certainly on the underside of some of the drums used by Altaic shamans was a bar representing the bow string. The shooting of arrows was also practised as a method of divination, with outcomes being determined by the flight and distance of the arrows being fired. The arrow contained much symbolic significance as it represented both the speed of ecstatic flight and shamanic action at a distance. The shooting of a chain of arrows symbolized the bridge to the Otherworld, which the shaman needed to cross in order to journey to the realm of spirits.

A by-product of the bear hunt was a divination method entailing the use of the bear's right paw. The Kets believed that the bear possessed the soul of a dead relative and so when the animal was hunted down, killed and subsequently taken back to the settlement, it had to receive treatment befitting a guest of honour. Since it was regarded as a deceased relative its name had to be known so that it could be properly welcomed. The bear's right paw was cut off and tossed up in the air as a name was called out. This was carried out three times and when the paw landed pad side up was it deemed that the correct name had been divined. At the end of the feast the paw became a talisman.

The tossing up of an object a number of times and the subsequent divining of an outcome from the way that the object landed is probably the simplest method of divination used by the Eurasian peoples. Many divined in this way using the drumstick. When doubts lingered after an ecstatic divination concerning the fate of a sick person, the Samoyed shaman of the Nganasan tribe would toss the drumstick up three times to further divine the outcome. Landing face upwards was regarded as a good omen in this case.

The Khanti (Ostyaks) and the Mansi (Voguls) used divination during a pregnancy to ascertain the health of the mother and the expected child. As soon as a woman became pregnant she made from birchwood a thumb-sized female figurine called a *sos*. This doll had a ribbon tied around its waist and the ends were used to suspend the *sos* between three fingers.

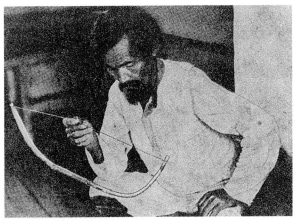

Siberian shamans use the bow as an instrument of divination by balancing it from the middle of the bow string, and then observing and interpreting the extent of any sway made by the bow in response to particular questions – one of a number of ways in which bows and arrows can be used as tools for divination purposes.

As the birth approached, the expectant mother would divine from the movements of the suspended doll whether she would survive and the health of the child. Hanging motionless or twitching erratically was deemed inauspicious, whereas a smooth swaying was a good omen.

Babies were believed to have the souls of ancestors reborn and so the name of the person who had in effect returned to the fold had to be determined. This form of divination was carried out by the eldest woman on the father's side, who placed a knife under the cradle containing the child and then attempted to lift the cradle off the floor each time a name was shouted out. Only when the correct name was called out did the cradle become too heavy to move, since the additional weight was a sign of the presence of the soul of the reborn ancestor.

The drum was also used by some Eurasian peoples, most notably the Saamis of Lapland, for divination purposes. The main method was to place a brass ring or a piece of antler on the membrane of the drum and then to start beating the drum frantically with the special antler drumstick. The movement of the ring across the images on the surface of the drum was keenly observed and the sound of the vibrating membrane was also noted. When the ring ceased to move in spite of the drumming, the image that it covered was taken to indicate the outcome to the immediate problem posed.

Amongst the *táltos* of Hungary a leather-covered sieve was often used for divining, with grains of maize thrown onto the surface and the outcomes read from the resulting positions.

There were various other ways of divining with rings. The Sakhas (Yakut) shamans were reputed to foretell a person's future by simply moving a ring around on the palm of the enquirer's hand. Of more importance was the role of the *eheken*, or 'spirit of hunting', which was represented by an irregular oval ring of antler horn covered with calfskin. Before the hunt, the northern Sakhas would smear the skin with fat and hold the ring near to a fire. When the fat melted in the heat and the face of the skin glowed, it was perceived that the spirit of the hunt was amongst them. The ring was tossed up and if it landed face upwards success in the hunt was assured. Landing face downwards meant that any hunting planned for that day had to be cancelled.

Scapulimancy, or the art of divination by shoulder-blade, was a method much favoured by the Altaic-speaking peoples. Sheep, goats and deer were generally the animals selected to supply the shoulder-blades. The bone was cleaned, warmed by a fire and smeared with fat. A northern Yakut diviner waved the bone around himself three times, spat on it each time and recited an incantation. He put some burning coals on the bone and fanned them to make them glow. As soon as the blade started to crack the coals were removed and the resultant lines were interpreted according to the accepted meanings. When the divination was completed the shoulder-blade was protected from subsequent desecration.

A method involving pieces of bone cut from the hooves of a deer was used by the northern Sakhas. The request was first whispered onto one of the bone pieces before it was waved around three times by the diviner. Next all the bone pieces were placed in three piles and then three bits at a time were taken away until only four were left in each section. The bones that were removed were laid out in the form of a human figure, which was then used as the divining map. The remaining bone pieces were thrown at the human image and the outcome determined from the resultant positions.

The use of bones for divination was particularly apt because to many of the Eurasian cultures bones symbolized the continual regeneration of life. The soul was possibly deemed to reside in the marrow and so the bones of animals killed in the hunt were carefully collected together and buried, thus enabling the animals to be reborn again from their essence. This practise mirrors the dismembering and resetting of the shaman's skeleton during some initiations in the Underworld. The skeleton was depicted on the ritual costumes of many Siberian shamans, thus emphasizing its symbolic power.

THE CELTIC AND NORSE WORLD

The number of parallels between the divinatory systems of the Norse and Celtic peoples is remarkable and perhaps suggests one reason why, when the two races came into conflict in the sixth century AD, they were in time able to fuse to become the Anglo-Saxon race. Both practised the art of throwing lots, and the description of the Norse augurs, drawn from the account of the Roman writer Tacitus, could equally well stand as a description of *Crannchur*, or 'Throwing the Woods', described in the chapter on the Celts.

Aside from this, there are strong parallels between the Norse Runic and Celtic Ogam alphabets – though each originated as an individual system and belongs to its own cultural milieu, despite various attempts in recent times to confuse the two.

Again, the reading of auguries from the flight and cries of birds seems to have been common to both peoples, and there are numerous references in the literature of the Celts and the Norse which testify to the sacredness of animals generally and the magical power of birds in particular.

We might also mention, while discussing such similarities, the importance attached to the reading of dreams by both peoples: both employed professional augurs to undergo a kind of temple sleep from which they returned with word of future events or the answer to a specific question.

Within a wider framework of world-wide divinatory techniques, we may note the close similarity between the accounts of Celtic diviners reading from the shoulder-blades of dead animals and those of the peoples of the Circumpolar region, who still practised this type of augury up to very recent times. The horse augury used by the Norse was, according to recent evidence, in all probability also practised in ancient Scotland.

Such common features help to reinforce the belief that at one time there existed a few basic divinatory systems using stones, twigs and the observance of natural events such as the fall of a leaf, the shapes of clouds, or the ever changing pattern of the stars. With the passage of time, these methods became more sophisticated and mutated into many different forms.

In the world of the Celtic and Norse peoples, as in the Circumpolar regions, we are able to look through a window in time to when divinatory systems were actually undergoing a period of development. We can therefore see the wide variety of types of divination practised by these people; as well as the common elements in their methods.

CHAPTER THREE

BY STICK AND STONE

Celtic Methods of Divination

John Matthews

The Celtic world once stretched from the far east of Europe to the edge of the Atlantic; now it is limited to Wales, Scotland, Ireland, Brittany and parts of Gallicia. The fascination with future events which existed among the people who lived in these areas from around the third century BC finds expression in many ways. Practitioners of the various arts of divination are recorded from the earliest times and are still recognized as part of a continuing tradition – though now it is those who possess 'the second sight' who predict the future, and the old methods of divining are virtually forgotten. However, references to a number of methods survive. We find these in medieval accounts of the 'Bardic schools' of Britain and Ireland, where such skills were taught as part of a 25-year curriculum. From them we can get a clear picture of how these methods worked and how they were practised, and gain fresh insight into the rich heritage of the Celtic tradition.

Among the systems and methods of which we find mention are divination by the throwing of *Ogam Sticks*; *Nealdoracht* or Cloud Reading; several kinds of *Incubatory Sleep*, in which the precognitive dreams of individuals were studied and interpreted; and three mysterious methods of divining events known by the enigmatic titles of *Imbas Forosnai* (Enlightened Manifestation), *Tenm Laida* (Illumination by Song) and *Dichetal do Chennaib* (Meditation on the Finger Ends). In addition are several methods of augury practised among the Gaels of Scotland. If we look closely at each of these we find that there is a surprising commonality to each and every one.

THE CELTIC WORLD
The Celts originated in the heartland of Europe, from where they migrated steadily westward, founding colonies in Spain, Gaul, Britain and Ireland. In time they migrated to Scotland and then back across the European continent as far as Italy and Greece, sacking Rome in 390 BC. A joyful and creative people, quick-tempered, energetic and great warriors, their art, religion and mythology had a powerful influence on the Western world; but they were more of a loose-knit confederacy than a united people, and when they met the might of the Roman Empire they gave way before it. Today the descendants of the original Celtic race can be found in Scotland, Ireland and Wales, as well as Brittany and parts of Spain. Their fascination with divining the future remains in the heritage of tradition and a strong belief in the 'Second Sight'.

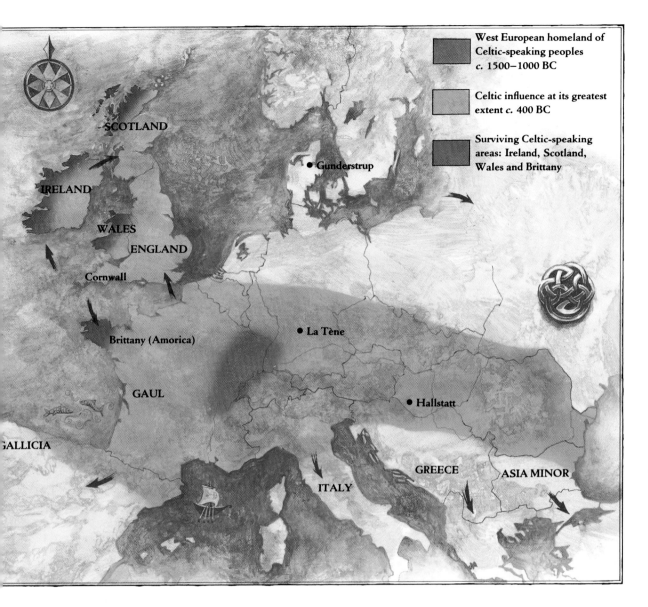

West European homeland of Celtic-speaking peoples *c.* 1500–1000 BC

Celtic influence at its greatest extent *c.* 400 BC

Surviving Celtic-speaking areas: Ireland, Scotland, Wales and Brittany

SCOTLAND

• Gundestrup

IRELAND

WALES

ENGLAND

Cornwall

Brittany (Amorica)

• La Tène

GAUL

• Hallstatt

GALLICIA

GREECE

ASIA MINOR

ITALY

OGAM: SECRET LANGUAGE OF THE POETS

Principle among the methods of divination that we know about is the use of Ogam (Ogham), a form of archaic alphabet put to many and varied uses. It has been called 'the Secret Language of the Poets' and formed an important part of the Bardic teachings in both Wales and Ireland. Hundreds of standing stones have been dis-

Across much of Ireland, Wales and Scotland, like curious fingers pointing to the sky, are large numbers of stones carved with inscriptions in Ogam. Using the edge of the stone as a stave, the combinations of lines that make up the letters are carved along the edges. They may have acted as grave markers or boundary stones. The one shown here is from Ireland.

covered bearing inscriptions in Ogam, some of which refer to famous heroes, while others are believed to have been boundary markers. But the uses of Ogam go far beyond this, being capable of sophisticated application and great subtlety of allusion. In the hands of a master it could be made to convey a wide range of meanings, and was almost certainly used to convey secret messages in a kind of code.

The Ogam alphabet consists of 20 letters, arranged in groups of five, which are constructed from series of straight lines incised across a single stave (five more letters of a more complex structure are thought to have been added some time after the original number). It

THE OGAM ALPHABET

OGAM NAME	LETTER	TREE
Beithe	b	birch
Luis	l	elm/rowan
Fearn	f	alder
Saile	s	willow
Nuin	n	ash
(h) Uathe	h	whitethorn/hawthorn
Duir	d	oak
Tinne	t	holly/elderberry
Coll	h	hazel
Quert	q	quicken/aspen/apple
Muinn	m	vine/mulberry
Gort	g	fir/ivy
(N) Getal	ng	broom/fern
Straif	str	willowbrake/blackthorn
Ruis	r	elder
Ailm	a	fir/pine
Ohn	o	furze/ash/gorse
Ur	u	thorn/heather

OGAM NAME	LETTER	TREE
Edhadh	e	yew/aspen
Ido	i	service tree/yew
Ebadh	eba	elecampane/aspen
Oir	oi	spindle tree
Uilleand	ui	ivy/honeysuckle
Iphin	io	pine/gooseberry
Emancoll/Phagos	ae	witch-hazel/beech

In the table above the names most generally attributed to the letters of the tree alphabet are shown along with their associated trees. (There is still some disagreement between the various attributions.)

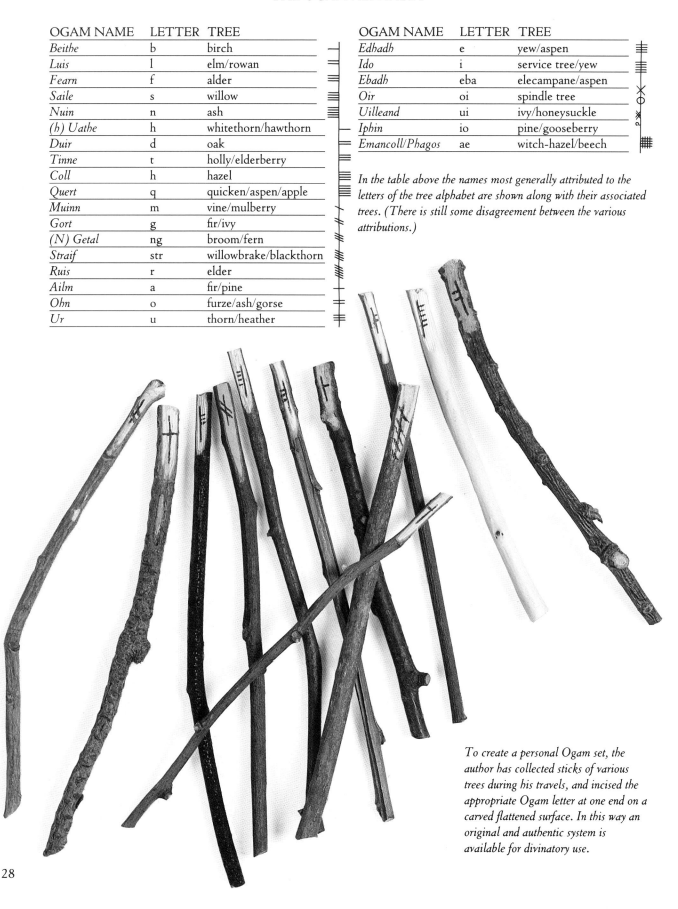

To create a personal Ogam set, the author has collected sticks of various trees during his travels, and incised the appropriate Ogam letter at one end on a carved flattened surface. In this way an original and authentic system is available for divinatory use.

was a simple matter to carve these enigmatic letters on the edge of stones, and it is from this source that the structure of the alphabet has been derived. The origin of the letters is given mythological status in several old Irish texts, among them *Cormac's Glossary*, which, although it was not compiled until the Middle Ages, is known to contain much earlier material. The passage in question reads as follows:

What are the place, time, person, and cause of the invention of Ogam? ... In the time of Bres, son of Elatha ...Ogma, a man well skilled in speech and in poetry, invented the Ogam. The cause of its invention [was] as a proof of his ingenuity, and that the speech should belong to the learned apart, to the exclusion of rustics and herdsmen. ... The father of Ogam is Ogma, the mother of Ogam is the hand or knife of Ogma. ... (Translation by W. Stokes.)

The figure of Ogma (sometimes called Ogmios) is well attested throughout Irish and Gaulish mythology. There, rather than being described as a man, he is very clearly identified as one of the Tuatha de Danaan, the primal gods of Ireland. Although the details of his discovery of the Ogam letters remain obscure, we may imagine that at one time there must have existed a story which told of his quest for the alphabet in much the same way as the Norse Odin is represented as having discovered the runes (see Chapter Four, The Message of the Runes).

Certainly Ogma was a master of the poetic mysteries, and it is in this area that Ogam finds its primary use. Each of the letters has a name, and is associated with a wide range of natural objects. The most famous example of this is the Tree Alphabet, in which each of the letters is identified with a tree. This has led some commentators to assume the existence of a complex tree 'calendar', with each month identified by an Ogam 'stave' (row) of letters. Whether or not there is any truth in this assumption it is an important example of the way in which the letters seem to have been used. The

names most generally attributed to the letters of the Tree Alphabet are shown opposite.

This points to the possible use of the letters in divining the future, though once again the evidence for their exact use is scarce. It would appear that twigs of wood from the various trees were inscribed with the appropriate letters and that these were then 'thrown' at random, the positions in which they fell and the relationships to one another then being read and interpreted.

How this was done is suggested by the many lists of Ogam correspondences found in a variety of ancient sources. Among others we find 'Sow Ogam', 'Bird Ogam', 'River Ogam', 'King Ogam', 'Colour Ogam' and 'Food Ogam'. It is evident from this that a truly vast range of associations existed, all of which had to be memorized by the Celtic shaman-poets, whose interpretive skills meant that Ogam divination was indeed a specialized activity.

'Finger Ogam' was used by those who possessed the knowledge of the alphabet and its hidden references. This involved using one finger as a vertical or horizontal stave against which combinations of other digits could be laid

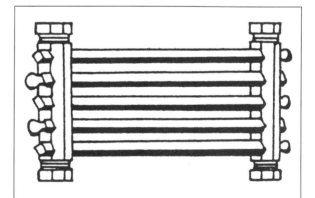

SPINNING THE FUTURE

In the Peithynen framework used by the Welsh Bards, five rods squared off to provide four surfaces, each carrying a carved Ogam letter, were placed into a wooden frame. By striking the rods with the palm of the hand, they were spun to give a combination of letters for interpretation. We must treat the authenticity of the Peithynen with caution, however, as it can be traced back no further than the eighteenth century, and may have been the invention of the great Welsh antiquarian and forger Iolo Morgannwg.

to spell out the Ogam letters. In this way messages could be passed that were undetectable by those who knew nothing of Ogam. The throwing of the sticks, called *Crannchur* or 'Casting the Woods', is referred to in a medieval text called the *Senchus Mor*, where it is said that when a decision was to be made, or a question asked, three 'lots' or slips of wood were placed in a bag, shaken and drawn forth again one at a time. According to the order in which they came forth (and, we may assume, the Ogam letter carved thereon), a decision to the question proposed was to be understood.

A later, almost certainly nineteenth-century system, is called *Coelbrenn*, 'Wood-Letters'. Despite its apparent lateness, the fact that the name of the system contains two ancient Celtic names, 'Coel' and 'Brenn' (possibly Bran, the Celtic God of Inspiration), suggests that it may derive from a much earlier source.

Other methods included the use of wooden dice, carved with *coelbrenns* on each side. These could then be palmed, shaken and thrown in a similar manner to conventional dice, but they could also be used by those informed in their symbolic values either to pass secret messages, or to foretell events in the future.

Taken together these references suggest that the Ogams were used as a divinatory system, and that this consisted in various methods of arriving at random combinations of the letters, which could then be interpreted by the skilled bard or shaman-poet.

That these methods, or ones similar to them, may also have been in use among the Druids is also a possibility, though we have only Julius Caesar's somewhat unreliable testimony to go on. Logic suggests that the Druids, who were certainly the keepers of the native wisdom in these islands, would have possessed ways of reading the future, but this is not enough to support the many fantastic theories proposed as to the methods they used. At least two specific means of divining the future may, with greater certainty, be attributed to Druidic practice. These are the reading of dreams and the interpretation of shapes in the clouds.

DREAM READING

Far and away the second most common method of divination practised by the Celts was the interpretation of dreams. Over and again we find references in the literature to people who possessed the ability to dream the future. This took a more specific shape in the accounts we have of Incubatory Sleep. This method seems to have originated in Classical Greece and to have sprung up independently within the Celtic world. It involved the person with a question regarding either past, present or future events, or with a problem to be solved, visiting a special temple dedicated to a particular god or goddess, in which a building containing a number of separate chambers was set aside. Here the querent was ritually prepared (probably by taking a purifying bath and being laved in sacred oils) and then left to sleep. If they had prepared themselves properly, and were in a correct state

During Incubatory Sleep the subject lay within a darkened chamber and received a healing dream or sometimes as visitation from a god. This is a depiction by Anglo-Danish artist Monica Sjöö.

of mind, they then received a dream, or sometimes a visitation from the deity of the place, in which the question they had proposed was answered. They were attended by priests or priestesses who were skilled in the interpretation of such dreams, rather like the oracles at Delphi or Eleusis in Greece, which also required interpretation.

Evidence for such practice among the Celts has been found at more than one site in Britain and Ireland. The best known is at Lydney in Gloucestershire, where a number of votive offerings have been found, as well as the foundations of a later temple complex consisting of numerous sleep-chambers clearly modelled on the type discovered in Greece and dedicated to Asklepios, the god of healing.

Related to this method of precognitive dreaming is a mysterious ceremony known as *Tarb Feis*, 'Bull Sleep'. This involved a trained shaman or priest being put to sleep in a darkened hut on a cured bull's hide. Invariably this seems to have produced the required trance state from which the practitioner emerged some hours later with the words of prophecy on his lips. A sufficiently similar description of this method exists from as late as the seventeenth century, suggesting the strength of this tradition and its survival and continuance until comparatively recent times.

READING THE CLOUDS

The reading of clouds is probably one of the oldest and most commonly practised methods of divination in the world. Among the Celts this method of precognition seems to have been carried to a fine art, judging by the existence of a specialized group of people whose task it was to practise the art of *Neladoracht*, 'Divination by clouds'. That this was a form of practice common to the Druids is shown in an ancient manuscript now in a Dublin library, in which it is told how a certain king asked his Druid to read the future for him. The priest did so by climbing to the top of *Crocna-Druad*, 'Druid's Hill', 'where he remained the night, returning at sunrise. He then addressed the king with these

words: "Are you asleep, O king of Erin and Alban? ....I have consulted the clouds ...and have discovered that you shall make a conquest of Alban, Britain and Gaul", which accordingly he did soon after.' (Translation by P.W. Joyce.)

FRITH

The *frith* (pronounced 'free') was a method of augury practised until recently in the Western Highlands and Islands of Scotland. Those practising the *frith* were usually people with the 'sight'. They were called *frithirs*, a title that has descended into modern usage as a surname: Freer. The Freers were the hereditary state augurs for the kings of Scotland. The method of augury was as follows: the *frithir* would fast on the first Monday of every quarter, and would stand before sunrise, bare-headed, bare-footed and blindfolded on the doorstep. She would put a hand on either side of the doorposts and make an invocation. On removing the blindfold, she would then make a prediction based upon the first thing she saw. An extensive list of possible sightings and their correspondences would have been part of the training of a *frithir*, but these are not available in any written text.

This was only one of several methods of augury practised among the Gaels of Scotland in particular. Although most of the information regarding them comes from comparatively recent times, the existence of these methods in folklore tradition suggests a much earlier point of origin.

SLINNEANCHACHD: SIGNS FROM THE SHOULDER

Slinneanchachd derives from the Gaelic word for shoulder, *slinnean*. The method involved the slaughter of an animal, usually a black sheep or a pig (the latter was sacred to the Celts). When the flesh had been boiled from the bones, the shoulder-blade was then studied and certain marks that appeared thereon were interpreted. An account dating from 1746 describes a soldier at the battle of Culloden predicting victory for the Hanoverian army after reading the shoulder-blade of a sheep.

DEUCHAINN: FIRST SIGHT

This is one of several types of augury involving the sight of significant objects, people or animals. It literally means 'trial' or 'proof' and in order to discover the outcome of some significant forthcoming event, such as a wedding, the person requiring to know this went up a hill or cairn which was too steep for an animal to climb. On the way down, or subsequently returning home, the first creature to be met with indicated what kind of person one might marry. Similarly, if it was required to know what kind of fortune might attend upon one at the start of a new year, the enquirer would walk to the end of their house, outside, with eyes shut. On opening them, the first thing to be seen was the omen sought for.

A similar form of augury was *Manadh*, generally translated simply as 'luck', which involved the observance of certain birds or animals that were said to bring either good or bad luck. Thus a cuckoo's call was said to predict the death of a child, while a cock crowing at midnight meant news coming next day. Each of these methods, though seemingly random, required skilled interpretation.

IMBAS FOROSNA: ENLIGHTENED MANIFESTATION

Perhaps the most mysterious of Celtic divinatory methods that we know something about is *Imbas Forosna*, which may be translated as 'Enlightened Manifestation' or more simply 'Illumination' and which is described in various Celtic texts as being widely practised among the Celts of Britain and Ireland. The technique involved entering a completely darkened place and spending some time alone and in a state of sensory deprivation. At the end of a specified time – ranging from several hours to three days – the seer was brought forth into bright light, which might either be sunshine or the light of a fire. Either way, the effect of the long enclaustration in darkness, followed by the sudden exposure to brilliant illumination, seems to have set free the tongue and enabled the diviner to utter inspired words and answers relevant to the question he or she had originally entered the dark place to discover.

DICHETEL DO CHENNAIB: MEDITATION ON THE FINGER ENDS

A number of explanations of this practice have been put forward in the face of sparse textual information. The most likely is that it refers to the use of Finger Ogam combined with a type of meditation that led the seer to conceive an inspired answer to the question asked. An alternate theory is that the words may be translated as 'The Cracking Open of the Nuts of Wisdom', these being the hazels that grew above the mystical Well of Segais in the Celtic Otherworld. Salmon swam in this well and were believed to eat the nuts, for which reason to catch and eat a salmon was considered one road to extreme illumination, and the great Irish hero Fionn MacCumhail is said to have acquired his considerable wisdom by this means.

TENM LAIDA: ILLUMINATION BY SONG

This refers to the chant of the shamans by which they passed into a trance state that enabled them to journey into the inner realms and bring back information not readily available to the rest of humankind. The account in *Cormac's Glossary* suggests a more elaborate ritual, in which the seer first chewed a piece of raw meat, which he then placed on the threshold of his dwelling, before entering an altered state of consciousness. It has been suggested that this may refer to the fact that when raw meat is chewed or consumed it releases endocrines in the brain, thus generally enhancing consciousness.

These then are the principal methods of divination practised by the Celts. We can be confident that a people with such a highly developed interest in the reading of the future had other methods. The information remaining may be scarce, but it is certainly sufficient to inform us of their dedicated pursuit of knowledge by these and other means.

THE MESSAGE OF THE RUNES

Divination in the Ancient Germanic World

Peter Taylor

The Roman orator and author Tacitus, writing in the first century AD, gives us in his *Germania 10* an account of the divinatory practices of the ancient Germanic peoples:

For divination and the casting of lots they have the highest regard. Their procedure in casting lots is always the same. They cut off a branch of a nut-bearing tree and slice it into strips; these they mark with different signs and throw them completely at random onto a white cloth. Then the priest of the state, if the consultation is a public one, or the father of the family if it is private, offers a prayer to the gods, and looking up at the sky picks up three strips, one at a time, and reads their meaning from the signs previously scored on them. If the lots forbid an enterprise, there is no deliberation that day on the matter in question; if they allow it, confirmation by the taking of auspices is required. (Penguin translation)

The signs marked on the strips of wood were probably similar to those holy-signs known to us as rune-staves. Although Tacitus had observed

The runic inscription on the eighth-century silver-gilt mount shown above, found in the River Thames in London, probably forms a chant.

this particular divinatory procedure being carried out by men, he makes it clear that the ancient Germanic people held the prophetic abilities of women in the highest possible regard: 'they believe that there resides in woman an element of holiness and a gift of prophecy; and so they do not scorn to ask their advice, or lightly disregard their replies' (*Germania 8*). Tacitus concludes *Germania 10* with an outline of various forms of augury which would have been used for the 'taking of auspices', the first being 'seeking information from the cries and flight of birds'. The patterns formed by birds flying would have played a part in determining the shapes of the rune-staves. Tacitus also tells us that pure white horses were kept at public expense in sacred woods and groves; they were yoked to sacred chariots, and note was taken of their neighs and snorts. The horse omens inspired great trust, 'not only among the common people, but even among the nobles and priests, who think that they themselves are but servants of the gods, whereas the horses are privy to the gods' counsels.' Sleipnir, the horse of Óðinn, had teeth that were graven with Runes, and the name of the nineteenth Rune is *ehwaz*, the horse.

In *Eiríks Saga Rauða 4*, there is a remarkable

description of an oracular priestess known as the *Vǫlva* or *Seiđkona*, who travelled around the country giving weather forecasts and prophetic advice. In the divinatory ceremony of *Seiđr*, the *Vǫlva* visited the Otherworld in trance, whence she was called back by chanting to give voice to her prophetic utterances. There are similarities here to certain shamanic practices of the Eskimo, Lapp and Finno-Ugric peoples (see Chapter Two, The Frozen North).

Seiđr is closely connected with the cult of the fertility goddess Freyja/Vanadis. On special occasions, the high seat was raised up on a sacred burial mound and those consulting the *Vǫlva* were clad in boar helms and masks: the ancestors and the goddess herself spoke through the *Vǫlva* from the Underworld.

The peoples of the ancient Germanic North also paid much attention to visions received in dreams. In an Underworld practice called *Útiseta*, they slept on the hide of a totemic beast in a pigsty, a sacred forest grove, or on a burial mound. This enabled oracular contact with the tribal ancestors or with female fertility powers.

RUNES

(In what follows it should be noted that 'Ur-Runes' refers to Runes before their systematization; 'Runes' to the essential oracular mystery beyond each symbol; 'rune-staves' or 'rune-signs' to the carven or inscribed shapes; and 'rune-names' to the mnemonic song-words which are the sonic keys to the Runes.)

The divinatory practices so far mentioned are those of a people living in close harmony with the environment, the ancestors, the seasonal and stellar cycles and the deities. All of these aspects coalesce in the mysterious symbols known as Runes, which provide us with the tools for a uniquely environmental form of divination. The word 'Rune,' which occurs in various forms in both Germanic and Celtic languages, means 'a Mystery' or 'holy secret' that is 'whispered'.

RUNE ORIGINS

Ancestral lore sings of an ancient tribe known as the Völsungr, who wandered out of the far

North with the last great Ice. They were guardians of the primordial forests and holysteads, and of the ancient trackways, the dragon paths, linking them. These 'Children of Freedom' offered help to any suffering deep need, bondage or oppression, thus engendering fear among human oppressors. Their direct memory of the timeless hoard of Ur-Runes provided them with the wisdom, power and compassion needed to carry out these tasks.

It was also the task of the Völsungr to seed knowledge of the Ur-Runes among those of the newer tribes who would maintain their Mysteries for the future need of the Land. This task complete, the Völsungr withdrew into the deepest and most hidden holy heart-woods of the diminishing Northern Forests, and passed beyond human knowledge.

THE GERMANIC 'FUÞARK'

In the fifth century BC, certain alphabets came into use in the Alpine Regions, known variously as North Etruscan, North Italic or Alpine. During the course of the following century, the *Alpengermanen* are thought to have come into contact with these alphabets and made some use of them. Evidence for this exists in the form of a bronze helmet, dating from the third century BC, found at Negau in Steiermark, south of the Danube. It is inscribed with a text in a Germanic language, but using Alpine letters. The text reads: *HARIGASTI TEIWA* – to the god Harigast (Wōđanaz).

ΛVIIΑ ⅂I⅂ ↑I↑ ʃΑΥⅠ(I Λ⅄

THE JOURNEY OF THE RUNES

The Völsungr fetched the Runes southward, treading out in the Land the pathway of the White Wyrm (dragon), and marking its backbone with the Runes. The shape of this growth in the wisdom of Land guardianship can be seen in the rune-staves on the map and expressed by the following key words, which represent the Runes in the order in which they appear on the map: free the Land; nurture; turn and let flow the blood of the Land; seek that which is; hear the holy Rede; kindle the inner fire; give; wish; hallow; follow the Pole Star; water the roots of the World Tree.

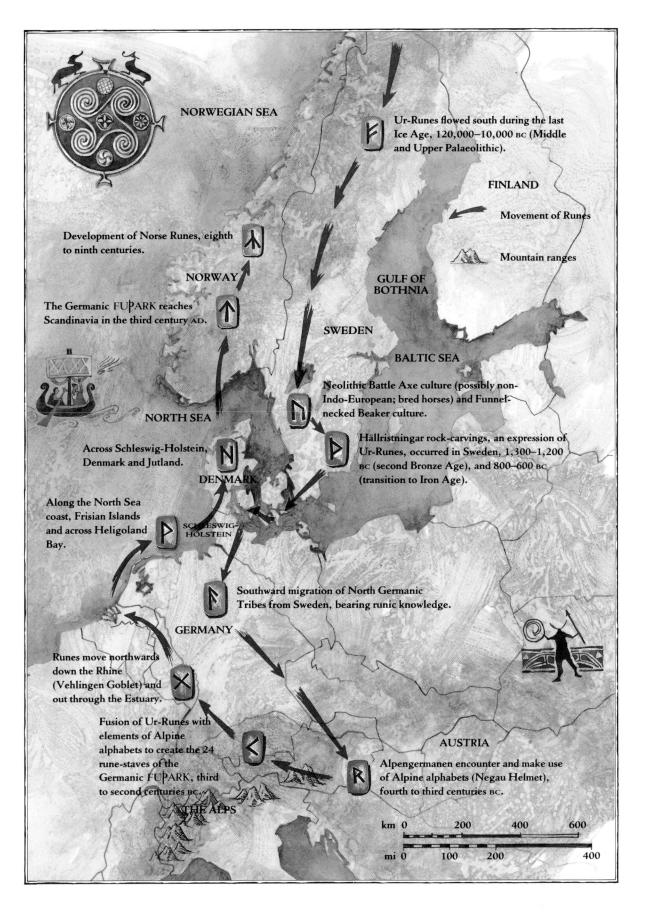

Ur-Runes flowed south during the last Ice Age, 120,000–10,000 BC (Middle and Upper Palaeolithic).

FINLAND

Movement of Runes

Mountain ranges

GULF OF BOTHNIA

NORWEGIAN SEA

Development of Norse Runes, eighth to ninth centuries.

NORWAY

The Germanic FUÞARK reaches Scandinavia in the third century AD.

SWEDEN

BALTIC SEA

Neolithic Battle Axe culture (possibly non-Indo-European; bred horses) and Funnel-necked Beaker culture.

NORTH SEA

Across Schleswig-Holstein, Denmark and Jutland.

DENMARK

Hällristningar rock-carvings, an expression of Ur-Runes, occurred in Sweden, 1,300–1,200 BC (second Bronze Age), and 800–600 BC (transition to Iron Age).

Along the North Sea coast, Frisian Islands and across Heligoland Bay.

SCHLESWIG-HOLSTEIN

Southward migration of North Germanic Tribes from Sweden, bearing runic knowledge.

GERMANY

Runes move northwards down the Rhine (Vehlingen Goblet) and out through the Estuary.

AUSTRIA

Fusion of Ur-Runes with elements of Alpine alphabets to create the 24 rune-staves of the Germanic FUÞARK, third to second centuries BC.

Alpengermanen encounter and make use of Alpine alphabets (Negau Helmet), fourth to third centuries BC.

THE ALPS

km	0		200		400		600

mi	0		100		200		400

There occurred at this point a remarkable fusion between the Germanic Ur-Runes and letters from the Alpine alphabets, resulting in the creation of the 24 Germanic rune-staves known to us. The reason for this fusion may have been to preserve the Runes for times when magical symbols would increasingly be used for written communications and records. But it should be said that, even after this systematization, rune-staves continued to be used primarily for magical purposes rather than for writing, and never developed a cursive form.

The 24 Germanic Runes – known as the 'FUÞARK' from the letter values of the first six Runes – are divided into three families (or *ættir*) of eight Runes. Each family of eight Runes can be linked to the eight directions on the horizon, to the seasonal festivals, and to various cycles of time and stars. To inscribe an object with the complete FUÞARK was a magical act of considerable potency.

The following pages (38 to 40) show the 24 Germanic rune-staves (together with the Anglo-Frisian form where it differs); the rune-name in Proto-Germanic and Old English; and the letter-value.

Also given for each Rune is a series of words, generated from the 'ancestral' Indo-European roots of the mnemonic rune-names, and from other Indo-European roots which are resonant in sound and meaning. (For a full appreciation of this magico-linguistic aspect of runic knowledge, it would be necessary to give the Indo-European roots and their derivatives in both Germanic and Old English. There is, however, only space here for derivatives in modern English.)

It should be emphasized that these words are not 'oracular meanings' of the Runes, but are extensions of the rune-names, to be meditated upon and uttered. Thereby are the sonic keys forged that will unlock the doors to the oracular and prophetic mysteries of the Runes themselves. It is important to distinguish between the Runes and the mnemonic names attached to them. The names are not only mnemonics, but also a means of stimulating the deep oracular

memory of the Runes themselves.

(Derivatives in capital letters have equivalents in other Germanic languages; those in lower-case have derived from Indo-European by different linguistic paths. Each numbered group of words derives from one Indo-European root. An asterisk indicates that the word has been reconstructed from the information available.)

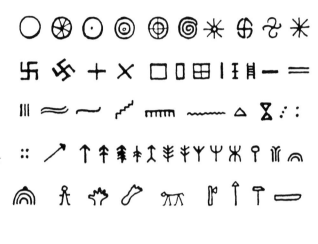

A formal expression of the 'Ur-Runes' is the Hällristningar rock-carvings (top), found in particular abundance in Sweden, dating from two periods: 1300–1200 BC (second Bronze Age), and 800–600 BC (transition to the Iron Age). Such pictorial symbols, together with their associated song-names and magical lore, were the ancestral inheritance of the North Germanic peoples migrating south from Scandinavia. They are to be seen above, inscribed together with Runes, on a lance-tip dating from the third century AD, found at Kovel, south-east of Brest.

This Swedish rune-stone from the Viking period was carved c. 1020 by Åsmund Karesson of Osla in Uppland. The inscription reads: 'BJÖRN, ÖDULF, GUNNAR AND HOLMDIS RAISED THIS STONE TO ULF, GINLOG'S HUSBAND, AND ÅSMUND HEWED [IT].'

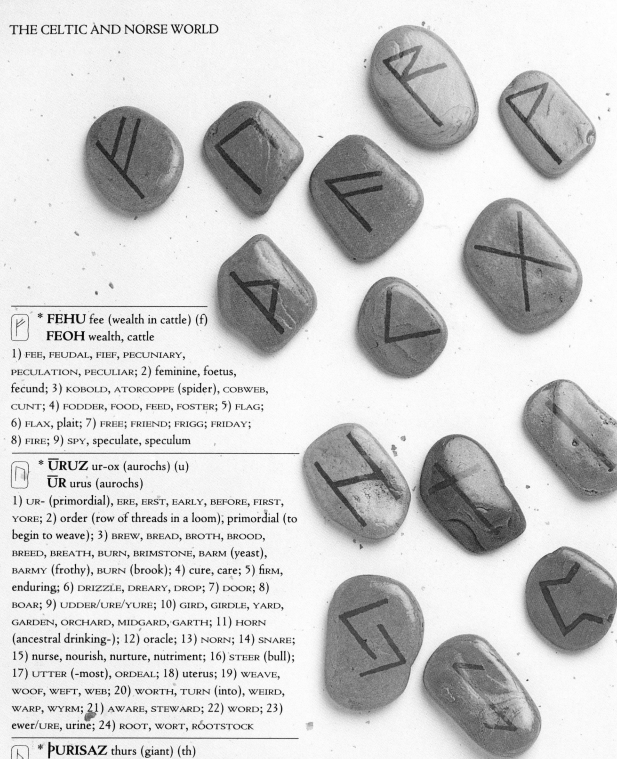

* **FEHU** fee (wealth in cattle) (f)
  FEOH wealth, cattle

1) FEE, FEUDAL, FIEF, PECUNIARY, PECULATION, PECULIAR; 2) feminine, foetus, fecund; 3) KOBOLD, ATORCOPPE (spider), COBWEB, CUNT; 4) FODDER, FOOD, FEED, FOSTER; 5) FLAG; 6) FLAX, plait; 7) FREE; FRIEND; FRIGG; FRIDAY; 8) FIRE; 9) SPY, speculate, speculum

* **ŪRUZ** ur-ox (aurochs) (u)
  ŪR urus (aurochs)

1) UR- (primordial), ERE, ERST, EARLY, BEFORE, FIRST, YORE; 2) order (row of threads in a loom); primordial (to begin to weave); 3) BREW, BREAD, BROTH, BROOD, BREED, BREATH, BURN, BRIMSTONE, BARM (yeast), BARMY (frothy), BURN (brook); 4) cure, care; 5) FIRM, enduring; 6) DRIZZLE, DREARY, DROP; 7) DOOR; 8) BOAR; 9) UDDER/URE/YURE; 10) GIRD, GIRDLE, YARD, GARDEN, ORCHARD, MIDGARD, GARTH; 11) HORN (ancestral drinking-); 12) oracle; 13) NORN; 14) SNARE; 15) nurse, nourish, nurture, nutriment; 16) STEER (bull); 17) UTTER (-most), ORDEAL; 18) uterus; 19) WEAVE, WOOF, WEFT, WEB; 20) WORTH, TURN (into), WEIRD, WARP, WYRM; 21) AWARE, STEWARD; 22) WORD; 23) ewer/URE, urine; 24) ROOT, WORT, ROOTSTOCK

* **ÞURISAZ** thurs (giant) (th)
  ÞORN thorn

1) THURS, STORM; 2) THORN; 3) THUNDER, THURSDAY; 4) THRESH, DRILL, TURN, TWIST, THREAD; 5) THRILL, THROUGH

* **ANSUZ** Áss/Ásynja (Holy Power or
  wielder of divine breath: 'Asura') (a)
       ŌS mouth (o)

1) OS (mouth of womb, divine utterance); 2) ASH (from fire); 3) IS, YES, SOOTH; 4) ASH (tree)

* **RAIÐŌ** riding (r)
  RĀD riding

1) RIDE, RIDING, ROAD, RAID, READY, STRAIGHT; 2) READ, REDE, RIDDLE ('riddle my rede'), RITE, 'ṚTA' (cosmic order); 3) TREE, TROW, TRUE, TRUST, TRUTH, TROTH, TAR; 4) RAW; 5) RIGHT, REALM, RULE, RECKON; 6) RED, ROWAN, RADDLE/RUDDLE, RUDDOCK, RUBRIC, RUST; 7) ROOT

* KAUNAZ ulcer
* KĒNAZ resinous pinewood (torch)
　(cf. German 'kien')
　* KANŌ skiff (k)
　CĒN or **CEĀN** resinous pinewood (torch) (c)
1) PINE, PITCH; 2) IGNEOUS; 3) CHINE, CLEFT, CHINK, SCION, KITH; 4) (Indo-European '* gen-'): KIN, KING, KIND, CHILD; 5) knee, kneel; 6) KNOW, CAN, CUNNING, KEN, KENNING, COUTH, KITH (kith & kin), KEEN (brave); 7) QUEEN; 8) candle, candour, incandescent, incendiary, incense; 9) SHINE, SHEEN, SHIMMER, KINDLE; 10) HEAP, HIP, HIVE, HIGH (cf. Lithuanian 'kaukas': swelling, boil, 'kaukarus': hill and Germanic 'Xau-xaz': High, a name of Wōðanaz), KNAP, KNOB, KNELL, KNOLL, KNOT, KNIFE, KNEAD; 11) GROUNDSEL ('pus-absorber'); 12) caustic, cauterize; 13) CAN (watering-), COBLE (boat for salmon fishing); 14) SHIP, SKIFF

* GEƀŌ gift (g)
GYFU gift
1) GIVE, FORGIVE, GIFT (for a wedding), GAVEL (tribute); 2) GOOD, TOGETHER, GATHER, GAD

* WUNJŌ 'winsome', joy (w)
WYN joy (clan-), pasture
1) WIN, WINSOME, WONT, WEAN, WEEN, WISH, venom, venery, VANADIS; 2) WIND, WEND, WANDER, WAND, WANDERER, VANDALS

* HAGALAZ hail, sleet (h)
HÆGL hail
1) HAIL; 2) GALLOWS, WINDLASS; 3) HAGGARD, HEDGE, HAWTHORN, quay; 4) HALE, WHOLESOME, WASSAIL, HEAL, HEALTH, HOLY, HALLOW; 5) HEL, HALL, HELE, HOLE, HOLLOW, HULL/HUSK, HAUGH, HELM (ritual mask); 6) HILL, HOLM; 7) HOLT, HALT (lame); 8) HOLLY; 9) HEW, HAY, HAYWARD, HAG

* NAUÞIZ need, necessity (n)
NȲD need
1) NEED, NECESSITY, NARWHAL, NAUGHT/NOUGHT, exhaustion; 2) nausea, nautical, nautilus, naval, nave, navigate, navy, argonaut

These stones were gathered by the author from the seashore in a storm, as is traditional. They were marked and reddened with the 24 Germanic runes, and are shown laid out in the three ættir, or families, of eight runes each.

* **ĪSA** ice (i)
  ĪS ice

1) ICE; 2) IRON (Celtic '* īsarno', the holy metal);
3) ICICLE

* **JĒRA** year, harvest (j – as the y in year)
  GĒR (fruitful) year or harvest (g)

1) YEAR; 2) HARVEST, pluck, carp (recite, brag)

* **EIHWAZ** yew (æ)
  ĒOH yew-tree (eo)

1) YEW (+ reddish and motley)

* **PERÞ** thorp (suggestion only) (p)
  PEORÐ

(this rune-name has yet to be satisfactorily translated, but
it is likely to relate to PERCHT, goddess of the Wild Hunt
and spinning) 1) THORP (village), TERP (village-mound);
2) EARTH; 3) BOAR (Indo-European '* eper-'); 4)
IRMINSUL; 5) HEARTH; 6) RUN, RUNNEL, EMBER DAY,
RENNET, RILL; 7) RAFTER, RAFT; 8) SPEAR, SPAR; 9)
SPROUT, SPURT, SPRIT, SPREAD, sperm); 10) BERTHA:
'the White Lady', Frau Wode

* **ALHIZ** elk
* **ALGIZ** protection (z)
  EOLHX-SECG elk (-sedge) (x)

1) ELM, ALDER, ELK; 2) ELL (45"), ELLEN, 'OUR LADY'S
ELLWAND'; 3) ELF, ELDRITCH; 4) SCYTHE, SICKLE,
SEDGE, SAXON; 5) SAY, SAW (a saying), SAGA, SKALD

* **SŌWULŌ** sun (s)
  SIGEL sun

1) SUN, SOL; 2) OE. SIGE (victory); 3) SWINE, SOW

* **TEIWAZ** Tīw (Shining One or deity of Pole
  Star, Deiwos, Tuisto) (t)
  TĪR Tīw/Tig

1) TUESDAY; 2) OE. STRÆLE (arrow); 3) STREW; 4)
STAR

* **BERKANA** birch twig (ᛒ)
  BEORC birch tree (b)

1) BRIGHT, BIRCH ('the White Tree'); 2) BEAVER, BEAR

* **EHWAZ** 'equine', horse (e)
  EH horse

1) equine, equerry, equestrian, equitation

* **MANNAZ** man (not male gender: human) (m)
  MAN human

1) HUMAN/S, WOMAN (OE. 'wīfman'), MAN (OE.
'wæpnman'); 2) MOUND, (hand); 3) MIND, MEMORY,
REMEMBER, MINDFUL, OHG. 'MINNA': love

* **LAGUZ** lake (water, sea) (l)
  LAGU water, sea

1) LAKE, LOCH; 2) LAW, LAY

* **INGUZ** Ing (god of fertility) (ng)
  ING Ing

1) groin; 2) kidney

* **ÐAGAZ** day (đ)
  DÆG day (d)

1) DAY; DAWN; 2) TIDE, TIDINGS, daimon, DEAL,
ORDEAL; 3) DAIRY, DOUGH, paradise; 4) DEW, HONEY-
DEW

* **ŌÞILA** odal (sacred ancestral land) (o)
  ĒÞEL inherited land (œ) (cf. Frankish '* fehuōd',
which reveals the close link between the Mysteries
of the first and last Runes)

1) ALL, PECULIAR; 2) ALLODIUM, ODAL, UDAL (although
these three words have become associated with false
notions of the ownership or holding of land, they in
reality refer to the holy guardianship and sacredness of
the Land. This is the key to the Mysteries of the Runes);
3) ÆÐELING (prince), EDELWEISS; 4) WŌÐANAZ,
ÓÐINN, WÓDEN

The Germanic rune-staves were not the end of
the Runes' journey. At the end of the second
century BC, there were present in the Alpine
regions Germanic survivors of the Battles of
Vercellae (the Cimbri) and Aquae Sextiae (the
Teutons). The Cimbri stayed in the southern
foothills of the Alps before recrossing to
Germany, and may have learned the Runes from
the *Alpengermanen*, later passing them on to the
Suevi.

During the first century BC, the Runes
journeyed northwards down the Rhine, possibly
carried by the Cimbri, Suevi or Teutons,
meanwhile also being taken eastwards by the
Marcomanni of the Upper Rhine. The Rhine
journey of the Runes is evidenced by a first
century BC goblet found at Vehlingen on the
Lower Rhine, inscribed with the following potent
runic formula: ᛏᛁᛁᛁᛚ

And so the Runes flowed out of the Rhine
Estuary, along the North Sea coastal routes by
way of the Frisian Islands and Heligoland Bay,
and from there across Schleswig-Holstein to

reach Denmark, Jutland and, by the third century AD, Scandinavia.

An early Scandinavian runic find is the lance-tip from Øvre Stabu in Norway, dated AD 200. The Runes inscribed thereon are: ᚱᚨᚢᚾᛁᛃᚨᛉ *raunijaz*, the tester. From the second century onwards, rune-staves were increasingly to occur on objects of metal, stone and bone, particularly in the regions close to the Baltic Sea.

The magical 'FUÞARK' order of the rune-staves first appears on a Gothic grave-slab at Kylver in Gotland around 400 AD (see Contents page), and on a golden medallion from Vadstena in Sweden (*c.* 550), which also shows the three families of Runes divided by double dots.

It also appears, in modified form, on an eighth-century Saxon 'scramasax', or short sword, found on the bed of the Thames in London. The Saxons first gained knowledge of the Runes in Schleswig-Holstein and north-west Germany; and later in Friesland there developed the 28 rune-staves of the 'FUÞORC', which the Saxons brought to England during, at the latest, the sixth century. The 'FUÞORC' continued to develop, reaching a total of 33 rune-staves in early ninth-century Northumbria.

NORSE RUNES

The use of the Germanic 'FUÞARK' came to an end early in the ninth century. After a period of transition, an entirely Scandinavian rune-row came into being, which in its development was at least partially independent of its predecessor. Unlike the Anglo-Frisian rune-staves, which gradually increased in number, the Norse Runes represent a magical concentration of the runic energies into only 16 staves. The earliest record of purely Norse rune-staves is an inscription on a fibula from Strand in Norway, dated 800. The inscription reads: '*siglis n a (nauða) hle*', the ornament is a protection against distress.

The Norse rune-staves, names and letter values, together with images derived from the Norwegian and Icelandic rune-poems (thirteenth and fifteenth centuries), provide further keys for unlocking the mysteries of the Runes.

Old English golden ring (eighth century), found on Greymoor Hill in Cumbria, England. The engraving is likely to be a runic chart or magical formula.

	FÉ
ᚠ	cattle, sheep, property, money (*f, b̶*) (*wolf in forest; sea-fire; serpent-path; gold*)

	ÚR
ᚢ	drizzle, flakes of metal (*u, y, w, ø, au*) (*slag; reindeer runs over hard-frozen snow; weeping of clouds; shower*)

	ÞURS
ᚦ	giant (*th – hard and soft*) (*giant: cliff dweller*)

	ÓSS
ᚬ	mouth of river or firth (*ą, ó*) (*scabbard of swords; god: ancient creator, king of Asgard, Lord of Valhalla*)
ᚨ	

	REIÐ
ᚱ	riding, chariot (*r*) (*Regin forged best sword*)

	KAUN
ᚴ	sore, boil (*k, g, ng*) (*ulcer; death: pale corpse; painful spot, dwelling of putrefaction*)

	HAGALL
ᚼ	hail (*h*) (*coldest of grains; Creator of primeval world; driving sleet; sickness of serpents*)

	NAUÐ
ᚾ	need, difficulty, distress, poverty (*n*) (*naked man chilled by frost; distress of bond-woman; oppression; hard labour; service*)
ᚿ	

	ÍSS
I	ice (on sea or water) (i, e) (ice: the broad bridge; bark of rivers, roof of wave; wild boar)

	ÁR
↑ / 1	year, good season (a) (harvest; good summer; fully ripe crops)

	SÓL
4	sun, sun goddess (s) (sun: light of the world; divine judgement; shield of sky; shining ray; destroyer of ice)

	TÝR
↑	Týr (divinity of lode-star) (t, d, nt, nd) (one-handed Áss; smith has oft to blow the bellows; leavings of wolf, king of temples)

	BJARKAN
⟡	birch (b, v, p, mb, mp) (greenest-leaved of branches; Loki lucky in deception; fir tree)

	MAÐR
Y	person, human (m) (increase of mould; great the claw of hawk; joy of humanity; adorner of ships)

	LǪGR
⌐	sea, water (1) (water: falls from mountain side; ornaments of gold; welling stream; broad geyser; land of fish; lake)

	ÝR
⅄	yew tree, bow of yew (R, y) (greenest of winter trees; sputters when burns; bent bow; brittle iron; giant of the arrow)

During the course of their heroic voyages (eighth to twelfth centuries), the Vikings seeded runic knowledge from the Arctic and North America (Newfoundland) to the Mediterranean. Inscriptions have been found as far apart as Greenland, Venice, Orkney and the Isle of Man.

Runes remained in use to a very late period in the North: sixteenth-century inscriptions have been found in Gotland; and in seventeenth-century Iceland, Christians deemed it necessary to burn people to death merely for the possession of rune-staves. Runic calendars were still in use in remote regions of Sweden in the nineteenth century.

ANCIENT TRIBAL USES OF RUNES

The wise women and men used the Runes on behalf of the tribe for these reasons: to determine the tasks to be carried out; to divine the pleasure and intentions of the deities for the tribe; to alter consciousness; and to bring about external events.

At a birth, the Runes were cast to find the name and life-path of the child. Runes were also used to assist members of the tribe when returning to the ancestors at death and to determine the course of tribal migrations.

They were used by the tribal magicians on their ecstatic journeys into the Underworld, as a means of gaining knowledge, for healing, and to bring back gifts to the tribe, such as wisdom, inspiration or courage. Rune-chants were used for the conception, gestation and birth of a child, and also for the celebration of the seasonal festivals.

If healing was needed, the Runes were cast and used as gateways in order to remember the means of healing that particular injury or sickness. This is going neither into the past nor into the future: it is entering into that condition where everything actually is, the eternal present moment.

A METHOD OF RUNIC DIVINATION

If you come to the realization that you have forgotten the reason for your presence on Earth, the Runes can be used to restore that memory. By using the Runes as gateways, you descend to the Underworld to regain lost knowledge and to find the spiritual tools that will enable you to carry out the task that you remember.

The Runes are not for fortune-telling in the modern sense. Wanting to know whether good or bad things are going to happen to you is alien to the consciousness out of which the Runes emerged. Runes can, however, help us towards achieving wholeness and act as a mouthpiece for the gods, goddesses, ancestors and non-human beings who will help us with the task of environmental regeneration. When casting the Runes, you are allowing the formation of a pattern, a map of the relationship between this world and the other worlds within Creation.

The method of runic divination given here is based upon the image of the Nine Worlds of Creation on the Web of Wyrd (Wyrd meaning the pattern of cosmic destiny), which is eternally spun between root and branch of Yggdrasil, the Tree of Cosmic Axis, by the dark weaving goddess Urðr. There is no suggestion that this is an ancient method, but it will be found to be in resonance with the nature of the Runes.

Ideally, the web pattern should be painted or embroidered on a white cloth, but this is not essential. If a specific question is being asked, ensure that it is framed with clarity and reduced to its essential kernel of meaning. The method may also be used with no question, in which case questions rather than answers are likely to be generated.

Commence the divination by kindling a sacred flame and making a short invocation to one of the Norse deities associated with Runes. Chanting based on rune-names might also be done at this point. Become aware of the eight directions on the horizon, of the sacredness of the Land, and of the central axis – pointing towards the Pole Star – about which all the worlds turn.

The rune-staves or stones (the signs are traditionally coloured red) can either be taken out of their bag, one at a time, and placed according to the numerical sequence on the diagram (or any other sequence that you are inspired to use); or, if preferred and a rune-cloth is being used, all the staves or stones may be cast onto the cloth, and the nine falling closest to the circles be allowed to form the pattern.

The nine circles form a map of the Nine Worlds of Creation delineated in Norse mythology. Their significance in this context is briefly indicated as follows:

1 *MIÐGARÐR* – Middle Earth: the land or environment; here might be encountered the earth goddess Nerthus and the ancestors.

2 *NIFLHEIMR* – the World of Mists and Ice, location of *Hvergelmir*, the Roaring Cauldron, which nourishes one of the roots of Yggdrasil:

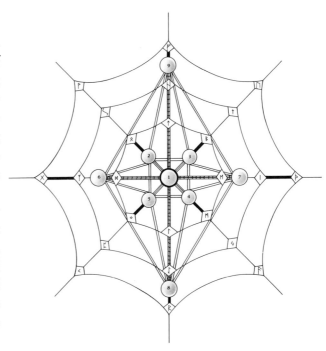

Key to the map of the Nine Worlds of Creation on the Web of Wyrd
1 *Middle Earth (the land or environment)*
2 *The World of Mists and Ice*
3 *Giant World*
4 *The World of Fire*
5 *The World of the Vanir*
6 *The World of the Elven Smiths*
7 *The World of the Star Elves*
8 *The World of the Dark Goddesses of Spinning and Weaving*
9 *The Realm of the Aesir and Asynjur*

an expression of the primordial realm of Cosmic Ice; here might be encountered the vast nurturing forces of the cow Auðumbla, from whose teats flowed the galaxies.

3 *JǪTUNHEIMR* – Giant World, location of *Mímisbrunnr*, the Well of Memory, which nourishes one of the roots of Yggdrasil: an expression of the vast primordial beings known as *Asuras*; here might be encountered the giantess Gerd, beloved of Freyr, of whom it is sung in *Skírnismál*: 'Her arms glistened so they reflected all the heavens and seas.'

4 *MUSPELLSHEIMR* – the World of Fire: an expression of the primordial realm of Cosmic Fire; here might be encountered 'the Keeper of the Oracular Flame'.

5 *VANAHEIMR* – the World of the Vanir (fertility

deities): here might be encountered Idun, keeper of the Golden Apples of Immortality, who carved Runes on the tongue of Bragi, god of poetry.

6 *SVARTALFHEIMR* – the World of the Elven Smiths: the realm of 'sub-atomic space'; here might be encountered Sunna, the feminine power of the Sun shining in Earth, and Íwaldi, guardian of the primordial Mead Cauldron and father of the Elven Smiths. They give teaching concerning the laws of chemistry.

7 *LJOSSALFHEIMR* – the World of the Star Elves: the realm of 'stellar space'; here might be encountered the Vanadis (Freyja) and her brother Freyr, Lady and Lord of the Star Elves. They give teaching concerning the laws of biology.

8 *HELHEIMR* – the World of the Dark Goddess of Spinning and Weaving: the deepest realm of the Underworld; here might be encountered Urðr, who eternally weaves the Web of Wyrd.

9 *ÁSGARÐR* – Realm of the Æsir and Asynjur, location of *Urðabrunnr*, the Well of Fate, which nourishes one of the roots of Yggdrasil: here might be encountered Frigg (who 'knows men's fates though she does not prophesy') and Óðinn seated on their thrones, from where they are able to look out over all the worlds. They give teaching concerning the laws of physics.

10 Return to the Land: at this point, the first stone can be reconsidered in the light of the entire pattern; and if appropriate, a tenth stone may be cast to indicate a process of regeneration in the Land.

Conclude the divination by bidding thanks to any beings contacted and by reaffirming the sacredness of the Cosmic Axis, the eight directions on the horizon and the Land. Return the rune-staves to their bag and extinguish the flame.

Viking runic inscription in Maeshowe, Orkney, made by 'that man most skilled in runecraft west over the sea' during the winter of 1151–2. The bottom row consists of kvistrūnir *(branch runes). The number of branches to the left of the upright indicates which of the three families the rune-sign belongs to; and the number of branches to the right tells us which rune-sign within the family is to be read.*

There are Ogams as well as Runes carved on this rune-stone. The rune-signs read: 'THÓRGRÍMR CARVED THIS CROSS'; *the Ogams read:* 'A BLESSING UPON THÓRGRÍMR.' *This is an example of a type of rune-stone where the talismanic potency is concentrated in the Runes forming the power-name (*THÓRGRÍMR*) of the magician who made the carving.*

EUROPE
AND
THE WEST

In the West the great civilizations of Greece,
Rome, Mesopotamia, Egypt and Babylon
developed their own divinatory systems, which
generally became more complex with the passage of time. Thus in the classical world a
number of state-funded oracles were established
at the great religious centres of Delphi, Delos,
Dodona and Rome; while in Mesopotamia the
study of the stars and planets evolved gradually
into the exact science we know today as
astrology. In Babylon, meanwhile, the study of
omens became increasingly sophisticated, with
vast collections of significant events recorded
and tabulated. At the same time, throughout the
classical world, extispicy, the study of entrails,
flourished (see Chapter Seven).

The melting pot of the Near East gave birth
to Tarot, a symbolic card game which grew to
be perhaps the quintessential divinatory system
of the West. And this in turn was influenced by
Cabbala, the Jewish mystical system which,
though it had nothing to do with foretelling the
future, did give rise to one such system, Galgal,
which is discussed in Chapter Eight.

In every case these were far more formalized
than the random casting of rune stones or Ogam
sticks, or the counting of bones and stones,
which developed into numerology and geomancy
on the one hand, whilst continuing to be used in
shamanistic fashion by grass-roots diviners of
the kind discussed in Chapter Nine, later in
this section.

Within all the complex divergences between
the main methods of Western divination, certain
common threads continue to emerge: the belief
that it was possible to enter into a state of being
in which one could communicate directly with
the spirit world (oracles); the belief that there
existed a store of wisdom deriving from most
ancient times, and which it was possible to tap
into through the study of complex symbols and
correspondences (Tarot, Galgal); and that the
movement of planets and the positions of
constellations at birth affected the lives of
everyone (astrology).

And still, while such systems as these became
ever more complex and refined, the practice of
the ancient shamanic techniques of divination –
the observance of natural events in the world
which surrounds us – continued largely unchanged and unabated. Village wise women
throughout the European world continued to
study the flights of birds, the lines in the palms
of hands, the embers of spent fires and all the
variations in the patterns of the weather, just as
today their descendants read patterns in tea-
leaves and the vague shapes that appear in the
cloudy depths of crystal balls.

In palace and court, as in village hut and
roadside, wizards, astrologers and fortune-tellers
delved ever deeper into the hidden secrets of
creation. Their methods were increasingly dis-
similar, but they still sought the same thing – to
find out what the future held in store.

THE KEYS OF TAROT

Divination by Cartomancy

Rachel Pollack

The Tarot is the classic divination system of Western European culture. Although more people know astrology, astrology originated in Asia, while, as far as we know, the Tarot began in Italy in the Renaissance. The Tarot's importance comes from more than its legendary accuracy as a tool of prophecy. Its symbolic pictures outline a deep spiritual teaching, and in recent decades Tarot readers and commentators have explored the Tarot as an almost infinite source of psychological understanding.

No one knows the exact origin of the Tarot, a problem that only adds to the mystery surrounding it. We do not even know the origin of the word. *Les Tarots* is the French name for a card game, an ancestor of bridge, known in Italy as *Tarocchi*. No information has come down to us as to why the game's players used those particular terms, although there is a Taro River in Northern Italy, not far from the Swiss border.

Many people have put forward theories of the Tarot's origin. These include Cabbala (see below), Egyptian initiation practices, Tantra (Indian esotericism), allegorical poems and processions, medieval Celtic traditions, underground Christian heresies, masters of Atlantis, Chaldean phases of the Moon, and so on. Most of these theories share a common assumption: that the Tarot contains so much coded wisdom it *must* originate in some ancient secret doctrine.

Historically, we know of the Tarot first as a card game. Cards of any kind first appeared in Europe in the fourteenth century, possibly brought by Crusaders from the Middle East. In the middle of the fifteenth century an artist named Bonifacio Bembo painted a set of Tarot cards as a wedding present for a marriage between the Sforza family and the Visconti family of Milano, Italy. One hundred and fifty years earlier, in 1300, Church officials burned to death one Maria Visconti, whom a sect of heretics had elected as the first woman pope. The classic Tarot contains a card titled the Female Pope.

The Renaissance was a time very given to allegories, spiritual development, alchemy and occult ideas (not unlike our own time). Whatever the Tarot's origins, the cards certainly contain allegorical images: Death, the Last Judgement, the Christian virtues of Temperance and Strength, the Wheel of Fortune, and so on.

When the Romanies ('Gypsies') came to Europe from North Africa they discovered the Tarot and began using it for fortune-telling.

Many people today still believe that the Romanies invented the Tarot, or that they brought it to Europe from Egypt. (The word 'Gypsy' derives from the mistaken belief that the Romanies, who in fact originated in India, come from Egypt.) Despite this early use in divination, the Tarot still existed primarily as a game. In fact, *Les Tarots* is still played today through much of Southern Europe and French-influenced Northern Africa.

In 1781 a man named Antoine Court de Gebelin made a startling pronouncement. In the course of a multi-volume study of occult teachings, Court de Gebelin claimed that he had discovered the 'book of Thoth', a legendary book of universal knowledge created by the Egyptian god Thoth for his magician disciples (according to Egyptian myth, Thoth was the inventor of magic and writing). This book did not lay buried in some secret library, but existed in plain view, as the game of Tarot. Inspired by Court de Gebelin, an occultist who called himself Etteila (his name, Aliette, spelled backwards) created a Tarot deck devoted to divination rather than game-playing.

In the mid-nineteenth century Eliphas Lévi (the occult name of Alphonse Louis Constant) extended Court de Gebelin's suggestions into a system. While continuing to use Egyptian images, Lévi linked the Tarot primarily to Cabbala (an idea first put forward by Court de Gebelin), a vastly complex Jewish system of mysticism, meditation, cosmogony, theosophy and magical practices. Originating in medieval Spain, Cabbala developed into the main structure of Christian as well as Jewish occultism in Europe.

The links between Cabbala and Tarot are certainly impressive. Cabbala derives from meditation on the 22 letters of the Hebrew alphabet (see Chapter Eight, Divination on the Tree of Life). The Tarot contains 22 trump cards. Cabbala teaches that God created the Cosmos in four steps, or 'worlds'. The Tarot contains four suits. Cabbala focuses on two primary images, the four-letter name of God in Hebrew, and the Tree of Life, with its ten

'Sephiroth', emanations of the light of God. The four suits of the Tarot each contain four 'court' cards, along with cards numbered from one to ten. No wonder Antoine Court de Gebelin and Eliphas Lévi considered the Tarot a systematic expression of Cabbalist wisdom. And yet, as far as we know, in all the thousands of pages of Cabbalist writing, no mention exists of anything like Tarot cards.

At the turn of the century an esoteric group named the Order of the Golden Dawn developed Lévi's ideas further. They linked the cards to magical rituals, and especially to astrology. The Order of the Golden Dawn existed for only a few years, but its influence continues today. Two of its members later designed the two most popular Tarot packs of the twentieth century. Arthur Edward Waite created the 'Rider' pack with painter Pamela Colman Smith. This pack has sold millions of copies world-wide. A great many contemporary Tarot creators base their pictures on Smith's drawings. Aleister Crowley designed *The Book of Thoth*, painted by Lady Frieda Harris. Although not as accessible as the Rider, Harris's elegant art and Crowley's dense symbolism have given this pack enormous influence.

The Tarot consists of two parts: the 22 trump cards, known as the Major Arcana (Arcana means secrets), and the four suits, collectively called the Minor Arcana. Traditionally, only the Major Arcana contained scenes and people. These are the allegorical images mentioned above. The Minor Arcana usually showed only the correct number of symbols from the particular suit. That is, the Ten of Cups would show ten cups arranged in a pattern, the Two of Swords depicted two crossed swords, and so on.

The Rider pack changed this, which is one reason for its great popularity. In Smith's paintings every card shows a scene. The Ten of Cups displays a family celebrating under a rainbow. The Two of Swords portrays a blindfolded woman holding a sword in each hand. This new begining – adopted by most contemporary decks – fundamentally changed

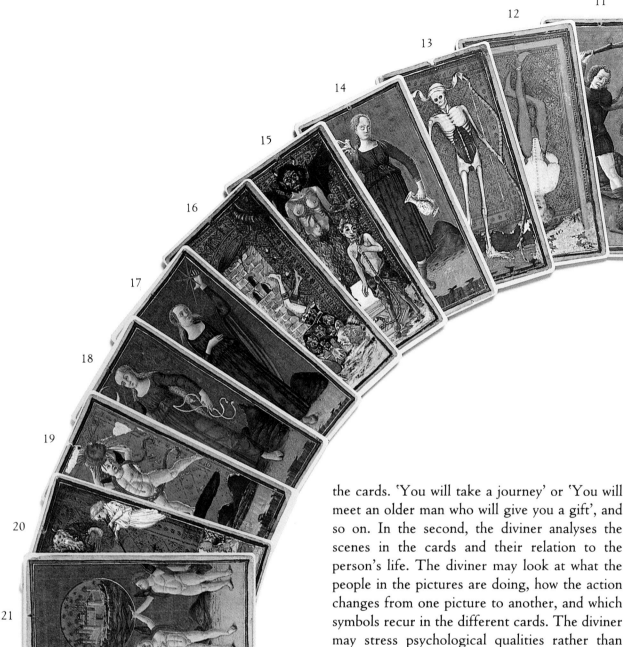

Tarot divination. Previously, the Minor cards carried formulaic interpretations, phrases like 'journey by water' or 'a message, hidden plans'. The Rider pack enabled diviners to interpret the events and actions shown in the pictures.

READING THE TAROT CARDS

There are three ways to divine with Tarot. The first involves memorizing the meanings (or looking them up) and applying them strictly to the cards. 'You will take a journey' or 'You will meet an older man who will give you a gift', and so on. In the second, the diviner analyses the scenes in the cards and their relation to the person's life. The diviner may look at what the people in the pictures are doing, how the action changes from one picture to another, and which symbols recur in the different cards. The diviner may stress psychological qualities rather than events. Finally, the 'psychic' approach involves giving no meanings at all to the cards, instead using them as triggers for internal revelations, for flashes of insight and knowledge. In practice, most modern readers combine elements of all these approaches. They will know a set of meanings for the cards, they will look carefully at the pictures and how they compare with each other, and they will allow understanding to come to them as they look at the images.

The modern approach to Tarot has brought together the spiritual and divinatory interpretations. Previously, those people who sought

The Bonifacio Bembo hand-painted Tarot cards of the Visconti-Sforza deck are among the oldest known in the world. We see the Major Arcana spread like a bridge of gold across the world. There are no numbers on these cards. The standard sequence, from the Fool, bottom right, to the World, bottom left, is first known on a French deck dated 100 years earlier.

wisdom in the pictures tended to spurn divination. Waite refers to the practice as 'a long insult'. Other books ignore divination entirely. Conversely, books on divination tended to give only the most cursory explanation of the cards' spiritual symbolism. Contemporary Tarot readers, however, try to apply the Tarot's spiritual lessons to interpretations in readings. In turn, the readings will lead to fresh understanding of the spiritual symbolism and how these symbols work in our daily lives. These spiritual lessons derived primarily from the Major Arcana.

The Major Arcana are shown here in their generally agreed order:

0 The Fool (some place this card at the end, or between 20 and 21)
1 The Magician, also called the Juggler
2 The High Priestess, also called the Female Pope
3 The Empress
4 The Emperor
5 The Hierophant, also called the Pope
6 The Lovers
7 The Chariot
8 Justice (in some modern decks Strength is 8 and Justice is 11)
9 The Hermit
10 The Wheel of Fortune
11 Strength
12 The Hanged Man
13 Death
14 Temperance
15 The Devil
16 The Tower
17 The Star
18 The Moon
19 The Sun
20 Judgement
21 The World

In general, most commentators agree that the Major Arcana depicts the soul in its journey from birth to enlightenment. Arguments centre on the specific stages of the journey, and on the particular doctrine – Cabbala, Egyptian, Celtic, etc. – outlined in the symbolism. For instance, many people have described the Magician as 'the male principle' and the High Priestess as 'the female'. But just what do these terms mean? Are they simply light and darkness, or the positive and negative poles of electromagnetism? Do they describe actual men and women? And is the Magician derived from the Egyptian god Thoth, and the High Priestess from the goddess Isis? Or do they symbolize the first two connecting pathways on the Cabbalist Tree of Life (or the

The Rider pack has become the world's most popular Tarot. Here it is shown in a simple, four-card spread. The four can be the four elements, or the four seasons of the year.

second and third, if the Fool signifies the first)? Or do they portray roles human beings can play, such as a ritual magician and the priestess of an occult order? Or perhaps modern descendants of tribal shamans and diviners? The Tarot gains much of its power from the fact that all of these interpretations exist simultaneously.

Unlike the *I Ching*, the Tarot images bear no official text. Even the names and numbers of the cards apparently developed some time after the earliest known paintings. The lack of an orthodox doctrine allows us to accept the accumulated wisdom of past interpretations while opening us to fresh possibilities each time we look at the pictures. And even though the cards now come in a specific order we can change that order simply by shuffling the pack. New juxtapositions open the way to new ideas.

The Minor Arcana consists of four suits of 14 cards each: Ace–10, plus the four 'Court' cards, Page, Knight, Queen, and King. The names of the suits have changed over the years. Most common are:

Wands, also called Staves, Rods, etc.
Cups
Swords
Pentacles, called Coins in earlier packs

Traditionally, Tarot commentators have paid more attention to the Major Arcana than the Minor. Most modern interpreters link the Minor suits to the four 'elements' of medieval philosophy and modern astrology. These elements are fire, water, air and earth. Some arguments exist over which suits belong to which elements. The most common attribution runs Wands=Fire, Cups=Water, Swords=Air, Pentacles=Earth. Some contemporary decks have renamed the suits in line with the elements, for example, Stones instead of Pentacles, Flames instead of Wands.

Divining with Tarot involves 'reading' the cards. Some people do this by turning over cards at random and seeing what inspiration rises from them. Most, however, lay the cards down in specific patterns, known as 'spreads', or 'lay-outs'. Hundreds of these spreads exist. Some serve particular purposes, for instance a 'year

The Tarot de Marseilles has become the classic Tarot. We see them here in a 12-card spread with several possible interpretations. We can see each card as representing one month of the coming year, for example. Alternatively, we can interpret them within the context of the 12 houses of the Zodiac.

spread' to look at issues likely to arise in the coming 12 months. Or various relationship spreads targeted to the particular problems and issues of romantic involvements. Or spreads to help people understand and recover from alcoholism and other special problems. Some spreads derive from particular shapes: a spread in the form of a six-pointed star, or a spread outlining a human body (with the 'brain' card showing what a person thinks, the 'heart' card what the person feels, and so on).

Whatever the spread, the principle remains simple. Each position in the spread carries its own meaning, such as 'past influences', 'unconscious desires', and so on. Since each card bears a meaning as well, the interpretation combines the card and the position. For example, the Five

TAROT READING USING THE CELTIC CROSS SPREAD

Question: The querent, a woman, has the possibility of a new relationship. What is the best way to react? Deck used: the Rider pack.

1 Central issue: the Fool. This indicates the person's desire to leap into this new relationship. She has an impulsive quality and an openness, which may lead to love but which also may get her in trouble.

2 Crossing influence: 4 of Swords. This card shows a counter desire to the Fool. The querent has been hurt in the past and feels a need to heal. Having such a clear conflict between this card and the Fool has led to her indecision.

5

4

0   1
2

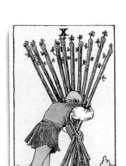

THE FOOL .

THE STAR .

6

6 Approaching influence: Star. This continues the theme of liberation. The person will experience a renewed optimism. She will stop holding back and will express herself very openly.

7 Self: 2 of Cups. She is ready for a genuine commitment with an equal partner.

8 Others: Page of Wands. The traditional meanings for this card include a faithful lover. It therefore indicates that the other person can be trusted and is eager for this relationship. The card is a good match for the Fool.

 10

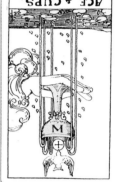 9

 8

3 Basis (influence of the past): Lovers reversed. This indicates a love relationship that went badly and is the cause of the hesitation.

4 Recent developments: 8 of Swords reversed. The reversed card says that this woman has begun to free herself emotionally from the damaging effects of the past relationship. This card and the Fool together indicate a liberation and a chance for a new beginning.

5 Possible developments: 10 of Wands. The 10 suggests the person has a tendency to take on herself all the burdens of maintaining a relationship. She will have to be aware of this attitude to make the new relationship work.

THE LOVERS.

3

PAGE of WANDS.

II   7

9 Hopes and fears: Ace of Cups reversed. The Ace is the gift of love and happiness. Reversed, it says the person fears the relationship will turn out badly, and that love will be an illusory hope. This fear is what holds her back. The reading is telling her it comes from past hurts, and not from the actual situation.

10 Outcome: 7 of Wands reversed. The card advises the woman to take action. Along with the cards which have come before (such as the 8 of Swords, the Star and the Page of Wands), it tells her that love is not an illusion and she can follow her feelings with confidence.

of Cups usually signifies loss. In 'past influences' the card would indicate a previous loss which still affects the person's life. In 'future events' the same card would show the possibility of facing such a loss in the coming time. And in 'influences of others' it might show someone else suffering from a loss.

Some Tarot commentators and teachers recommend various rituals for reading the cards. These might include ways to hold them, phrases to say while mixing them or laying them out, and so on. However, the basic procedure remains simple. The 'querent' (the person seeking the reading) mixes the cards. Often, they will end the shuffle by separating the pack into three piles. The reader then lays out the cards in the particular spread. Turning each card face up, the reader interprets their meanings in the light of whatever questions the querent has brought to the reading.

The power of the reading lies first of all in the reader's ability to see and communicate the message shown in the cards and their combinations. Secondly – and perhaps more importantly – the power lies in the querent's response to the pictures.

In traditional fortune-telling the querent said very little. The reader was supposed to discover hidden knowledge and predict future events. Many Tarot readers still follow this approach, and many people who go for a Tarot reading expect such revelations. However, in the past few decades the emphasis has shifted to self-knowledge for the querent, and the possibility of using the Tarot as inspiration for positive change. In such a model, the reader first seeks to help the querent understand the issues involved in the situation, and then to make good choices and act on them. Of course, this method still requires the reader to trust that the cards will reveal truths not apparent on the surface. The difference is a matter of emphasis. For instance, if a querent asks 'Will my husband remain faithful to me?' the reader may avoid making a prediction and instead help the querent to look more closely at the problems in her marriage, at the reasons for her worry or insecurity.

As a result of these shifts many readers involve the querent much more directly in the choice of an appropriate spread and the interpretation of the cards. Some readers do not use any standard spread patterns, but will make up a spread on the spot based on the querent's issues and questions. When interpreting the cards, the reader will still explain the symbolism and rely on her or his own intuition as to the meanings. But she or he also may ask the querent, 'What does this picture say to you?' or 'Does this scene remind you of something you've experienced in your own life?' The reader will then take the querent's responses, combine them with the traditional meanings and the reader's own inspirations, and finally help the querent understand the possibilities and choices arising out of the reading as a whole. Some readers will end the reading with a meditation on a particular card, or by asking such questions as 'Which card symbolizes for you what you want to achieve in this situation?' In these ways, the reader attempts to take the reading beyond predictions. The cards and their symbolism become tools for the querent to gain more control of her or his life.

The Tarot is not only the most developed and complex of Western divinatory systems, it is also the most dynamic. New Tarot packs appear constantly, and many of these have taken the Tarot – and Tarot divination – in new directions (see the Appendix, Modern Restatements). For example, a number of new packs adapt the traditional Tarot pictures to a particular cultural context. These include a Native American Tarot, a Norse Tarot, an Aztec Tarot, and so on. Divination with these cards involves the reader with the concepts and traditions of those cultures.

Readers also have found new ways to use existing packs. These include dream interpretation, psychodrama, fiction writing, even musical composition through divination (the process involves assigning a note to each card, and then choosing cards at random). Whatever the Tarot's origins, it has evolved into a powerful tool for knowledge and inspiration.

CHAPTER SIX

SHAPES IN THE STARS

Patterns of Western Astrology

Prudence Jones

Astrology is a method of correlating events on earth with the positions of the planets in the heavens, in order to explain the significance of these events and to predict future ones. Astrologers think that earthly events are timed by the cycles of the celestial bodies, and that each of these celestial bodies – the Sun, Moon, planets and other phenomena such as asteroids and comets – is associated with a particular kind of event or situation. The planet Mars, for example, is connected with matters of initiative, pugnacity, breakages and disruption, with social groups such as gangs of young men, and with engineers, surgeons and soldiers. The two-year cycle of its apparent path around the Earth coincides, interestingly enough, with the standard length of posting in the armed forces in the UK. Such curious coincidences are the routine stuff of the astrologer's trade, and the skill of astrology lies not only in predicting when such coincidences are likely to happen, but in explaining why an apparently random, meaningless event was (or will be) in fact meaningful and able to serve the greater wisdom and understanding of those whom it involves.

Astrology is a unique mixture of precise scientific method (observation, measurement, prediction and verification or falsification) and the religious, magical or (more politely) 'synchronistic' outlook used in the other divinatory arts. Astrologers do not simply attempt to correlate events on Earth with the cycles of the celestial bodies, as applied astronomers do (for example in meteorology). They also assume that each moment, particularly the 'birth' moment of

any entity, from a human being to a building to a political party, has a potentially fated quality which will fix the nature of that entity for the rest of its lifetime. Certain moments are seen as intrinsically powerful, whether they correspond with a 'birth' or not, in particular the times of eclipses, solstices and equinoxes.

AN ANCIENT ART

Most ancient cultures used a certain amount of applied astronomy in order to regulate their calendars, from the simple observation of the lunar cycle and the seasonal variation in the sunrise point on the local horizon, to the more elaborate calculation of the solstices, the equinoxes and the true solar year (exactly 365 days, 6 hours, 9 minutes and 9.5 seconds). Many ancient cultures also included some method of interpreting celestial events such as eclipses, which were thought to be omens – direct communications from the divine powers to those who could interpret them. Modern Western astrology, however, descends directly from just one of these cultures: the celestial omen-lore of ancient Mesopotamia.

The Mesopotamians – the Sumerians, Akkadians, Babylonians and Assyrians who lived in what is now Iraq, the land between the rivers Euphrates and Tigris – were assiduous inter-

This cuneiform tablet is one of the early Babylonian records of celestial omens. It was carved in the reign of King Ammisaduqa, c. 1700 BC, and records observations of the planet Venus. Hundreds of such astronomical records have been preserved in stone.

preters of omens. Hundreds of clay tablets, inscribed between the nineteenth and first centuries BC, have come down to us, recording the observation and interpretation of various classes of omen. These omens included the shapes formed by molten lead when poured into cold water, the pattern of veins on the liver of a sacrificed animal (see Chapter Eight, Consulting the Oracles) and, relevantly for our purposes here, the appearance of the stars, eclipses and planets in the night sky. Here is one of the celestial omens:

> *There will be an eclipse which is evil for Elam, Aharou, lucky for the king my lord, rest happy. It will be seen without Venus, to the king my lord I say there will be an eclipse.* (Translation by Dorothea Wender.)

Although celestial omens were recorded by reference to their position in the night sky, for example 'in the east' or 'against the constellation of the Fishes', there is no evidence that regular cycles of occurrence were taken into account. Each omen seems to have been interpreted individually, like tea-leaves in a teacup, rather than being seen as a particular instance of a regularly occurring natural cycle, as it is in astrology proper.

SCIENTIFIC METHOD AND THE EMERGENCE OF WESTERN ASTROLOGY

What turned Babylonian omen-reading into astrology was its increasing association with scientific method. A curiosity about the existence of mechanical processes which unfold according to intrinsic rational laws, independently of the whims of personal choice, whether divine or human, seems to have grown in the eastern Mediterranean during the last 800 years BC. The Greeks are its most famous exponents, but in Mesopotamia as well we see empirical method developing, with the so-called Astronomical Diaries beginning in the mid-seventh century BC. The 18.6-year eclipse cycle was calculated with some exactitude by scholars in Athens and in Babylon, and it was a Greek, Euktemon, who first identified the solstice and equinox points at about the same time (the mid-fifth century), thus creating a framework of observation within which an exact solar calendar could be drawn up. This framework of observation, known as the ecliptic, or Sun's annual path against the constellations as seen from Earth, is also the framework of modern astrology.

The earlier celestial observations, whether for omen-reading or for calculation of the seasons, had been located in the sphere of the local observer, the set of orientations based on the four compass points which surrounds a person looking at the heavens from anywhere on Earth.

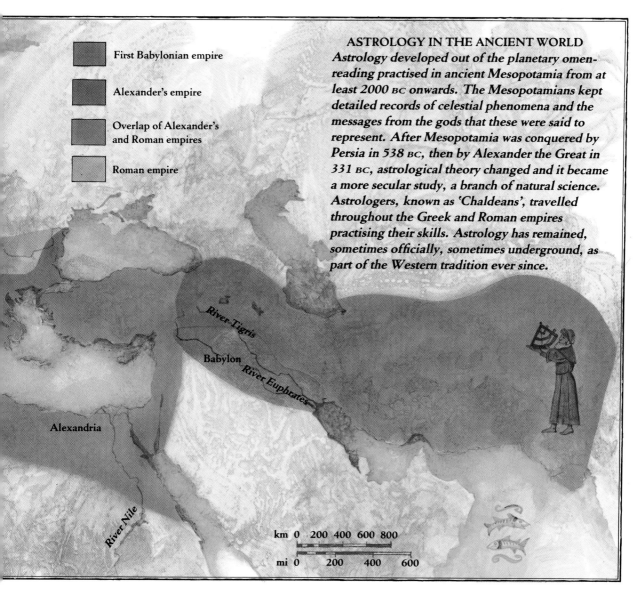

ASTROLOGY IN THE ANCIENT WORLD

Astrology developed out of the planetary omen-reading practised in ancient Mesopotamia from at least 2000 BC onwards. The Mesopotamians kept detailed records of celestial phenomena and the messages from the gods that these were said to represent. After Mesopotamia was conquered by Persia in 538 BC, then by Alexander the Great in 331 BC, astrological theory changed and it became a more secular study, a branch of natural science. Astrologers, known as 'Chaldeans', travelled throughout the Greek and Roman empires practising their skills. Astrology has remained, sometimes officially, sometimes underground, as part of the Western tradition ever since.

First Babylonian empire

Alexander's empire

Overlap of Alexander's and Roman empires

Roman empire

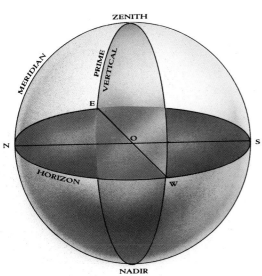

The six spatial co-ordinates of any location on Earth (the four compass directions, above and below) are the earliest framework for locating celestial phenomena. This is the observer's sphere. The earliest Babylonian omen text, apparently foretelling the destruction of Ur by Enneatum in 2400 BC, tells the king: 'You shall look to the South and observe the eclipse.' Much later, in about 750 BC, the poet Hesiod times the seasons in this way:

When Orion and the Dog Star move
Into the mid-sky, and Arcturus sees
The rosy-fingered Dawn, then Perses, pluck
The clustered grapes, and bring your harvest home.

With the discovery that the Sun's path (the ecliptic) is inclined to the Earth's equator at about 23½°, the Greeks were able to identify the constellations which marked its highest and lowest points (the two solstice signs, Cancer and Capricorn), and the points where it cuts the equator in the spring and autumn (the equinoxes, Aries and Libra). These four, together with the celestial pole and its opposite point in the southern sky, allowed planets to be located against the fixed co-ordinates of celestial space, not simply against individual constellations in the local sphere of observation.

With the mapping of the ecliptic onto the fixed points of the solstices and equinoxes, what is called the celestial sphere could be calculated. Planets could be located in the celestial sphere, i.e. relative to the solstice and equinox points, rather than simply relative to the local sphere of the four compass directions, zenith (the point directly above the observer at right angles to the horizon) and nadir (the point directly below). The way that this was done was simply by dividing up the Sun's annual path into 12 × 30° sectors, calculated originally from the point of the summer solstice, but later, as is still the case today, from the spring equinox. The 30° arc following the spring equinox was called after the constellation which occupied it at the time, i.e. Aries, the Ram, the next arc was called after the next constellation, Taurus, the Bull, and so on.

This system of dividing the Sun's annual path into 12 sectors, which also defined the 12 months of the original solar calendar, was developed at the same time that the solstice and equinox points were located in the sky. Because of what is known as the precession of the equinoxes, i.e. the slow wobble of the earth's axis over about 26,000 years, the signs of the Zodiac, the 30° arcs beginning with the spring equinox point, no longer coincide with the constellations after which they were named. When early astrologers referred to a particular sign, such as the sign of the Fishes (Pisces), sometimes they meant the constellation called the Fishes, sometimes (as nowadays) the 12th 30° arc of the ecliptic following the equinox. Until the Greek astrologer Ptolemy, writing in the first century AD, decided in favour of the latter, astrologers' usage was variable. Nowadays, however, Western astrology follows the so-called 'tropical' pattern, with the signs measured from the 'tropics' or seasonal turning-points marked by the solstices and equinoxes, whereas astrology in India locates the planets by reference to the actual constellations (see Chapter Eighteen, Star Lore in the East).

After the fall of the Roman Empire, leading theologians in the Church, which had continued the Imperial plan of dominating Europe through a universal civilization, unfortunately condemned the predictive aspect of astrology. The art went into decline for many years in Christian Europe, being pursued almost entirely outside Christendom by the Arabs and the Jews. Then, when the Christians clashed with the Arabs in eighth-century Spain, the emperor Charlemagne took up the study of astrology himself, as well as employing a full-time astrologer. Astrology remained among the regular political resources of the crowned heads of Europe, although periodically debated and restricted by the Church, until after the Reformation, when it slowly fell into disrepute in mainland Europe,

not being revived until the Theosophical Movement of the 1880s. Strangely enough, the years following the Reformation were the time when astrology began to be popular (as opposed to élitist) in Britain. Astrologers were busy dealing with personal queries and with political predictions throughout the seventeenth century, and during the Age of Reason in the following two centuries astrology retained near-respectability among the common people, with regular sales of almanacs, textbooks and even magazines.

Astrology remains popular in the West today, particularly in the simplified fortune-telling form of the 'Sun-sign' column, but also among a growing number of people who are looking for a more elaborate philosophy to explain their place in the universe. Like the Hindu and Buddhist systems of thought, which have also been adopted by Westerners (and which themselves accept astrology's validity), astrology satisfies both the age-old need for philosophical explanation and the modern demand for scientific justification. It is, however, shunned by both the religious and the scientific Establishments, being too fatalistic for Christians and for atheists alike, and being (so far) insufficiently validated to satisfy the scientific community. Astrology challenges the cruder forms of Western belief in absolute individual self-determination, but as yet it has not found a language that will allow it to be incorporated into mainstream Western thought. It therefore remains part of a lively and articulate subculture.

ASTROLOGICAL INTERPRETATION

A horoscope is an accurate diagram of the positions of the Sun, Moon, the planets Mercury, Venus, Mars, Jupiter, Saturn, Uranus, Neptune and Pluto, located by reference to the ecliptic (the Sun's annual path against the constellations as seen from Earth) as this intersects the local sphere of the observer.

The basics of astrology are summarized in beginners' textbooks. Their synthesis into a chart reading demands skill and experience, and astrological theory is constantly being modified through feedback from practitioners.

THE PLANETS

These celestial bodies are the motive forces of the horoscope, the people, groups, forces, drives and emotions that make things happen in our everyday world. They were originally seen by the Babylonians as deities, and are named after these deities in their Roman form. Each has a particular symbol that represents it in the horoscope diagram.

SUN ☉	Genuineness, authenticity, nobility. Ostentation and magnificence. The monarch, presiding authority.
MOON ☽	Instincts, reactions, needs. Mothers, brewers, those who work by the sea. Populism. The general public.
MERCURY ☿	Observation, communication, skilful knowledge or action. Letters, telephone calls, short journeys, cars. Solicitors, broadcasters, journalists, statisticians, small businesses.
VENUS ♀	Attractiveness, beauty, victory, attainment, love. Purses, cash in hand. Jewels, works of art, young women. Sculptors, painters, singers, dancers.
MARS ♂	Pugnacity, vigour, initiative, courage. Competitiveness. Iron, weapons, young men. The armed forces, surgeons, butchers, engineers.
JUPITER ♃	Magnanimity, generosity, aspirations and success. Judges, teachers, ecclesiastics, merchants and foreign travellers. Large gentle animals. The legal establishment, educated or informed opinion.
SATURN ♄	Sternness, inflexibility, limitations. Lead, deserts, bones and borders. Old men, farm labourers, beggars, hermits. Hierarchies, control mechanisms.
URANUS ♅	Genius, inventiveness, disruption. Electricity and computer technology. Space technology, aircraft. Revolutionaries, inventors, earthquakes.
NEPTUNE ♆	Compassion, idealism, merging and dissolution. The ocean, mist, pharmaceuticals. Musicians, dancers, the fine arts. Visionaries, alcoholics, dependent and helpless people. Socialism.
PLUTO ♇	Hidden power, transformation, destruction and regeneration. Biological imperatives. The underworld, miners, sewage workers, criminals. Surgeons and psychiatrists. Big business.

THE HOUSES

These are divisions of the local sphere of the observer (see the diagram on page 57), in which both planets and signs are located. They are usually shown on the horoscope diagram as sectors of the circle. There are many ways of dividing up the local sphere, and their relative merits are a subject of increasing debate. Four constant points are important: the ascendant, the point where the ecliptic cuts the horizon in the east; the descendant, its opposite point in the west; the midheaven, or MC, the highest point of the ecliptic (which in northern hemisphere charts is usually high in the southern sky); and its opposite point, the lower midheaven or IC, the lowest point of the ecliptic. These points and the 12 spaces between them (in most systems of division), which are the houses, identify the area of life within which the signs and planets are active.

FIRST HOUSE	Beginnings, physical appearance, self-interest.
SECOND HOUSE	Possessions, resources, values.
THIRD HOUSE	Neighbourhood, siblings, all communications and local travel.
FOURTH HOUSE	Home, origins, land. Father, ancestors. Unconscious resources, buried treasure.
FIFTH HOUSE	Creativity, children, recreation, pleasures, play. The arts.
SIXTH HOUSE	Health and illness, routine and maintenance activities including work. Workers, carers.
SEVENTH HOUSE	Partnership or enmity. The opposite of self: spouse or partner, and enemies.
EIGHTH HOUSE	Shared resources. Other people's values. Loans and credit. Taxes. Letting go of pure self-interest.
NINTH HOUSE	International communication. Philosophy, dreams and visions. Lawyers, ecclesiastics.
TENTH HOUSE	Prestige and standing in the community. Career. Authority and responsibilities. People in charge.
ELEVENTH HOUSE	Ideals, hopes, hobbies, friends. Legislative assemblies.
TWELFTH HOUSE	Unconscious impulses, hidden enemies, solitude, sleep and meditation. Institutions and confinement.

THE SIGNS

The signs are divisions of the celestial sphere: 30° divisions of the ecliptic, beginning from the spring equinox point. They add information about the nature of the houses and the planets in them. Thus, for example, the planet Jupiter in the sign Aries in the fifth house indicates success and the expansion of understanding (Jupiter) through a vigorous, enterprising attitude (Aries) to creativity or recreation (fifth house).

ARIES	♈	With initiative, aggressively, impulsively.
TAURUS	♉	Steadily, thoroughly, with gusto.
GEMINI	♊	Rapidly, skilfully, with versatility.
CANCER	♋	Emotively, protectively, with feeling.
LEO	♌	Magnificently, with style, in an overbearing manner.
VIRGO	♍	Prudently, with an eye to detail.
LIBRA	♎	Elegantly, fairly, rationally.
SCORPIO	♏	Intensely, passionately, with secrecy.
SAGITTARIUS	♐	Magnanimously, idealistically, without animosity.
CAPRICORN	♑	Methodically, with determination, authoritatively.
AQUARIUS	♒	Objectively, democratically, through communication.
PISCES	♓	Vaguely, passively, with sensitivity.

THE ASPECTS

The angular relationships between the planets, as seen from Earth, describe the interaction of the forces which the planets represent. When two planets are in roughly the same place in the sky ('conjunction'), their forces are said to merge; for example, Moon conjunct Mars gives a militant attitude to mothering, or perhaps a nurturing attitude to initiative. Planets separated by 90° ('square') frustrate each other's influence, planets 120° apart ('trine') work smoothly and effortlessly together, and planets opposite each other in the Zodiac are expressed through contrast, whether by enmity or by partnership and co-operation.

APPLICATIONS OF ASTROLOGY

NATAL HOROSCOPES

The bulk of a modern astrologer's work is concerned with personal horoscopes for individuals. The natal chart, i.e. the horoscope for the moment of birth, tells the astrologer what sort of person he or she is dealing with, with what talents, what liabilities, what characteristic relationships and life situations. Then, by calculating the movements of the planets as they leave their natal positions, the astrologer can also see how this natal potential unfolds, and in particular on what dates certain aspects of the natal blueprint will be emphasized (the predictive side of astrology). Whether these developments of the natal pattern manifest in the person's life as a change of outlook, a change of friends or situation, or as a seemingly external 'accident', the astrologer cannot say. For most astrologers, the so-called 'outside' world is simply a reflection of the so-called 'inner' world. Both are manifestations of the unfolding of the cosmic pattern, which is measured by the cycles of the stars and planets and a phase of which is embodied in each individual's natal chart.

HORARY CHARTS

Astrology can be used in a more specifically divinatory way, to answer questions such as 'Where are my lost keys?' The horoscope is cast for the moment of asking the question, and the position of the planets and signs are interpreted according to the highly specific rules of horary, in much the same way as the yarrow stalks or coins of the *I Ching* are read. The expression 'to cast a horoscope' is derived from the medieval method of determining some kind of ascendant, in the days before regular tables were available, by casting stones, the resulting geomantic figures each being taken to represent a particular part of the Zodiac. The bulk of astrologers' work in the English astrological renaissance of the seventeenth century (by which time accurate ascendants were generally calculated) seems to have been horary, and this technique was revived in the early 1980s.

MUNDANE ASTROLOGY

The astrology of the 'mundus', the physical world ruled by science and mass psychology, is usually contrasted with that of the psyche, the individual soul, which is generally considered to have at least some free will and moral responsibility. In modern terms, mundane astrology is concerned with the collective, with groups and organizations, particularly with nations, empires and other political groupings. Nations and organizations have natal horoscopes just as individuals do, and these can be analysed by the same techniques. In addition, eclipses, solstice and equinox horoscopes, and the cycles of the planets through the signs and relative to each other can be interpreted as giving what we would nowadays call a psychological climate to the times. The study of mundane astrology received a boost in the 1980s as the availability of computer technology has made the rapid analysis of horoscopes possible.

EVENT CHARTS

A horoscope for the occurrence of a particular event, whether a physical one such as an earthquake, or a mental one such as an inspiration or discovery, will show the astrological factors operating in that place at that time. For instance, the horoscope for the bombing of the conference of Britain's ruling Conservative Party in October 1984 shows a conjunction of Mars and Jupiter – someone taking the law into their own hands. Such astrological factors are nowadays interpreted as the unconscious forces of mass psychology, which become embodied in pressure groups as well as in the personal psychology of charismatic leaders. The analysis of event charts gives a useful insight into the hidden background of the events, and can help people to deal skilfully and accurately with their effects. In particular, the chart for the time when a person falls ill and takes to their bed ('decumbiture') has traditionally been used to diagnose and predict the course of an illness. The use of decumbiture charts for medical diagnosis is, however, restricted by law in many Western countries today.

ELECTIONAL ASTROLOGY

Because the natal chart describes the nature of an entity for the whole of its life, astrologers have often been asked to choose, or 'elect', the most favourable possible time to begin an enterprise, found a company – or even to time conception or induce a birth. The most famous example of a (probable) election is that for the Royal Observatory at Greenwich, drawn up by the Astronomer Royal, Flamsteed, in 1675. More recently, in the USA, the astrologer Joan Quigley elected the times for various meetings, journeys, signings, etc., on which the course of President Reagan's presidency hung. The success of her endeavours is obvious: Ronald Reagan stayed in office for the maximum two terms, remained hugely popular throughout, presided over *détente* with the Soviet Union, and successfully disproved allegations similar to those that had plunged Richard Nixon into utter disgrace. Despite this recent example of the art, the theory of electional astrology has not been developed in any detail during the twentieth century.

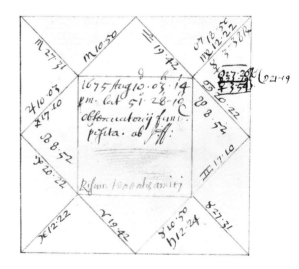

This horoscope was drawn up (in the square format of the times, now replaced by circular diagrams) by the first Astronomer Royal, John Flamsteed. It records the moment when the Royal Observatory's foundation stone was laid: 10 August 1675, 3.14 p.m. Was the time chosen deliberately, or was the horoscope merely done on impulse? Flamsteed's comment, 'May this keep you laughing, my friends', is ambiguous, just as we might expect from serious Saturn in the horoscope's fifth house of games and pleasantries.

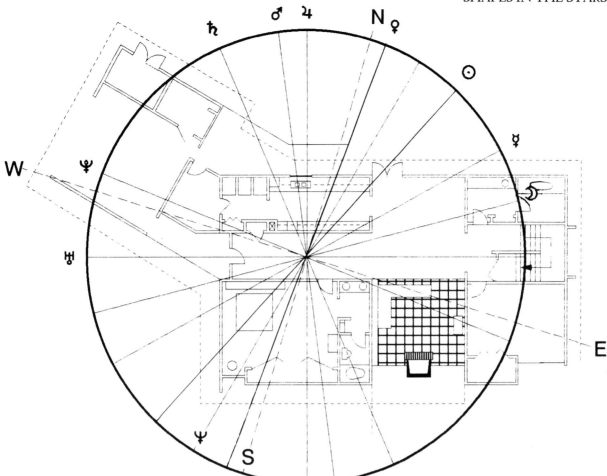

LOCAL SPACE ASTROLOGY

This is an ancient branch of astrology, familiar in China as an aspect of Feng Shui (see Chapter Seventeen, Dragon Lines in the Land), which has become available again through computer technology. The horoscope diagram normally locates planets on the plane of the ecliptic, but the local space chart shows where the perpendiculars of the planets' altitudes cut the local horizon. The local space derivative of the natal horoscope, for example, gives its owner a set of expectations about any place where they live. Energy, strenuousness and strife lie on the Mars line, and the person who wants excitement should go in that direction from their present home in order to find it. One person was amazed to find that her Mars line led directly to the port where she was called up for her annual military service. Within the home, the various activities of life are best located according to their lines of planetary rulership, or, as Ben Jonson's Abel Drugger put it:

Here the circular map of the local horizon, with azimuths showing the sighting lines to and from the planets in a natal horoscope, is superimposed on a floor plan of the horoscope owner's house. Notice the Moon line going through the kitchen, an ideal location for it, and the Uranus line going through the staircase. This is less suitable: light bulbs in the hall and on the stairs will probably have a short life, and the stairwell might behave as a natural lightning conductor for as long as the owner of that particular horoscope lives in the house.

I would know by art, sir, of your worship,
Which way I should make my door, by necro-
mancy,
And where my shelves, and which should be for
boxes,
And which for pots. I would be glad to thrive, sir,
And I was wished to your worship by a gentleman
. . . that says you know men's planets.

This ancient application of astrology has been brought up to date by modern researchers since the 1970s, but is as yet little used in routine practice.

ASTRO*CARTO*GRAPHY

By contrast, a different application of astrology to the landscape, made possible only through accurate geographical surveying and easily accessible computer mathematics, has become widely used over the last 15 years. The Astro*Carto*Graphy map is a two-dimensional summary of all possible local observation spheres (see the diagram of the observer's sphere). It shows all the places on Earth where, for example, the planet Jupiter was seen at the midheaven at the time of the chart owner's birth, the places where it would therefore be easy for them to make a career (midheaven) as a teacher, entrepreneur or ecclesiastic (Jupiter). In places where, by contrast, Uranus was rising, the person would appear to others as an erratic, eccentric, probably brilliant individual who would disrupt any situation they came into. Astro*Carto*Graphy thus makes it easy for people to choose (or at least to know) the astrological effect of their new location when they move house.

The technique is also used in mundane astrology to locate the prevailing astrological influences at each seasonal ingress (solstice or equinox). It gives mundane astrologers an idea of what kind of events to expect in the different areas of the world. For example, the winter solstice A*C*G chart for 1978, forecasting the year 1979, showed Venus, the planet which traditionally rules Islam, and Uranus, the planet of revolution, at the midheaven in Iran. It was, of course, during the following 12 months that the Shah was deposed and an Islamic republic took his place.

At the exact moment of the winter solstice, 1978, certain locations on Earth saw one or more of the 10 planets either rising, culminating, setting, or at inverse culmination. This map displays those locations, with rising and setting planets identified by 'R' and 'S' against their glyphs (at the end of the curved lines), planets at upper and lower culmination noted at the top and bottom respectively of their straight lines. Hence, for example, a person born at the exact moment of the winter solstice 1978 in southern Mexico, with the sensitive, impressionable Moon rising, would lay themselves open to some abrasive experiences by relocating to western Scotland, which would put flinty, no-nonsense Saturn at the midheaven point which describes authority figures. Note the culminating position of Venus and Uranus in Iran, analysed in the text.

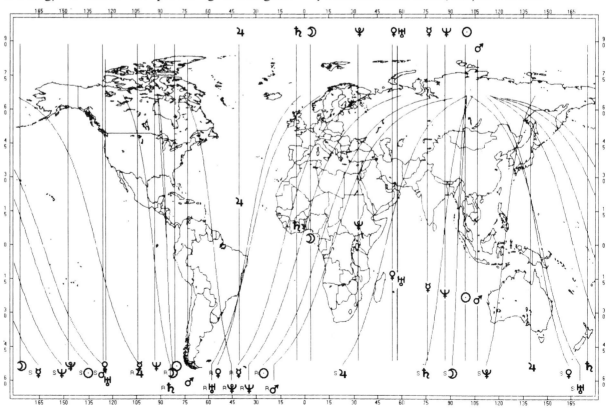

CONSULTING THE ORACLES

The Classic Systems of Greece and Rome

Robert Temple

When we think of ancient Greece and Rome we tend to think of the great classical philosophers such as Plato and Aristotle, the supremacy of the intellect and the rule of reason. It is not generally realized that divination was an important part of classical life and was practised on a daily basis. We could even go so far as to say that the whole of classical civilization was based on divination as the foundation of all its actions. No major decision of state, such as going to war, was made without consulting the gods through divination. Few personal undertakings, such as financial investment, getting married or making a journey, were embarked upon without divination. Even the great Socrates consulted the oracle at Delphi.

The classical civilizations had many forms of divination which they used constantly: divination by lightning, by the flights of birds (augury), by the chance words uttered by idiots or passers-by (cledonism), by thunderbolts, by the manner in which chickens pecked at corn, and so on. Divination by lightning and augury by the flights of birds were both very complex systems. The sky was generally divided up into 16 sections: if birds flew from one section to another, that signified one thing; if they then flew from that section to another, it meant something else, and so on. The same applied to streaks of lightning. There were 'textbooks' to consult so that people could look these things up. In a surviving ancient Greek dream book by Artemidorus, there are hundreds of different dreams listed alongside their prophetic meanings.

Inferior forms of divination, lacking in official sanction and prestige, were practised by wandering fortune-tellers. Farmers had much folklore about what they called 'omens', namely calves born with two heads or even children with webbed fingers, all of which portended various sorts of coming events and disasters. Other methods included an early form of roulette, which was connected with the oracle at Delphi and gave answers to enquiries rather than winners in a gambling game; both lots and dice were also used to consult the future. The Greeks were keen on an early form of crystal-gazing, whereby maidens gazed into pools of water or bowls of liquid and sought visions of the future. The Babylonians had voluminous Omen Books, many fragments of which survive, and much of

Greek terracotta from South Italy, c. 480 BC. A diviner is about to remove the entrails from a sacrificial pig in order to consult the future.

that lore entered into folk wisdom, which probably survives in peasant societies today. There is certainly a very strong tradition in modern Greece among the country folk about fairies, the evil eye and prophecy.

EXTISPICY: AN EXAMINATION OF ENTRAILS

It is often assumed that the main divination system of the Greeks and Romans, as well as of the Assyrians and Babylonians, was astrology. But in fact astrology was a very late technique, and it can be said without the slightest doubt that the main divination system of the classical cultures was extispicy, which is divination by the entrails of sacrificial animals.

Extispicy was a mania with the Greeks, Romans and Etruscans. Of the last, Cicero, who was himself an official Roman augur, said in his book *On Divination*: 'the whole Etruscan nation has gone stark mad on the subject of entrails.' The animal that was sacrificed was usually a lamb, although occasionally oxen were used, especially by the Romans.

Extispicy was in fact the main divination system of Western man for many thousands of years, and because of its remote origins in Stone Age antiquity or earlier, the millennia of its continuous use, and its widespread geographical extent, it can probably be regarded as the main divination system to have been used on this planet during the entire history of humanity.

I re-created the ancient extispicy techniques by going to an abattoir and personally removing the entrails of freshly slaughtered lambs, following the directions of the ancient Babylonian tablets which set the pattern for the later Greeks and Romans. Generally, in the modern age, only butchers can be expected to know much about entrails as they emerge from animals, but I decided it was necessary to re-create the ancient setting in order to see just what it was that the ancients were doing. In this way I was able to resolve many enigmas.

The two main organs used in divination were the liver and the intestines. I discovered that if you pull the liver out of a freshly slaughtered lamb it will act as a perfect mirror; I could see my face in it clearly for fifteen or twenty minutes, after which it went dull and ceased to act as a reflector. Because the ancients were somewhat literal-minded when they wanted to figure out what internal organs were for, they decided the purpose of the liver in the body was *to act as a mirror* of the divine rays that the gods were thought to be shining down on us continually. The liver was therefore thought to be the seat of the soul. There is plenty in such sources as Plato and Plutarch on this subject to satisfy the most curious. Since the gods have foreknowledge, it follows that the divine rays bring us intimations of the future if we can only discern them. So the premise of extispicy was that if you scrutinize the liver of a sacrificial animal carefully enough, it will yield foreknowledge traces left behind by the divine rays which have streamed into it up until the moment of the sacrifice. The Babylonians divided the lamb's liver up into 55 separate 'zones' where, if marks were found, they portended various things. The Greeks tended to look for broader indicators such as the presence or absence of various main fissures and protrusions. The most important was the 'head', or 'lobe' or 'finger' as the Jews

This Babylonian baked-clay model of a sheep's liver, c. 2000 BC, would have been used for reference and instruction. Lying across the liver on the right is the gall bladder. The liver is divided into 55 sections for divination purposes and covered with cuneiform texts commenting on the sections.

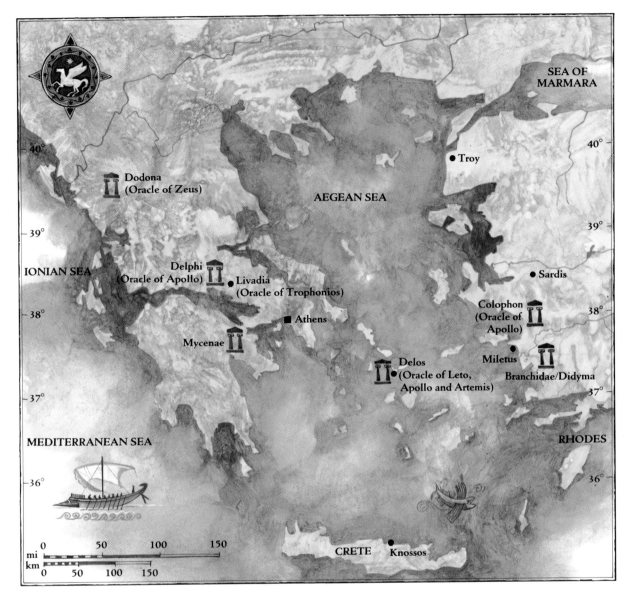

SACRED SITES OF THE ORACLES
*The main oracle centres of the Greeks
were established at particular geodetic
locations, marking latitude lines. Hence
Dodona, Delphi and Delos are one
degree apart (39° 30', 38° 30', 37°
30') in succession, and were matched by
corresponding Eastern oracle centres on
the same latitude lines: Metsamor beside
Mount Ararat (see inset map), an oracle
near Sardis beside Mount Sipylus, and
the Oracle of Apollo at Branchidae/
Didyma near Miletus (also 39° 30',
38° 30', and 37° 30'). The oracle
centres preceded the age of classical
Greece, and the sacred sites may in
turn have preceded any oracular function.*

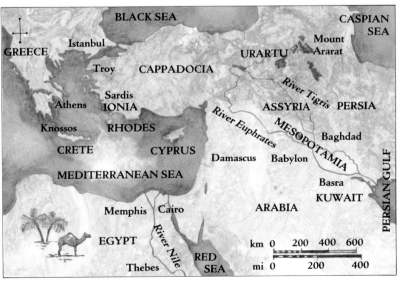

still call it; its absence was a dreadful sign, and it was said to have been absent just before the deaths of both Julius Caesar and Alexander the Great. Its anatomical name is the *processus pyramidalis*, and it is shaped like a protruding tetrahedron, which was considered significant by the Pythagoreans and the Platonists, for whom the shape was the elemental particle of fire.

The scrutiny of the intestines also revealed mystical connections. The lamb's intestines, when laid flat for inspection, form a spiralling labyrinth which has been depicted on stones and in clay for millennia as a sacred symbol. The pattern was also connected to the orbital motions of the planets, and the writings of Martianus Capella make this connection explicit. The Etruscans were the ones who, in Roman times, were the experts in extispicy, and they especially drew these connections between celestial motions and the complex pattern of the coiled intestines.

The retrograde motions of Mercury in particular were connected with the twist-and-return pattern of the intestinal spiral; this connection was made as early as 2750 BC by the Sumerians of the Middle East, who based their 'Mask of Huwawa' on intestinal convolutions, and this Mask was also meant to represent the planet Mercury.

Divination by the intestines was based upon a

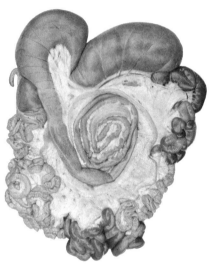

The intestines and caecum of an unhealthy lamb. In the centre is the 'spiral colon', which was the part consulted by the Babylonians, Greeks and Romans for prophecy. In this instance a single arc of the spiral colon is inflamed as a result of gastro-enteritis, causing it to become practically invisible. The 'count' of the arcs, which can be plainly seen, is thus an odd number, which was considered an unhappy omen.

close examination of which arcs of the spiral may have been inflamed by infection, such as in gastro-enteritis. When an arc of intestines is inflamed, as I have personally seen, it goes white and matches the colour of the surrounding intestinal fat, thereby becoming essentially invisible. The 'count' of the arcs then becomes odd rather than even in many cases, which yields an unfavourable prognosis for the future.

In both the intestines and the liver, disease will have been at work, causing the unfavourable signs. The disease, and therefore the inauspicious signs, will often have come from unwholesomeness of the environment. In very ancient times our nomad ancestors used such indicators as cues to move on to healthier pastures. This earliest tradition is explicitly preserved in the text of Vitruvius, the Roman architectural writer, for whom the choice of a sound geographical location was the necessary preliminary to building anything at all. Inspection of the entrails of animals thus comes down in the end to using the technique of the autopsy to look for signs of internal disease, which may indicate that things in the environment are not as well as they seem.

THE ORACLES: SEERS OR FRAUDS?

Amongst the Greeks the form of divination of second importance after extispicy was certainly the use of oracles. Whereas extispicy was revered as of primary value, and practised by most people very frequently indeed, the institutional and formal divinatory establishment was represented by the oracle centres, primary among them being Delphi. Delphi, Dodona and Delos were the primary oracle sites used by the Minoans prior to 1200 BC in Greece proper.

The original purpose of these sites seems not to have been for oracular uses primarily, but rather for geodetic ones, that is, for measuring the Earth. The oracles were founded as sacred expressions of key points established by surveying techniques that marked out latitude lines. For instance, Dodona, Delphi and Delos form a descending scale of geodetic points precisely one degree of latitude apart. The geodetic points seem to have been correlated with musical notes in the heptatonic diatonic scale (which archaeologists have established existed as early as 2500 BC), somewhat in the manner that the later Pythagoreans revered the musical notes and spoke of a 'harmony of the spheres'. It is therefore presumed that the original purpose of the oracle sites was connected with a reverence

In contemporary Ethiopia the intestines of animals are still consulted by the native inhabitants as indicators of future events. The Mursi tribe are a cattle tribe, so divination by entrails is easily accessible to them. This is a survival of the ancient practice of extispicy, which has been continuously used for several thousand years, longer than any other form of divination.

for the earth spirit, and that the meticulous measurements were not merely for navigational purposes, but for elucidating the deep mysteries of the measurement of the Earth as a sphere and its cosmic motions, which to the ancients were the profoundest mysteries of all. As the centuries wore on, however, the oracles achieved increasing prominence and the geodetic function was forgotten.

The oracle at Dodona had the official primacy, with Zeus as its patron, but because it was so distant and difficult to reach in the far north-west of Greece, Delphi took on the role of the major arbiter of Greek affairs in classical times. In connection with the manner in which the oracle of Delphi worked, there is much misinformation, some of it purposely circulated by the priests at the time. It was claimed that the sybil, or prophetess, sat on a tripod over a chasm in the earth from which intoxicating fumes (supposed to arise from the rotting corpse of a mythological monster called Python) rose up to send her into a prophetic trance. She would then utter poems which told the enquirer what his future held. In practice, the utterances of the sybil were taken down and systematically rendered in verse by poets resident for the purpose. But as the French excavators discovered earlier this century when they commenced their digs at Delphi, no chasm in the earth existed. In fact the original site of the Delphic oracle was two miles (three kilometres) further up the mountain in a small cavern. The classical site, which had been adopted as easier of access, was a secondary one and not the 'real thing', a fact that its custodians were probably anxious to keep to themselves.

The whole tale was probably invented as a cover-story to explain the strange smell of the intoxicating fumes from burning drug-plants. Inhaling fumes or swallowing drugs can induce states which bring visions of various kinds. Shamans all over the world from the earliest times have done this in order to obtain insights and glimpses of the future. There is much clear archaeological evidence that the Minoans used opium routinely in their religious rituals. The sybil of Delphi was fumigated by drug plants and

possibly swallowed them as well. Iamblichus tells us that the priest of the oracle of Apollo at Colophon drank a drugged potion before prophesying, and that the prophetess of the oracle of Apollo at Branchidae passed out after inhaling drugged fumes from boiling potions, after which she could prophesy in a trance.

There is no doubt that states of trance and self-hypnosis, whether drug-induced or not, were used frequently in connection with many of the ancient oracles. This practise existed in Egypt as well, and the foundation of the main Greek oracles may have been done in connection with the Egyptians, for Herodotus records a tradition that Dodona was founded from Egyp-

At the dramatic and remote site of the ancient Greek Oracle of Dodona, in the north-west of Greece, the Oracle of Zeus was situated. The original site was probably on the nearby Mount Tomaros. The answers to questions about the future were said to be conveyed by the rustling of the leaves in Zeus's sacred oak trees, and were interpreted by the priests.

The Castalian Spring, situated at the entrance to the Castalian Gorge, is one of several springs at Delphi. Although water from it was apparently used in preparing the drugged potions for the prophesying sybil, the Spring of Kassotis above the temple is supposed to have been the actual divinatory spring proper during classical times. But the Castalian Spring takes its name from another spring two miles higher up the mountain, where the original site of the oracle was prior to 1000 BC.

tian Thebes, and the oracle at Delos is thought to have been founded by the son of Cecrops, an Egyptian who became King of Athens, in 1558 BC. A good deal of evidence survives from Egypt, Mesopotamia and Greece about trance inductions. One Hellenistic papyrus from Egypt suggests words that will invariably produce a prophetic trance and advises: 'Say the formula seven times into the man's ear, and right away he will fall down. Sit down on the bricks and make your enquiry, and he will describe everything with truth.' At certain periods in the history of Delphi there were probably sybils who had genuine prophetic visions. The difficulty arose when such a sybil died and could not be replaced; the institution could not simply be shut down, so stronger drugs would be used and eventually organized fraud was the only answer.

It was also a regular practice amongst the Greeks to drug those who came to consult certain of the oracles. This was not the case at Dodona or Delphi, but it was most definitely the case at the oracle of Trophonios at Lebadea, now known as Livadia. Pausanius has left a minute description of this harrowing experience. After fasting and being made to drink mysterious potions, the drugged client was led to a chute down which he slid into the underground chambers where he was assailed on all sides by a mass of serpents. In a state of utter terror and total suggestibility, he would hear someone tell him a prophetic message. Often he would stay underground for days, where cells evidently existed to enable clients to 'sleep it off'. If the client expressed scepticism he might be murdered and never 'reappear from the Underworld'. The actual drugs regularly used were extremely powerful and included henbane, thorn apple, and black and white hellebore. Henbane was so important that Pliny tells us its name was *apollinaris*, named after Apollo, patron god of Delphi and of prophecy in general.

The most eerie and bizarre of all the ancient classical oracle centres was undoubtedly the pre-Roman oracle of the Dead at Baia on the western coast of Italy. It is near the present city of Naples, and was linked with the oracular cave

and sybil of nearby Cuma, which is reputed to have been the earliest of the Greek settlements on the Italian peninsula. In 1967 a retired English engineer named Robert F. Paget rediscovered the fantastic underground sanctuary of the Baian oracle, which was blocked up in the reign of Augustus. The underground complex has never been opened to the public, and only a handful of scholars and archaeologists have ever been allowed access. What is so extraordinary in this artificial underground complex carved a fifth of a mile into the solid rock is that it actually contains an *artificial River Styx* across which clients were rowed in a coracle. They were presumably meant to believe that they were genuinely visiting the Underworld. Seances appear to have been staged in the inner sanctum. The description of the descent into Hades given in Book VI of Virgil's *Aeneid* is in fact a description of the descent into the Baian oracle, near which Virgil lived for some time. The Inner Sanctum has never been fully cleared of the rubble with which it was filled by Agrippa, a henchman of Augustus who had a special hatred for the oracle for some personal reason, and swore that no one would ever use it again.

Much of the oracular set-up in Greece was therefore phoney. A network of carrier-pigeons and carrier-swallows carried secret messages from all over the Mediterranean world to Delphi and the other oracular centres, notifying the priests of the latest events, the results of battles, the deaths of kings, and so forth. These were then 'uttered by the god' as prophecies. The 'prophetic doves' so often used as symbols of the oracle centres were the bird-telegraphy which made accurate political prophecies possible and gave centres such as Delphi immense wealth and political power. Delphi took the side of Sparta against Athens in the Peloponnesian War, and one reason may have been that the Spartans were so conservative in their religious piety that they were easier to fool. But the phoniness of the oracular institutions was a peculiar form of pious fraud, which was often perpetrated by intellectuals 'for the good of the masses', and it would be wrong to think that the only motives were

sordid. For after all, one High Priest of Delphi was the author Plutarch, and of him at least we can be quite certain that he was as upright and honest a man as ancient Greece ever produced. Indeed, much of what we know of Delphic lore comes from his profound and learned writings. He lived during Roman times, though he wrote in Greek, and already much of the history of Delphi in the earlier Greek classical era was as remote to him as it is to us.

Oracular responses were often phrased in enigmatic form or posed as riddles. While maintaining arch-conservative positions with regard to cult matters, these responses by the oracles often stretched the minds of the Greeks in creative ways and stimulated fresh modes of thought, even occasionally setting mathematical problems! As the philosopher Aristotle, who made a special study of riddles oracular and otherwise, said of them: 'The thoughts were startling and they did not fit in with the ideas already held.' It is because the Greeks were courageous enough to think fresh thoughts that we still honour them today, and it takes no act of divination to predict that we will continue to do so as long as there are thinking men about.

Lake Avernus (top), near Cuma and Baia in Italy, is within the crater of an extinct volcano. The ancient Greek geographer, Strabo, wrote of it: 'The inhabitants affirm that birds, flying over the lake, fall into the water, being stifled by the vapours rising from it ... the oracle of the dead was situated somewhere here....'

The cave of the Sybil of Cuma in Italy (middle), not far from the location of the Oracle of the Dead at Baia, was visited by countless enquirers in antiquity. The prophesying Sybil sat in the far niche. Her replies to questions are said to have been written on leaves laid on the floor; when the door was opened, the wind blew the leaves into confusion, symbolizing the state of our knowledge of the future. Cuma was a Greek settlement in Italy, established long before the rise of Rome. This cavern was excavated in 1932.

On one side of this Etruscan bronze (left), c. sixth century BC, an augur scans the skies to study the flights of birds for clues to the future. On the other side, a diviner studies the liver of a sacrificial animal to predict the future by the divinatory science of extispicy.

THE TREE OF LIFE

Galgal, A Cabbalistic Method

Cherry Gilchrist

The letters are without question the root of all wisdom and knowledge, and they themselves are the substance of prophecy. In a prophetic vision, they appear as if they were solid bodies, actually speaking to the individual.

Rabbi Abraham Abulafia, *Life of the Future World*, 1280

The Hebrew alphabet is a sacred language. Its 22 letters are seen as the key to the secrets of creation; every letter has a meaning, and is a word in its own right. Letters within words can be reordered, giving rise to new meanings. This is more easily done in Hebrew than in most languages, and can be used as a way of reinterpreting holy scriptures. The letters themselves are said to have power, and in deep contemplation may be visualized turning into fire or angelic beings, as the esoteric texts tell us, bringing prophetic revelation to the meditator. Letters are the spirit through which God speaks to man, and through which man may understand and even influence the world.

In the medieval schools of Jewish Cabbala, letter magic and meditation was carried on to an extremely advanced degree, and many texts of instruction were circulated secretly, for fear of endangering the uninitiated. Cabbala, though at that time a part of Judaism, was nevertheless regarded with suspicion by many of the orthodox, as it leaned towards the occult and the mystical, and towards a direct personal experience of the divine.

Galgal is a relatively new flowering of the Cabbalistic tradition, but it lies in direct descent from these earlier schools. It is, in a sense, a divination system that took hundreds of years to grow. Combining the Hebrew letters and the Tree of Life, the two main lines of Cabbalistic teaching, Galgal has evolved from that first burning concern with prophecy and revelation and with discovering hidden knowledge through letter permutation and Tree magic. We can see here how spiritual impulses may still be at work centuries later, producing new tangible evidence of their existence as time goes on. Because Galgal cannot be divorced from the Cabbalistic tradition itself, it will be helpful to look at certain aspects of this first before turning to the divination system in detail.

CABBALA: THE HIDDEN TRADITION

Like most schools of wisdom, only so much can be charted. Cabbala is chiefly an oral tradition, the teachings handed on from teacher to pupil, and what finds its way into the books is only a part. The scholars are prepared to authenticate the existence of Cabbala only from the medieval period onwards, where it took root, following the dispersion of the Jews, in North Africa, Spain, Italy and other parts of Europe. But it is considered to be much older, and may not, in fact, have originated within Judaism at all, for

The symbol held aloft on this carving from the Egyptian temple of Kom Ombo, constructed about 300–200 BC, represents 'order and stability'. It bears a marked resemblance to the Cabbalistic Tree of Life, hinting at Cabbala's long history, which may have wound its way through various religious mythologies.

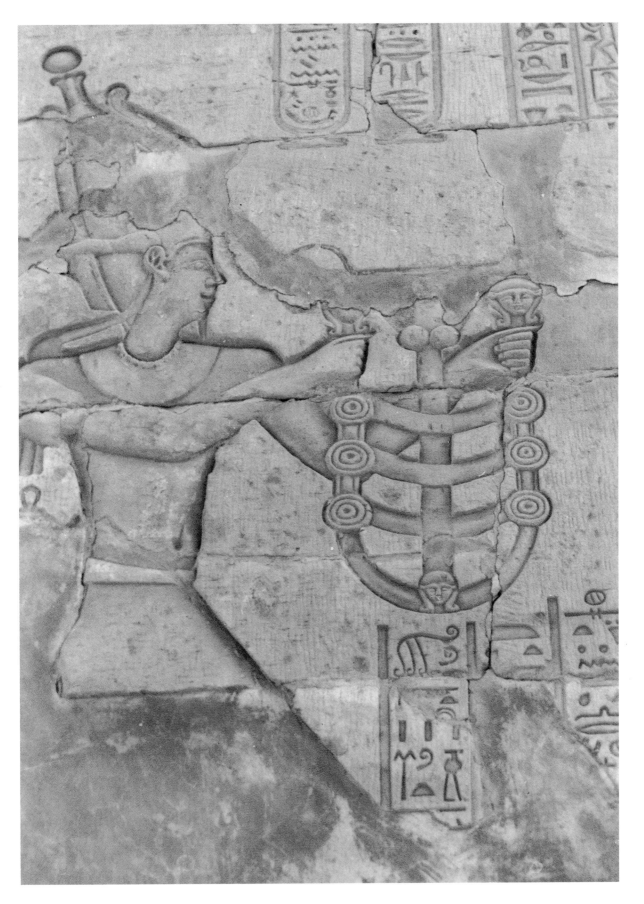

the symbolic representation of the Cabbalistic Tree of Life is found in a very similar form in certain Assyrian and Egyptian carved reliefs.

Cabbala is a way of knowledge; like other schools of wisdom it may find a home within orthodox religion, but it is not bound to remain there. It is recognized by many as having a universality, so that it is possible to understand the various major religions within its framework. The power of Cabbala to cross cultural boundaries was witnessed in Renaissance times, when its teachings were eagerly seized upon by men such as Giordano Bruno and Marsilio Ficino, leading lights in the philosophic and artistic renewal of Christian Italy; and since then a strongly Westernized, Christian form of Cabbala has developed.

Cabbala means 'to receive'. This implies that each human being is capable of receiving directly from God; but how we receive is dependent upon how we are, and so it also implies that we may have to do a little work upon ourselves first before we can expect this to happen. Most Cabbalistic schools promote a thorough training, which encourages individuals to meditate, to observe, and to work with both their hearts and their minds. This can also include ritual and magical work, and visualizations known nowadays as 'path-working', where images are allowed to arise as the practitioner concentrates on one particular path of the Tree of Life. Although the work of such schools is usually carried out behind closed doors, participants today are encouraged to live and work in the world. Cabbala might have attracted more religious recluses in earlier times, but the need for integrating worldly and heavenly experience has always been recognized.

'Receiving' also implies a structure, so just as you need a prism to refract light, and a radio set to pick up transmissions, Cabbala provides a framework that finely tunes the sensibilities, generating more experience and offering a means of understanding it. The Tree of Life and the Hebrew alphabet are the structures most commonly used by Cabbalists, sometimes together, sometimes independently.

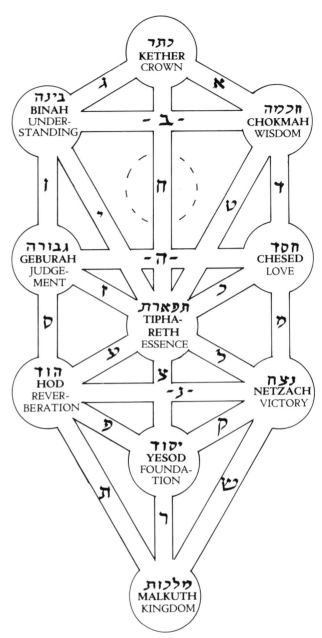

The Tree is a map of creation which has been in a process of continuous development for at least 1,000 years, and probably much longer. Although representations vary, it is usually portrayed as a glyph, a stylized form with ten Sephiroth (spheres) marking the ten different levels of creation, starting with Kether, the Crown, and finishing with Malkuth, the Kingdom. Twenty-two paths connect the Sephiroth, which are arranged on the three pillars of Force, Consciousness and Form. The three highest emanations, of Kether (the Crown), Chokmah (Wisdom) and Binah (Understanding), are the supernal triad of forces which shape the whole of life. The Lightning Flash of Creation then passes through the hidden Sephira of Daath (the Abyss) to reach the manifest world of Chesed (Love) and Geburah (Judgement), the two great rulers of human life. With Tiphareth (Essence), this creates the 'soul'

א	ALEPH	OX (TAME)
ב	BETH	HOUSE
ג	GIMEL	CAMEL (FRUITION)
ד	DALETH	DOOR
ה	HEH	WINDOW (BE)
ו	VAV	HOOK (NAIL)
ז	ZAYIN	SWORD (WEAPON)
ח	CHET	FENCE (FEAR)
ט	TET	SERPENT (MUD)
י	YOD	HAND
כ	CAPH	PALM OF HAND
ל	LAMED	GOAD (LEARN)
מ	MEM	WATER
נ	NUN	FISH
ס	SAMEKH	SUPPORT
ע	AYIN	EYE
פ	PEH	MOUTH
צ	TSADI	FISH HOOK (JUST)
ק	KOOPH	BACK OF HEAD (MONKEY)
ר	RESH	HEAD
ש	SHIN	TOOTH
ת	TAV	SIGN

The Tree is both a map of the universe and of the individual; 'as above so below' is a favourite maxim of Cabbalists, and it is said that we each contain the complete Tree within ourselves. It lends itself readily as a kind of Jacob's Ladder which we can climb towards the source of creation, each step bringing new experiences, new challenges and responsibilities. Each Sephira has attracted a wealth of correspondences to itself: astrological, cosmological and, in modern times, scientific and psychological. There are colours, images, qualities ascribed to each one which are used in various forms of Sephirothic meditation, or as a basis for ritual magic, depending upon the orientation of the practitioner.

The tradition of working with Hebrew letters, the sacred alphabet, is obviously more pertinent within Jewish Cabbala, though it certainly has not been neglected in Western Mystery schools. It will not have escaped the eagle-eyed that with 22 paths upon the Tree, and 22 letters in the Hebrew alphabet, we have an excellent opportunity to marry the two. This is, in fact, the basis of Galgal. There are also versions of Cabbala that concentrate more intensely upon the letters, and these are direct ancestors of the Galgal system as they imply an active use of the letters, rather than simply ascribing them to the paths.

THE SOURCE OF GALGAL DIVINATION

The main antecedents of Galgal are the teachings of Abraham Abulafia (*b.* 1240 and quoted above) and Chaim Vital (1543–1620). The *Sefer Yetzirah*, one of the key medieval Cabbalistic texts, emphasizes how the world is created through the permutation of letters. These fundamental permutations can thus be said to form a series of divine names, and it is these which constitute the backbone of Abulafia's work. (His name has recently gained new popularity through being given to the endlessly-permutating computer in Umberto Eco's best-selling novel *Foucault's Pendulum*.)

Abulafia's intense, magical system of medi-

triad, which must be activated and purified in our journey through this world. Next come Netzach (Victory), signifying feelings and desires, and Hod (Reverberation), signifying mental powers of communication and analysis. Yesod, on the central pillar of consciousness like Tiphareth, is our personality and our foundation in the world, and Malkuth, which is often said to be the hardest Sephira of all to understand, is the physical world of the senses.

The Hebrew alphabet (above) is shown with the transliteration and meaning of each letter. The letters themselves have power and are understood to be a way to unlock the secrets of the universe, bringing revelation to those who contemplate them.

Older forms of Jewish divination include the interpretation of dreams. Here Joseph is seen giving advice to the puzzled Egyptian Pharaoh as to the prophetic meaning of his dreams. Any specific ancient techniques associated with such divination are lost to us today.

tation, involving breathing techniques and ritual movements, outraged his more conventional contemporaries. His claim to true prophecy was denied on the grounds that prophecy could only occur in the Holy Land; his reply, characteristically, was that he had attained the Holy Land of the Spirit and could thus claim to be a prophet. His outlook was broad, and he stated that any language could be used for mystical purposes, not just Hebrew, and that Christians as well as Jews could attain spiritual enlightenment. However, he plainly believed Judaism to be the best religion, since his most perilous exploit on record was when he set out on a mission to convert the Pope, an adventure from which he was lucky to return alive!

Rabbi Chaim Vital, born in 1543 and thus heralding a later development of Cabbala, was a man of brilliant intelligence and extraordinary learning. His interests extended to alchemy, astrology and all current forms of divination. His methods were directed towards gaining entry to the Gates of Understanding, another key Cabbalistic concept associated with the Sephira of Binah, the Great Mother, and they included ritual purification, mantric repetition of holy texts, and visualization of a Holy Name in letters of white fire tinged with the colour of the appropriate Sephira. After careful preparation, the initiate is told to:

> *Strengthen yourself with a powerful yearning, meditating on the supernal universe. There you should attach yourself to the Root of your soul and to the Supernal Lights. It should seem as if your soul had left your body and had ascended on high. Imagine yourself standing in the supernal universe.*

Like Abulafia, Vital recognized the potential dangers of his system, and left instructions on discriminating between fantasy and revelation.

The work of these two schools, along with the tradition of work with the Tree of Life, are the main source of inspiration for Galgal. Cabbalistic astrology is also woven in; Vital's interest in astrology has already been mentioned, and a long association between the planets and Sephiroth exists – both, in one sense, are 'heavenly spheres'. The elegant framework of the Tree of Life, with its geometric structure and different numberings (10 Sephiroth, 22 paths, three pillars, four worlds, and so on) lends itself to astrological interpretations, astrology being itself based upon pattern and number. Galgal uses a method, common among Cabbalists, of equating the Sun with the central Sephira of Tiphareth, the Moon with Yesod, Earth with Malkuth, and the planets with the outer Sephiroth of the Tree. Unique to Galgal, however, is the ascription of the 12 houses of the zodiac with 12 triads upon the Tree of Life (see page 76).

Galgal was first published as a set of 56 cards with an accompanying text in 1972 (Scot o' the Covert, London). The immediate cause of its creation was a discovery made by its originators, Wilfred Davies and Gila Zur, while experimenting with letter permutation in the time-honoured fashion. Until then, no system of placing the letters upon the Tree had proved entirely satisfactory. Cabbalists of different schools argued the merits of different orderings, and some went so far as to say that any letter on any path would give at least some illumination – a statement hard indeed to disagree with.

However, two traditional oral teachings of Cabbala provided the clue that was to result in Galgal. Firstly: 'The Tree emanates forth in the order of the Lightning Flash' (the order of the Sephiroth as given above); and secondly: 'The Tree is complete at every point'. Thus, if it is taken that the Tree begins with Kether and ends at Malkuth, and if at every new Sephira the potential pathways to the pre-existing Sephiroth are mapped in, in descending order, this gives a numbering of 1–22 for the paths, and a placing for the letters following their natural order through the alphabet.

The proof of the validity of this method came when the two researchers began to form the 'wheels' of Galgal. Each card consists of a segment of the Tree which is given a circular shape; the name Galgal itself means wheel, and the term has been used in Cabbala since the Middle Ages to refer to a particular technique of permutating letters. The outer rim of the wheel will thus contain a short sequence of letters, one for each path that forms the rim. These particular combinations of letters began to throw out a remarkable series of meanings; without any extra manipulation, in nearly every case the sequence of letters contained several words within it. Other possible orderings of the letters upon the paths were tried, with minimal results being achieved.

HOW GALGAL WORKS

In Galgal, four of the meanings from the letters around the circumference of each wheel create four separate cards. These are in each case assigned to the four worlds, named in Cabbala as Assiah, the physical, Yetzirah, the formative or psychological, Briah, the creative, and Aziluth, the abstract. In astrology they are known as earth, water, fire and air. So, for instance, for a wheel with Tiphareth (translated as Know: Adorn) as its centre, and with five Sephiroth at the rim (named Crown, Wisdom, Mercy, Judgement and Understand), we have four cards: in ascending order of worlds they are the Gambler, Concern, Pride and the Society. Another, with Yesod (Found: Experience) at the centre, gives rise to the Locksmith, the Eater, the Witness and the Wanderer.

The complete set of 56 cards parallels the number in the Tarot pack, but here the resemblance ends, for whereas the Tarot is vividly imaged, portrayed in bright colours, Galgal is a series of patterns drawn in stark black and white, framed against the deep red of the board on which the cards are laid out. Just as the Cabbalistic letter meditation was designed to draw one through to deeper and deeper levels of understanding, so too Galgal leads the practitioner past the imaginative and intuitive level to the place of 'true thought', the place of the abstract, in the sense that sacred geometry is abstract. Not everyone finds it easy to use for this reason.

Each Galgal card has as its centre one of the

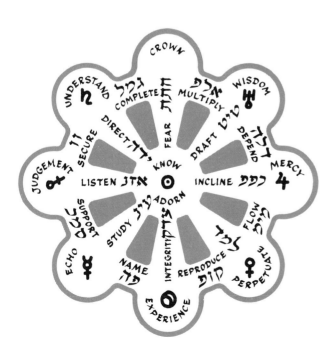

This is one of the 14 wheels of Galgal. Each wheel appears on four cards, once for each element.

Sephiroth from the pillar of consciousness. This means that the divination reading itself centres upon the human capacity to create and, if necessary, to make changes. This offers hope, as opposed to a fate-bound, mechanized view of the universe. The whole Tree, with its letters and Sephiroth, shows us the complete map of creation; the Galgal layout, each card a partial representation of this, shows us the world we have created at this moment in time.

Fourteen cards are laid out with 12 placed around the outside of the board, a schema which equates the mundane houses of astrology (see Chapter Six, Shapes in the Stars) with the twelve external triads of the Tree of Life. Two central cards give the essence and the appearance of the matter enquired about, the Tiphareth and the Yesod of the situation. The twelve astrological houses, which are also used for divination in certain forms of geomancy (see Chapter Twenty-three, Ancient Secrets of the Earth), cover every aspect of human worldly life: family, money, work, ideals, lovers, speculation, travel, health, and so on. Economic, social and psychological aspects are incorporated too and so the houses provide a comprehensive basis for framing the matter to be answered.

The interpretation of each card is thus partly defined in terms of the 'house' it is placed in. The manual that accompanies Galgal gives a clear guide to using the system, and some hints as to the essential meaning of each card, but, as with other major divination systems, the real art of interpretation lies with the practitioner. The title of each card taken at face value is enough to kindle a response, and it is certainly not necessary to be a student of Cabbala to use Galgal, but those wishing to penetrate further can take account of the 'element' of each (earth, water, fire or air), the portion of the Tree represented in the wheel, and the words engraved on each separate path, which are derived from the root meaning of the single letter that belongs there.

Galgal can therefore be used not only as a system of divination, but as a way of entering into the living tradition of the Cabbala. If we think of certain major divination systems, such as astrology and the *I Ching*, as having an out-flow and an in-flow, it can be seen that we can either stay on the tip of the out-flow, using the system simply for practical purposes, or we can choose to be drawn in on the in-flow, following the system right to its very heart and finding it thus a way of knowledge as well as a way of reading the past, the present and the future.

The author, Cherry Gilchrist, lays out the cards for a Galgal reading, in the order of the Lightning Flash of Creation. The board is inscribed with correspondences that help the practitioner to read the 'story' that the cards spell out, according to Cabbalistic and astrological symbolism.

CHAPTER NINE

WISE WOMEN COUNSELLORS

Popular Methods of Divination

Marian Green

In this age of instant communication with friends, relatives and events around the world, it is easy to forget that in the past people had to rely on the services of sensitives, seers, oracles and clairvoyants to glean any information about distant events. From the courts of kings down to the humblest peasant whose loved ones were away at war, there was a desire to know what was happening and to be kept abreast of battles, invasions or the coming of a flood. Because the technologies we take for granted did not exist, all kinds of methods, rational and irrational, were used. Thus both couriers on horseback and those who could fly beyond their bodies gathered information, and conveyed it through time and space to those who needed to know.

In many parts of the world, the training of seers and the places where they practised their arts were within the confines of religious temples or royal palaces, permitting access to only a chosen few. The Wise Women of the past may originally have been chosen as oracles or seers in the temples of the Classical world – chosen because they had a different capacity for far-seeing than men, perhaps due to that inherently female sense of awareness that enables such women to keep track of their children or loved ones when those people are out of sight.

Over time, this capacity to see beyond the immediate view became the province of Gypsies and country women, who learned their skills from other women in their families: by watching mother or grandma reading a palm and later enquiring as to what the symbols marked on their own hands meant. These women did not study books, nor did they write them; most of the accounts of folk fortune-tellers come from notes in their clients' diaries and day-books. For this reason, there are few books that detail their simple, intuitive, but extremely accurate and varied arts of divination and far-sight. Being 'weather wise' or able to 'talk to animals' were abilities women would inherit and then build upon. Most of the methods that have come down to us as amusements and folksy ways of foretelling the future have provided extraordinarily exact and relevant information that could not have been discovered in any other way.

Many of the methods that have gradually made their way down into the mystic arts of Gypsies, wise women, witches and fortune-tellers are ones in which the practitioner causes her vision to be focused on other levels of reality by means of a speculum or scrying glass, by the random scatter of tea-leaves, pebbles or other small objects, or by the shapes formed when molten wax is poured into water. In all cases, her attention has to be redirected away from the everyday world into that cross-dimensional space within the pattern or glass. To achieve this altered level of perception, the scryer (that is one who 'descrys' or far-sees) has to shift her consciousness quite deliberately so that other times and places may be shown to her. The pictures do not actually appear within the sphere of the crystal ball itself or in the tea-leaves, but in the mind of the fortune-teller. That art can be learned by most people, given patience and concentration.

81

SCRYING WITH A CRYSTAL BALL
OR OTHER SPECULUM

Since the earliest times certain individuals have discovered that, whilst in a dreamy state, they can begin to see images, shapes, symbols, numbers, figures or complete events apparently reflected in some shining surface. Cave-paintings in France, Australia, South Africa and elsewhere seem to show animals and human figures surrounded with 'haloes' or jagged auras, and this is exactly how many modern seers perceive images within a scrying glass. The pictures seen within the shiny surface are not real, not ordinary reflections, but always differ in intensity, colour or some other feature.

Still, dark pools of water, black stones, such as coal or jet, and wet slabs of slate have been

A collection of scrying instruments (from the top, anti-clockwise): 1 A lighted candle; 2 A glass of dark wine; 3 A concave black mirror; 4 Coloured and clear glass marbles; 5 A crystal of natural clear quartz; 6 A glass or crystal ball on its stand.

the mirror in which 'psychic' visions may be projected. The embers of fires, the flames of burning candles or lamps, the shimmer of the sun on a river, or even a wetted finger-nail may have been the oldest glittering media which helped those with the innate skill to discover other sights within the mind. At Wookey Hole Caves in Somerset, England, recent archaeological excavations uncovered a woman's skeleton dating back to the Stone Age. With her bones was an artificially polished sphere of crystalline granite about the size of a baseball. This appeared to have no other use than as a magical instrument, with which, in the confines of the dark cave, lit by a flickering fire, she may have been able to see visions of the whereabouts of game, and many fossilized animal bones lay scattered alongside hers.

In ancient Egypt there were sacred lotus pools used by priests for scrying, and shallow bowls carved of dark stone have been found in many parts of the world. When filled with water, ink or dark red wine they too became mirrors in which the future could be descryed. The crystal sphere that modern practitioners use is more recent; the earliest examples, used primarily for divination, date from about AD 1500.

To make any such speculum work you need to be able to distract your awareness of the world around you and become mentally and physically still. Often a period of quiet contemplation with the eyes closed will attune the psychic vision to see within the glass or crystal or black mirror when the eyes are opened again. Almost anything can be used: a bowl of water, a wine glass painted black on the outside, a polished sphere of dark or transparent quartz, lead crystal or even a hollow, glass sphere. Within the ball, which acts as a doorway through time and space, pictures will begin to swim out of a swirling mist. Often it is hard to relax enough to see even the swirling fog of astral matter, but eventually, given endurance, a darker area will appear within, and through that time-tunnel, or window of the mind, letters, shapes, symbols, images and information will begin to flow.

This engraved gold disc was made by John Dee, the astrologer and advisor to Queen Elizabeth I, and worn as a magical symbol to enhance the abilities of the scryer. It shows the four protective watch towers of a magical circle.

The author, using an eighteenth-century glass speculum backed by black velvet, seeks answers to questions. Reflections of light have to be ignored so that inner visions can appear within or beyond the sphere. It is necessary to change the level of awareness to achieve effective results.

A heart shows the love in your life, of which you will become more aware. This can be a future partner or children's affections if close to a toy symbol.

A snake shows underhand behaviour in business or professional work and you should be careful of trusting someone. If it is coming towards the top of the cup the threat implied is getting worse soon.

A dagger shows you have an enemy or rival who will make a sudden attack. It could be a new colleague or jealous underling who envies your position and will try to harm your reputation or self-esteem.

A moon, in this case waxing, shows an increase within a project, or new customers. A full moon can indicate a potential romance within a month. A waning crescent can indicate the end of difficulties, or minor, delaying troubles.

A clover leaf shows good luck, even if other symbols in the cup are less positive. It is especially lucky if there are four leaves. The nearer the top of the cup, the faster good fortune will reach you, cancelling other difficulties.

A broom is a positive indicator. If you are a witch it shows interesting journeys. If you are thinking of moving house a change is on the way. Spring-cleaning or brushing away difficulties is suggested.

A Victorian tea-leaf reader's cup and saucer, marked with common symbols and planetary and Zodiac signs, gave a deeper meaning to any tea-leaf patterns that had settled there after the ritual that preceded a reading.

When the client had drunk her cup of tea, made from loose leaves, she would consider the question to which she sought answers. She would take the cup in her left hand, swirl it clockwise three times and upturn its contents into the saucer. Sometimes this was repeated again, to ensure that all the wet tea-leaves had taken up the most auspicious positions for the tasseomancer to interpret.

A horseshoe is a symbol of good luck. If money or travel symbols accompany it, they show the area in which Fortune is smiling upon you.

A cat's head indicates peace and contentment, perhaps the chance to settle down. If the whole cat is in a fighting pose, it can mean strife or conflict. The shape of this symbol determines the good or bad implications.

Initials point you to look at anyone to whom they apply. If other symbols are those of love or contentment, this could be a life partner; or, if business signs, then that would be the affected area of your life.

Parallel lines point to a long journey. The longer and straighter, the more pleasant the journey, and symbols like palm trees or exotic objects could show a delightful holiday destination.

A saw can show a break with a friend or situation. It can also indicate hard personal work, which can also cut you off from the people with whom you usually spend time.

An anchor shows success, especially if close to the handle or rim. It indicates stability and success in home or work, but it is less fortunate if broken or surrounded by broken lines.

TEA-LEAF READING

Tasseomancy – the art of divining with tea-leaves – was introduced into Europe only as recently as the eighteenth century, for that was when the practice of drinking tea as a hot beverage drifted westwards from its original home in China and India. The observation of random patterns of small things has been part of the shaman's system of divination from ancient times; seeing patterns in tea-leaves is an eroded form of the shamanic priest or priestess's art. It is something our grandmothers used to do, or the Gypsy woman calling at the door, for nearly all tea-leaf readers are women.

It is probably because of the kind of questions one might ask over a cup of tea that it has fallen to female diviners to learn and carry on this art. The ritual method of using whole leaf tea in a pot without a filter, poured into a shallow-bowled cup and drunk whilst considering the question in the mind of the querent is still performed according to a traditional rite. When most of the tea has been consumed, another little ritual follows, in which the questioner swirls the cup three times clockwise, then tips it into the saucer. The tea-leaf reader then looks into the bowl of the cup at the patterns made by the residual leaves. Their positions towards the rim or bowl concern time, the quarter of the cup in which they fall gives an indication of the area of life they affect, and the clarity of the symbols adds weight to the interpretation.

The kind of tea we drink in the West provides the raw materials for the sorts of symbols that we can relate to: birds signifying journeys, a house for security, a dagger for danger, a tree for growth, a horseshoe for good luck, or a nail hinting at trouble. There are thousands of symbols, signs, shapes, letters and representations that have a definite interpret-ation. Because of the intimacy with which this divination would be performed – in the home, usually among friends – the questions are normally about love, family, home, career, progress in activities and partnership matters. Most traditional symbols produced by tasseo-mancy in the West respond to these questions.

In China, where the art developed perhaps 2,000 years ago and the tea is more stick-like and twiggy, the symbols discovered in the emptied bowl are more like the ideograms used in Chinese writing: not letters as we know them, but hieroglyphs with a pictorial meaning. The symbols could also form as the 64 hexagrams of the *I Ching*. In India the patterns are both symbolic and in letter form, as they traditionally use a more leafy form of tea, and the symbols are used in conjunction with astrology to predict the timing of future events.

Today all manner of teas are available and both Indian and China tea-leaves, as well as herbal teas and coffee grounds, can be used ritually to produce a pattern of scattered symbols from which the outcome of wishes or the train of events can be determined by someone with the skill to read them.

PALMISTRY

The 'form' of things has often been used to symbolize wider concepts, so in this way the human hand – the lines upon the palm, the shapes of the fingers, the colour and texture of the nails – has, from ancient times, been used to discover the nature of the individual whose hands are being examined. Although the fact that the whorls, loops and bridges of lines at the fingertips of every human being are unique has been known only since the middle of the last century, diviners have always known how distinct every hand is. Cave walls across the Earth are decorated with hands: handprints in red or white ochre, outlines and hand-shaped paintings.

In the Old Testament of the Bible it is written 'God sealeth up the hand of every man; that all men may know his work' (Job 37:7), but in far more ancient Vedic texts from India and in Chinese scripts some 3,000 years old, allusions to telling a man's fate from the shape, lines and patterns on his hand have been deciphered. In the West, it is the writings of the Greek philosopher Aristotle that first confirm people's interest in their hands and the existence of those especially skilled in reading the palm for its future prognostications. Aristotle is believed to have gained his knowledge on the matter of hand-reading from earlier Egyptian texts, found on an altar dedicated to Thoth (Hermes), the god of wisdom and writing, which he described in a letter to Alexander the Great. In classical Rome there were hand diviners, some lauded by Pliny, others satirized by the playwright Juvenal.

Once again the wandering Gypsies may have brought this most portable form of divination to the common people during the Dark Ages. When books became more readily available there were a number of texts in Latin, Greek, Sanskrit, Hebrew, German and, later, English detailing the significance of the lines, mounts, phalanges and shape of the hand. In the sixteenth and seventeenth centuries a wide variety of books by scientists, alchemists and philosophers contained material on palmistry and the hand. In Britain the art of hand-reading may have existed since the time of the Druids, who seem to have had a kind of language or method of communication known as Finger Ogam, based on the phalanges, palm and movements of the hand, by which they could silently talk to each other in the presence of others without betraying their secrets (see Chapter Three, By Stick and Stone).

Much of the symbolism of palmistry is based on astrology, with mounds on the palm and individual fingers attributed to planets and their symbolism. The ring finger, for example, is associated with Apollo, the Sun god: the wedding ring – usually made of gold, the metal of the sun – is placed there during marriage because the ancients believed a line of energy ran directly from that finger to the heart.

The lines show the many markings that need to be taken into account when a reading is given. Traditionally, the pattern of lines, grooves, wrinkles and soft cushions of flesh on the left hand (in right-handed people) represents the raw talents, the inherited traits and the potential of the individual, while his right hand shows what he has done with them. If you look at your own hands you will see distinct differences in the clarity, depth and patterns of the lines on each hand, although the general layout will be similar.

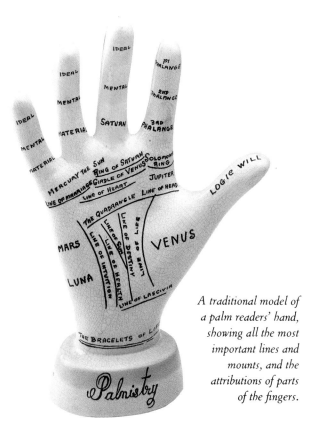

A traditional model of a palm readers' hand, showing all the most important lines and mounts, and the attributions of parts of the fingers.

People who suffer from Down's Syndrome have a combined head and heart line, a reflection of the way that their thinking tends to come from their feelings. Other characteristics such as colour, the texture of the nails, the shape of the mounts and the numbers of fine lines can be seen as clear indications of disease or potential illness. Like some other seemingly improbable forms of alternative diagnosis, this is being scientifically studied to see whether it can yield results before conventional methods are used.

The overall shape of the hand gives guidance as to the practical nature of the individual, and there are generally considered to be eight forms: the elemental or simple hand; the spatulate or active hand; the conical or temperamental hand; the square or practical hand; the philosophic hand with knotty joints; the pointed or spiritually idealistic hand; the hand with two basic characteristics; and the truly mixed hand. The shape of the palm is also important, and whether it is narrow or square, regularly shaped or curvy all determine specific aspects of the owner's personality, or predict future trends in his affairs.

The primary lines are: Heart, telling of love; Head, showing practicality and intelligence; and Life, showing how long the individual might be expected to live and the times of danger from ill health or accidents. The line of Destiny, in the centre of the palm, may indicate factors beyond the control of the person, or influences on him. The mounts of Venus, the Moon and Mars indicate aspects of strength: Venus is physical vitality and sensuality; the Moon shows sensitivity, creativity and inner or psychic strength; while Mars shows courage. The other mounts associated with the planets are Jupiter, showing self-confidence and self-esteem; Saturn, showing the stabilizing effects of relationships and business partnerships; the Sun, showing artistry and imagination; and Mercury, showing a wide span of interests, including science, eloquence, enterprise and business acumen. These mounts may have indented rings, chains, stars, crosses or squares on them, some enhancing the owner's abilities, others showing difficulties on their path through life.

The study of each individual feature on both hands – the interconnections of the lines, the softness of mounts, the varying lengths of the phalanges of the fingers, the flexibility of the thumb – all add up to an extremely complex subject. Every land has its traditions and there are numerous books of interpretation of each feature. Part of the essential skill of any divination, however, is the personal interaction between the reader and the client. There has to be trust and honesty on both sides. Because the palm reader actually has to hold the hands of her client, there is a very close connection through which a great deal of background information can be gained psychically, and this can greatly expand the reading. Confidence is essential, and this seems to be the main reason why most palmists are women: it gives female clients assurance and also pleases young men, who like to hold hands with wise or witty seeresses.

Readings still take place at fairs where Gypsy readers ply their traditional skills of 'dikkering' or fortune-telling, or in the parlour where friends meet to chat about their futures.

A palm reader in Mali uses the same method of close touch and examination with his client as that used by European and Indian palmists. The palmist spreads out his client's hand to point to features concerning marriage or family.

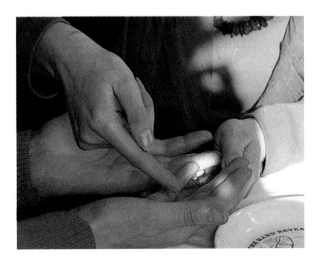

In this consultation, the author, Marian Green, shows a client some of the important lines and markings on her hands. It is the sense of psychic touch, as well as the inherent meanings of these signs, which gives value and depth to any such reading.

CHAPTER TEN

THE SEASONAL ROUND

The Folklore of Divination in Britain

Jennifer Westwood

At different times and in different places divination has been the province of experts: shamans, soothsayers, prophets, priests, astrologers, Gypsies and village Wise Women and Cunning Men. Today this strain of professional divination survives – indeed flourishes – but so does the traditional divination of the peasantry, even if somewhat less conspicuously. These country folk were only occasionally able to afford the services of the local 'Star Reader' and mostly sought for themselves through portents and signs some certainty in an uncertain future. Country people, and people in isolated work groups such as fishermen and miners, have been less touched by outside influences than the rest of the community and have remained more conservative. Consequently, divinations known in sixteenth-century England were still practised in the nineteenth, and even in the twentieth century old divinatory formulae may be part of our daily lives without our knowing it.

WEATHER PROGNOSTICATION

Weather 'saws' mostly fall into the category of divinations that have been absorbed into proverbial lore: 'Red sky at night, shepherd's delight', for example. This is a prediction based on observation, as are many prognostications taken, in the manner of the Roman augurs, from the flight of birds: if swallows skim low to the ground, storms will spoil the crops, but if they fly high, there will be drought.

Such saws were the product of collective experience reaching back many years, handed on as a rule of thumb to the greenhorn, as were prognostications based on the weather of a particular day of the year. If St Paul's Day (25 January) was wet, corn would be dear, and if it rained on St Swithun's (15 July), 40 days of rain would follow. This type of weather forecasting on the basis of observed natural phenomena was useful to a wide audience and found a place in print in, for example, the prognostications published by John Claridge, 'the Shepherd of Banbury', *The Shepheards Legacy: or, John Clearidge, his forty years experience of the weather* (1670).

It is doubtful whether countrymen separated this fundamentally rational lore from much that had a quite different intellectual basis. It cannot have been forecasting based on observation, for example, but a presumption of the benign influence radiated by a doubly holy day over the whole of the next twelvemonth when farmers predicted a good year if Christmas Day fell on a Sunday.

THE DIVINATORY RHYMES OF BRITAIN

Divination was once practised all over Britain and many of the rituals were accompanied by a rhyme. Most of those on the map are explained in the text of this chapter. 'Oak before Ash' is a typical weather prognostication, and the invocation 'O good St Faith' was recited on 6 October, St Faith's Day, by girls performing the Dumb Cake ceremony. 'If you love me, bounce and fly' accompanies an old Hallowe'en charm. Though hazelnuts are used in the ritual described in the text, this version uses apple pips. If the sweetheart is faithful, the pip will burst on the fire, otherwise burn quietly. 'If you love me, cling all round me' accompanied the old Oxfordshire game of 'lovelaces' played with four blades of grass. The blades were held in one hand, and knotted at each end. The omens were read according to whether they formed a ring, came apart, or fell separately.

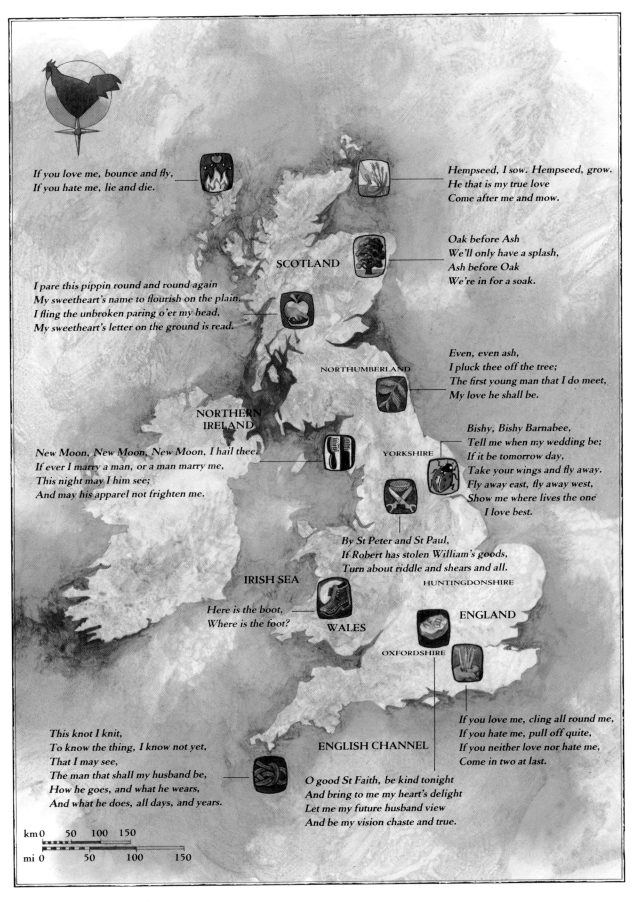

If you love me, bounce and fly,
If you hate me, lie and die.

Hempseed, I sow. Hempseed, grow.
He that is my true love
Come after me and mow.

Oak before Ash
We'll only have a splash,
Ash before Oak
We're in for a soak.

SCOTLAND

I pare this pippin round and round again
My sweetheart's name to flourish on the plain.
I fling the unbroken paring o'er my head,
My sweetheart's letter on the ground is read.

NORTHUMBERLAND

Even, even ash,
I pluck thee off the tree;
The first young man that I do meet,
My love he shall be.

NORTHERN
IRELAND

Bishy, Bishy Barnabee,
Tell me when my wedding be;
If it be tomorrow day,
Take your wings and fly away.
Fly away east, fly away west,
Show me where lives the one
    I love best.

New Moon, New Moon, New Moon, I hail thee.
If ever I marry a man, or a man marry me,
This night may I him see;
And may his apparel not frighten me.

YORKSHIRE

By St Peter and St Paul,
If Robert has stolen William's goods,
Turn about riddle and shears and all.

IRISH SEA

HUNTINGDONSHIRE

Here is the boot,
Where is the foot?

ENGLAND

WALES

OXFORDSHIRE

This knot I knit,
To know the thing, I know not yet,
That I may see,
The man that shall my husband be,
How he goes, and what he wears,
And what he does, all days, and years.

ENGLISH CHANNEL

If you love me, cling all round me,
If you hate me, pull off quite,
If you neither love nor hate me,
Come in two at last.

O good St Faith, be kind tonight
And bring to me my heart's delight
Let me my future husband view
And be my vision chaste and true.

km 0   50   100   150
mi 0   50   100   150

THE SIEVE AND SHEARS

A commonly practised divination was the Sieve and Shears, used to discover thieves. The points of the shears were thrust into the wooden rim of the sieve so that the handles stood upright and the sieve hung from the points. Two people supported the handles with the middle fingers of their right hands. Once the sieve was suspended, the names of suspects were recited:

> By St Peter and St Paul,
>
> If (such-and-such) has stolen (so-and-so's) goods,
>
> Turn about riddle and shears and all.

When the thief's name was mentioned, the sieve turned or fell to the ground. Faith in the method was absolute.

DIVINATION OF LENGTH OF LIFE

Although even treasure-divining by the raising of spirits was long tolerated at official levels, forecasting the length of the king's reign was not. As important in politics as calculating through opinion polls the likely 'life' of a government is today, it was the province of the professional astrologer and expressly forbidden by law, as in popular estimation it came perilously near conjuring to take the king's life. Several astrologers were executed for it and in 1581 Parliament made it a statutory felony to cast nativities or calculate by prophecy how long Queen Elizabeth I would live. None the less such prediction continued: the Gunpowder Plotters employed it, and the astrologer John Heydon was allegedly imprisoned for predicting the death of Cromwell.

Outside the propertied classes – where there would be impatient heirs – people were less concerned with life expectancy as such than with the very real chances of dying in the coming year. To ascertain that likelihood, there was both a generalized reading of death omens – the howling of a dog round the house or the hooting of owls, or birds beating their wings against the window near a sick-bed – and more specific divinations.

Most often the recommended dates for divinations of any kind were the 'eves' or vigils before certain feast days of the pre-Reformation Church calendar, especially St Agnes's Eve (20 January), St Mark's Eve (24 April), St John's or Midsummer Eve (23 June) and All Hallows' Eve or Hallowe'en (31 October). All Hallows, the Christian feast of the dead, falls on 1 November, the beginning of the old Celtic year. In Wales *Nos Galangaeaf*, Winter's Eve, was one of the three Ghost Nights (*y Tair Ysbrydnos*) – the others being May Eve (30 April) and St John's Eve – when the spirits of the dead, the 'fetches' (doubles) of the living and the fairies walked the Earth. Because the dead were believed to know the future, all over Britain these three were particular nights for divination.

'Watching in the church porch' itself was most often practised on St Mark's Eve. The procedure was to go to the porch and wait for an hour before and an hour after midnight. At some moment during the vigil, the forms of those in the parish destined to die in the ensuing twelvemonth would appear.

'Cauff-riddling' was the Yorkshire name for a divination likewise performed mainly on St Mark's Eve, whose purpose was specific enquiry into one's own future. The enquirer went to a barn at midnight and, leaving the doors standing wide, riddled chaff (i.e. sifted husks of corn). If nothing was seen while he did so, the omen was good; but if a coffin carried by two bearers passed across the doorway, he would die within the twelvemonth.

Anecdotes like this – whether true or 'witness legends' designed to support a belief – raise the question of auto-suggestion, one reason perhaps why divining the future was commonly regarded as risky. Whether people thought of such ceremonies as the raising of apparitions (i.e. witchcraft) or as blasphemy (prying into the secrets of God) is unclear. Few, perhaps, drew distinctions.

MARRIAGE DIVINATIONS

Well into this century, marriage was the only career open to most women. Because of this, of all forms of popular divination the ones that survive in the most variety are those to do with marriage, and most were performed by girls.

Many of the rituals resemble conjurations, though often they leave some doubt as to whether the future partner is to be seen in the flesh, in a dream or as a 'fetch' or *doppelgänger*. In Northumberland, a girl had to find an ash leaf with an even number of leaflets and say:

> *Even, even ash,*
> *I pluck thee off the tree*
> *The first young man that I do meet,*
> *My love he shall be.*

She then put it in her left shoe. The first man she met after that would be her husband. This is apparently an encounter in the flesh, but what of the man who scattered ashes along a quiet lane on Hallowe'en in the expectation of seeing his destined wife following the trail?

A divination from north-west England takes the form of a salutation to the Moon. When the first New Moon of the year was seen, a girl was to take a brush in one hand and a comb in the other, and go in silence and secrecy into the garden. There she was to say:

> *New Moon, New Moon, New Moon, I hail thee.*
> *If ever I marry a man, or a man marry me,*
> *This night may I him see;*
> *And may his apparel not frighten me.*

She was then to return to the house in silence and go to bed, whereupon she would see her future husband in a dream, though the lingering apprehension in this charm suggests that originally he was expected as a fetch.

This was certainly so in a very old ritual once practised all over the country. Going at midnight to the churchyard, the enquirer (usually female) had to walk round the church sowing hempseed and saying:

> *Hempseed, I sow. Hempseed, grow.*
> *He that is my true love*
> *Come after me and mow.*

Looking back on the stroke of twelve (from the church clock), she would either see a coffin — meaning that she would die an old maid — or else a man's form would appear behind her with a scythe, mowing. St Mark's Eve, Midsummer Eve, Hallowe'en and Christmas Eve were all

suitable dates for the divination.

A man could find out who he would marry by going out to his barn and winnowing corn three nights running at midnight with both doors open. On the third night he would see the apparition of his future wife.

Midnight was also the critical time in the making of the Dumb Cake usually confined to Christmas Eve, St Agnes's Eve, St Mark's Eve or Hallowe'en. The Dumb Cake was a simple bannock (a round, flat loaf) – the traditional formula was an eggshell full of salt, one of wheat flour, and one of barley-meal. It had to be prepared alone, fasting and in ritual silence – hence the name. In Oxfordshire, girls pricked their initials on it and left it on the hearthstone to bake. Then they went to bed, leaving the door of the house open. At midnight the future husband's fetch was expected to enter through the door and add his initials. In the North of England, solitariness was not a requirement: two or three girls met together to bake the cake, divided it equally, and walked backwards upstairs holding it in their hands. They ate it just before getting into bed, in the hope of seeing the man they would marry in a dream.

The eating of the cake was probably originally required everywhere as the mechanism for inducing dreams and visions. In some parts of Northumberland, instead of the Dumb Cake, the girls ate an eggshell filled with salt, and on Tyneside men consumed a red herring, bones and all, for the same purpose.

MAGICAL ELEMENTS IN MARRIAGE DIVINATION

Darkness, secrecy, silence, the expectations raised by performance at the witching hour and on special 'ghost nights' - all played a part in creating the right context for these ceremonials. Others depended on magical factors. An old marriage divination recorded by Aubrey in the seventeenth century and still in use in the nineteenth could be used to see either a future wife or a husband, but only if you were away from home. 'You must', says Aubrey, 'lie in another county, and knit the left garter about the right-legged stocking (let the other garter and stocking alone) and as you rehearse these following verses, at every comma, knit a knot.'

> *This knot I knit,*
> *To know the thing, I know not yet,*
> *That I may see,*
> *The man (woman) that shall my husband (wife) be,*
> *How he goes, and what he wears,*
> *And what he does, all days, and years.*

The magic of knots – often employed in witchcraft – is involved here, as well the garter's possession of some sexual meaning: a bride's garters were snatched for luck at weddings.

In Wales, enquirers would walk seven times round the house carrying a boot, saying 'Here is the boot, where is the foot?' expecting to see the future partner appear. In Glamorgan in the 1950s a girl would scratch her boyfriend's initials on a leaf and put it inside her shoe. After a day and night, if the initials appeared plainer, she would take it as a sign that he was the one she would marry. In both rituals, the significant feature is the shoe, traditionally connected with marriage.

Plant material with magical significance was also often used. In Huntingdonshire, on May Eve, a girl would hang a branch of flowering May (hawthorn blossom) on a signpost at a crossroads and leave it there all night. In the morning she would look to see which way the wind had blown it, in the belief that her future husband would come from that direction. Not only was the crossroads traditionally a no-man's-land between the everyday and the supernatural, but the hawthorn was a fairy tree: their coming together is not coincidence.

John Gay, author of *The Beggar's Opera*, gives in *The Shepherd's Week* in 1714 a version of a game probably already old in his day. The enquirer suits his action to the words:

> *I pare this pippin [apple] round and round again*
> *My sweetheart's name to flourish on the plain.*
> *I fling the unbroken paring o'er my head,*
> *My sweetheart's letter on the ground is read.*

This is still played as a game in Scotland at Hallowe'en and by children at any time of the year, but an underlying seriousness is shown by the fact that the peel is thrown over the left shoulder – the (in the original sense) *fatal* side. The apple was regarded as a magical fruit.

In some places Hallowe'en was known as Nutcrack Night. If a girl wanted to be sure her lover was true, she took two hazelnuts and set them on the bars of the grate or on a log in the fire. If they burnt away together, he was faithful; if they flew apart, faithless.

DIVINATION AND CHILDREN'S GAMES

It is likely that a playful element was present in some marriage divinations from the first, and that it was the seemingly innocent, Arcadian appearance of such customs that has allowed so many to survive. Children still play 'He loves me, he loves me not' by pulling the petals off a daisy, one of several divinations of a simple counting-out kind. While some test the affections of a sweetheart, others sift through possibilities, like 'Tinker, tailor', originally played with cherry-stones: 'Tinker, tailor, soldier, sailor, rich man, poor man, beggar man, thief.'

Even more specific is the address to 'Bishy Barnabee', the ladybird, for obscure reasons named after St Barnabas. Blowing a ladybird off his or her hand, the enquirer says:

> *Bishy, Bishy Barnabee,*
> *Tell me when my wedding be;*
> *If it be tomorrow day,*
> *Take your wings and fly away.*

If he or she also wants to know the direction the lover will come from, action and words are the same, with the addition of:

> *Fly away east, fly away west,*
> *Show me where lives the one I love best.*

Marriage divination still flourished in the 1950s, when Welsh schoolgirls believed that if you counted nine stars on nine successive nights, on the ninth night you would dream of your future boyfriend. It remains to be seen if in the long term the force of the old drives will be enough to withstand the sexual revolution.

AFRICA

On the African continent divinatory systems have probably had a more continuous existence than in almost any other part of the world. The systems described in the two chapters that follow derive from very ancient times, possibly as far back as the Stone Age, and, remarkably in a time when Western influence is increasingly felt, they are still widely practised today.

As in the Celtic and Norse systems discussed in Chapters Two and Three, there is a direct link to deity. The diviners are not simply looking to the natural world, or to random events, or even to spirits, but directly to the gods; though it is also evident that they were in most instances either 'priests' or 'doctors', and thus fit within the category of shamans.

One also catches glimpses, in the accounts of anthropologists, of traditions that relate to 'families' of diviners, who passed on the knowledge of their skills from generation to generation. Although such instances are less well documented in the European world, it is more than likely that the same traditions were upheld within Western culture.

The similarities that obtain within individual tribes in the names attributed to the bones used for divination point to an ancient and widespread usage, and it is interesting to speculate whether bone divination was arrived at individually or was imported. There are clear similarities between Ifa and the various systems of geomancy, especially Sikidy and Raml (see Chapter Twenty-three), which is not surprising since these entered the West through the gate of North Africa. Other similarities are to be seen between the use of divination symbols drawn in sand and the allusive marks from which Saami diviners foretell events in the Far North (see Chapter Two).

The sheer diversity of places in which variations of the bone oracle are found suggests that this method is, indeed, the oldest and most basic of all the divination systems. It is in fact found in areas as widely separated as Europe, Scandinavia, Australia, New Zealand and the Americas, as well as all over Africa and throughout the East.

Although both of the chapters that follow concentrate on the particularly rich area of Southern Africa, similar systems exist throughout the rest of the continent. Aside from tribal variations, they are substantially the same as those described here.

CHAPTER ELEVEN

ORACLES IN BONE

Divination in Southern Africa

Kunderke Kevlin

In 1507 the Portuguese missionary Joano dos Santos observed the throwing of four 'bones' for the purpose of divination in Mozambique. Today, despite repeated attempts by white missionaries and governments in the colonial era to stamp out the practice, this same divinatory system is still widely prevalent in the industrial cities and rural areas of Southern and South Central Africa. The bone diviner continues to be a familiar figure, consulted whenever misfortunes threaten or have occurred, or whenever there is a need to have certainty about future events. People will consult him (it is usually a man) with questions such as 'What is the cause of my illness? Is there witchcraft involved? If there is, who is the witch?' or 'Will my cattle multiply and my crops be bountiful this year' or 'What will be the outcome of the court case?' As it is believed that virtually all misfortune is caused by witchcraft, most questions ultimately come down to a basic anxiety about witchcraft.

THE ORIGINS OF BONE DIVINATION

The tribal peoples of the vast area that comprises Southern and South Central Africa are not of the same cultural stock, so where and with whom this divinatory system originated is an intriguing question. The answer is hard to establish as it goes back in time long before written records existed. We can know only more recent events with certainty: that in the nineteenth century, for instance, the custom was brought to what is now Zambia by a migrating tribe from the Transvaal.

It has been suggested by some authors that the custom of bone divination of the first type described below originated with the old Zimbabwe culture and/or from the Arab trading influence in this same area. They supply no firm evidence for their view, but I found information in the ethnographic writing which does provide some circumstantial evidence.

It is certain, for example, that the names of the principal bones are of archaic origin and refer to cultural heroes or ancestor gods. The tribes of the Venda and Lemba, who live in the Transvaal province of South Africa, have traditions that link them strongly to the names used for the bones. In a famous legend it is told how Mwali, the great god, king of heaven, but also the ancestor god of the Royal Singo clan of the Venda, had a son called Tshilume and one of Tshilume's successors was called Hwami. Hwami and Tshilume are the names of two of the principal bones of the divination set among the Venda and Lemba and most of the tribes recorded as having the custom. The Venda names for the other two principal bones, Thwalima and Lumwe, are also widely distributed among the other tribes.

We know that the Venda and Lemba migrated together from Zimbabwe to the Transvaal (Zimbabwe was the magnificent capital of an ancient kingdom from which present-day Zimbabwe takes its name), and that the Lemba are a tribe of mixed origin, resulting from the intermarriage of Arabs and Africans. Other tribes make frequent reference to Lemba and Venda in the 'praises' attached to the bones, which tends to confirm them as the originators of the system.

In this chapter I focus mainly on the traditions of bone divination among the Sotho, Tswana, Venda and Lovedu tribes, who live in the South African provinces of the Transvaal and Orange Free State and in Botswana and Lesotho. The tribes further north, such as the Shona, differ quite significantly in their culture, although the basic principles of their system of bone divination appear similar. Other South African tribes, such as the Swazi, Zulu and Xhosa, who live in Swaziland, Natal, Transkei and the Cape Province, are again quite different culturally and tend to use a different form of bone divination, of which there are fewer eyewitness accounts. They also place greater emphasis on another form of divination, based on clairvoyance and usually carried out by women.

THE BONES

There are two different types of bones, which are used either separately or in conjunction with

THE SPREAD OF BONE DIVINATION
Bone divination probably originated in Zimbabwe. It became established in Southern Africa through the migration of tribes southwards and the acceptance of the custom by the tribes already resident there. Today it is found as far north as Zambia and as far south as the Cape Province.

each other. There are thus also two different forms of bone divination.

The first is divination by means of a set of four bones, which are differentiated into a senior male, a junior male, a senior female and a junior female. These bones consist either all four of ivory, bone, horn (of cattle) or wood, or two of the bones may be cut from the tip of the hoof of an ox or cow and thus be pyramid-shaped. Each of the bones has a positive, decorated side and a negative, undecorated side, so that they can form 16 different combinations when thrown together on the ground. Each combination or 'fall' has a name, a 'praise' (the poem that is recited when the fall is identified) and a standard general interpretation, and the diviner interprets this meaning in relation to the problems at hand. Thus the system is based on three oppositions – male/female, senior/junior and positive/negative – and the meanings produced by combinations of these categories.

The second is divination by means of a large number (up to 60) of *astragali* (knucklebones) of various animals and sometimes also a few other objects, such as seashells, tortoiseshell and special stones. In general the aim is to have a male and female bone of each species, with a few significant exceptions: for instance, among the Lovedu the antbear is represented by only one bone as it digs in the ground where the dead are buried and is thus associated with the ancestors. Again, each bone has a positive and negative side so that the diviner can 'read' the fall in terms of the position of the bones in relation to each other and according to which side faces up.

The Nguni peoples and the tribes of Southern Mozambique use only this second form of divination, while the Sotho, Tswana, Venda, Lovedu, Matabele and Kalanga use both types of bones, but consider the *astragali* of secondary significance.

THE DIVINER

The person who wants to be a bone diviner usually does this in combination with learning the skills of doctoring. The better-known diviners are also herbalists and base their

diagnosis, not on an examination of the patient, but on what the bones tell them.

Anyone who wishes to learn the skills of the doctor-diviner may ask a diviner to instruct him. As a rule the diviner, before commencing to teach another person, will consult his divining bones to ascertain if the prospective pupil is worthy of admission into the profession. If the bones reply in the affirmative, but only then, the pupil is taught how to divine. He learns the names of the divining bones and the meanings of

the various positions and combinations in which they fall, with the appropriate praises to each.

At first the teacher uses his own divining set, but after some time he tells the pupil to kill an ox, from whose bones he carves a set of the four principal pieces. The bones must be cut out of the raw flesh and doctored with various medicines. An appeal is made to the ancestors to give the bones the power of divination. The process may involve the use of white objects or substances, for example, placing the bones under white ash, or under white leaves on a growing tree beneath white moonlight. In some tribes the apprentice drinks a concoction of water in which the bones plus various roots, powders and the

Seeking advice on his health, a Tswana man has thrown the bones. The diviner – dressed in white, the colour of the spirits – studies the throw and will soon give a reading. The presence of a female healer indicates that she will also be involved in effecting a cure once the diagnosis has been made. In this case only a few of the pieces of a divining set have been used, i.e. two ivory tablets, six astragali *and one cowrie shell.*

flesh of a white goat have been boiled, so that he will eventually understand 'inside his heart' how to read the bones.

The period of instruction may be from one to three years, according to the ability of the pupil and the extent of the teacher's knowledge. The pupil may also extend his training by becoming an apprentice to other diviners after his initial training has been completed.

Learning bone divination is in many ways a logical process, rather than one requiring psychic ability. Definite rules of interpretation are taught and it is the bones, not the diviner, who are in direct contact with the spirit world. The diviner has to learn the rules in order to understand what the bones are telling him. Although the application of these rules to particular cases also requires intuition and creativity, as the rules have to be interpreted according to the complexity of each case, it is not requisite that the diviner himself develops psychic abilities.

THE MEANING OF THE BONES

The bones are believed to have an intrinsic power, which is strengthened, but not determined, by the ritual doctoring they have received. Different suggestions have been made as to where their power derives from. Some say they reveal the will of God, others that the ancestors speak through them, yet others that they reveal a more or less impersonal cosmic power. It is likely that all these viewpoints are true. The Bantu concept of God is very different from the Christian one, so that the first and the last suggestions are one and the same thing. And, as noted earlier, the ancestors are asked to 'strengthen' the bones and impart of their wisdom to them, but that does not mean that they are the ultimate source of the divining power. The ancestors are part of and bound by the same cosmic and moral order as man is. It should be noted that the term *bola* or *bala* or *bula*, which is used to refer to the divining set, has also been translated as 'the word', implying a relatively impersonal cosmic power.

The power of the bones lies in the fact that they represent important categories that are used in the ordering of the social and cultural world. It could also be argued that these same categories or ordering principles are found at the cosmic and natural levels. In other words, there are principles of order in the universe which manifest at both the human and non-human levels.

As mentioned previously, the divinatory set is based on the oppositions of male and female and junior and senior. These are also the key principles of the social order and cultural activities. The division between and the complementarity of male and female pervades nearly every social and ritual activity. Much of tribal life is divided into male and female spheres of influence, competence and experience. Often there were prohibitions against crossing from one sphere to another and where the two unavoidably met, as in sexual activity and procreation, there was considered to be both great danger and great creative potential. Symbolism constantly reinforces this basic division. For instance, when a boy is born the father will be told by a man hitting him with a stick across the shoulders, but if it is a girl a woman will pour a calabash of water over him. The earth is female, the sky is male; the left side of the hut is female, the right side of the hut is male; and so on. Even diviners were typically divided into the male diviners who used the bones and the female diviners who instead used clairvoyance.

The senior/junior opposition is equally significant. The whole of society is ranked within the sphere of each sex – the ranking often falls away when it applies to people of a different gender. Siblings of the same sex are ranked as senior and junior to each other, and this is extended to lineages, villages and totemic groups.

These rules are the basis of the kinship system and the bones are directly linked to specific positions within the family. Thus the simplest designation is father, mother, son, daughter – but this can be extended according to the case presented. Thus, the senior male bone can represent the paternal ancestors, the grand-

THE PRAISE-POEMS AND
THEIR READING

The four principal bones of the divinatory set combine into 16 different falls, each of which has its own name and praise-poem. The names of the bones and the falls show a striking similarity among the different tribes, if allowance is made for linguistic variation. This suggests that the meanings and interpretations of each fall might also have a single system of meaning. Unfortunately, this does not appear to be the case. Many praise-poems are virtually impossible to understand for a cultural outsider, and it can only be hoped that one day an African researcher/diviner will give a more understandable and thorough account. The meanings of some falls are, however, relatively accessible to Western diviners.

The fall in which all the four principle (senior male) bones fall positive is called *Mphirifiri* or *Mufirifiri*. It indicates too much action or feverish activity and is associated with fire and 'hotness', which is considered a dangerously overenergetic state.

The following is a Sotho praise for this fall:

Unrest of a multitude makes the dust rise; they have cut the cord that goes through the nostrils of the ox. At Phalaborwa, near the Olifants river, where the blacksmiths live, sounds the hammer, the morning bird sings, in the east the day shines.

This fall is generally interpreted as a negative one, associated with strife, illness, death and withcraft. A patient whose health is in question, for instance, will die; or there will be quarrels between the people and attempts to bewitch each other.

The fall that is negative for the senior male and female and positive for the junior male and female is called *Thlapadima* among the Kgatla, a Tswana tribe. The praise goes:

I am the cheater of the children, of the children who have no parents, of the rain; it is a person who cannot cross the river, it says one who sinks in and jumps out, it says the biter in the river (water)

father, the father's brother, the chief or simply a senior or elderly man. The junior male can represent the mother's brother, the maternal ancestors or any junior ranking male.

The meaning of the *astragalus* bones varies between clusters of tribes. With those tribes that have totemic groups they represent them, with the others they represent social categories. An account of the bones used by the Lovedu tribe illustrates that the full divinatory set represents the Lovedu social universe:

The Lovedu set is fairly stereotyped, consisting of about forty pieces, most but not all of which are bones.... Dominating the usual Lovedu set are four flat pieces of ivory or bone, two male and two female, which fall in sixteen different combinations.... There are other sets of four: pieces from the ventral surface of a tortoise, each with two easily distinguishable sides, and shells, two Olwa standing for males and two Cypraea standing for females. Having thrown the dice, the diviner looks first at the ivory pieces and gives the praises of their disposition, which indicates the general situation.... But this general situation must be related to the lie of certain other bones, particularly malope, *the knuckle-bone of the steenbuck-...from which, as representing the chief, the diviner next orientates the situation. The procedure thereafter involves linking this situation, on the one hand, with events of specific prognostications of good or evil and, on the other, with people playing a part in these events.* Thakadu or mudimo, *the talus of an antbear, represents the ancestors, who, like the antbear, live underground, shows whether they are angry or not, and is diagnostic of the health or life of a person, which in the last resort lies in ancestral hands.* Dau, *the phalanx of a lion,* phiri, *the knee-bone of the hyena... and* tshweni, *male and female knee-bones of the baboon, all stand for the evil power of witches and their familiars.... Two or three sheep bones stand for important or respected people, such as district or village heads, and goat bones...for mere commoners.... Different totems are shown by the bones of the animals revered.* (E. Krige, The Realm of the Rain Queen, 1943, pp. 226–7.)

when there is no rhinoceros or crocodile. What are you washing frog, why do you wash as if you will be taken by the rhinoceros or crocodile. The reeds are on the bank of the river, you are in the water, when the river takes you it will sweep you away, roots and all, and sweep you into the big rivers; it says we are just the same, you will be burned outside in the grass, and my body will be burned but when the first rains fall I shall grow again. (From the research notes of Professor Isaac Schapera.)

The first part of this praise has been said to refer to illegitimate sex, but no comment is supplied for the clearly much more profound statement about life and death in the latter part. This fall is also considered a negative one: it might mean that the patient will recover, but his blood has thickened and he is shivering; or a wife is deceiving her husband with other men in his absence; or a pregnant woman keeps miscarrying.

The meaning of the fall can differ according to what category of problem is presented. A fall that is generally negative may be propitious for one type of problem, for example rainfall in the case of *Mufirifiri*.

BONE DIVINATION IN A CHANGING WORLD

Bone divination originated in a tribal culture that was founded on close contact with the natural world. Today, the wild animals are confined to game reserves, and industrial cities dominate the economy. Many Africans now live their whole lives in an urban environment and even more spend the greater part of their time working in the cities and mines as migrant labourers. Tribal culture has undergone profound changes in the twentieth century, and these changes will inevitably have led to new developments in the symbolism and interpretation of the bones. It is unlikely, however, that the reasons why people consult a diviner have changed. The belief in witchcraft is certainly as strong as ever, and in fact the incidence of witchcraft accusations may have increased as a

Although lifestyle and customs have changed within many African tribes, belief in the power of divination remains strong. Here, Zulu mystic and diviner Laduma Madela prepares for a reading.

result of the psychological insecurities of this time of rapid social change. Today's African still turns to the diviner when beset by anxieties or difficulties, and so the sight of the diviner taking out his little bag of bones and shaking them out onto the ground remains a common one.

Note
I want to express my gratitude to Professor Isaac Schapera, who kindly allowed me to study his unpublished research notes concerning Kgatla divination.

CHAPTER TWELVE

IFA

A Yoruba System of Oracular Worship

John Turpin and Judith Gleason

Ifa, teacher of gods, of men, and the means of communication between them, is an oracular worship-and-belief system rooted in the spiritual history of the Yoruba people of south-western Nigeria. Despite social change, consultation of Ifa through its traditionally instructed practitioners continues to be a vital part of Yoruba life. Variants and derivatives of Ifa exist most notably in the Republic of Benin (formerly Dahomey) and in Togo. Across the Atlantic, Cuba became the stronghold of Ifa-in-diaspora, and today hundreds of Ifa priests, trained in Cuba and Africa, are practising throughout the United States.

There are five principal deities or divine beings associated with Ifa. Orunmila is the deity who manifests the spiritual essence of Ifa. Throughout the divination literature of Ifa one finds Orunmila verbally linked to a mysterious spirit or principle known as Ela, 'the preserver'. An indispensable companion of the divination process is Elégba, trickster spirit and messenger, who conveys the necessary offerings and sacrifices for well-being that human beings make, in accordance with oracular prescription, to the ancestors and to the various gods of the Yoruba pantheon. A second crucial companion of the process is Osanyin, divine herbalist and medicinal healer. Olodumare, the Yoruba creator, also known as Olorun, 'owner of the heavens', although out of respect invoked and at times depicted in the sacred verses of Ifa, cannot be said to play an active role in the

divination process, even on the sacrificial level of placation; for Olodumare is beyond responding to gifts of food and drink from humans.

The containers of Ifa's wisdom are called Odu, and they can be described in various ways. All practitioners consider the 16 major Odu to be divine personalities in their own right, and there are some practitioners who so conceive the entire group of 256 Odu. Because an extensive and elaborate traditional oral literature is associated with each Odu, they can be thought of as sacred 'books' belonging to a library housed in the collective memory of Ifa priests, who are known as *Babaláwo*, or 'fathers of secrets'. We can also imagine Odu that appear in the process of divination as signatures of prototypical events, apt to occur and recur in a

A divining tray (Opon Ifa) with the face of Eshu, intercessor, guardian and messenger, at the top of the board. This tray is from Ijebu, Nigeria, and has a diameter of 14 inches.

variety of ways in the experience of human beings. At the most tangible level, Odu are graphic figures: a series of 256 octograms resulting from the casting and notation of Ifa's lots.

1	2	3	4
Èjìogbè	Òyèkú Méjì	Ìwòrì Méjì	Òdí Méjì

5	6	7	8
Ìrosùn Méjì	Òwónrín Méjì	Òbàrà Méjì	Òkànràn Méjì

9	10	11	12
Ògúndá Méjì	Òsá Méjì	Ìká Méjì	Òtúrúpòn Méjì

13	14	15	16
Òtúrá Méjì	Ìretè Méjì	Òsé Méjì	Òfún Méjì

In this diagram the major Odu are listed in their usual ranking order. Each of the 16 configurations taken separately (rather than in a pair, as is the case here) may combine with any of the remaining 15, thus generating 240 more Odu, each with its own core meanings and attendant obligations.

ORIGINS

What is the origin of Ifa? According to myth, Orunmila came down to Earth at the beginning of time along with the other divinities, but in a period of great disorder (dramatized by the disrespectful bahaviour of his youngest son) the divinity of oracular wisdom retreated. Later, responsive to universal entreaty, Orunmila sent the Odu down to make order among gods and people in his stead.

This emphasis on order and reorganization

Babalorixa Balbino, founder of Ile Ase Opo Aganju (a Yoruba cult house) in Salvador, Brazil, performing a divination in February 1983 with cowrie shells, whose combinations coincide with those of Ifa. The rim of the divining tray is symbolically represented by necklaces of all the Orisha (Yoruba divinities).

may well be a coded way of referring to an incorporation by the earliest Ifa priests of an archaic and indigenous system of cowrie-shell divination known today as Dilogun. Dilogun, which in turn has incorporated much of the Ifa nomenclature and which contains recognizable permutations of many of its paradigmatic stories, continues to be practised widely by priests and priestesses of the various divinities

IFA IN AFRICA AND IN EXILE

Ifa divination originated among the Yoruba people, ten million of whom presently live in south-western Nigeria and parts of the neighbouring republics of Benin (formerly Dahomey) and Togo. Ifa was probably practised in Dahomey as early as the late seventeenth century. During the slave-trading era, Yoruba diviners were carried to Cuba in sufficient numbers to keep the practice alive there. In recent times Cuban Babaláwo in exile have introduced Ifa to the continental United States; and even more recently many African-Americans have been going directly to Nigeria for training. In Nigeria, Cuba and elsewhere in the Caribbean a system of cowrie-shell divination called Dilogun, with cultural and metaphysical links to Ifa, is standard practice. Other forms of cowrie-shell divination, based on a different numerical system, are widespread in West Africa, as is the Islamic method of 'sand cutting'.

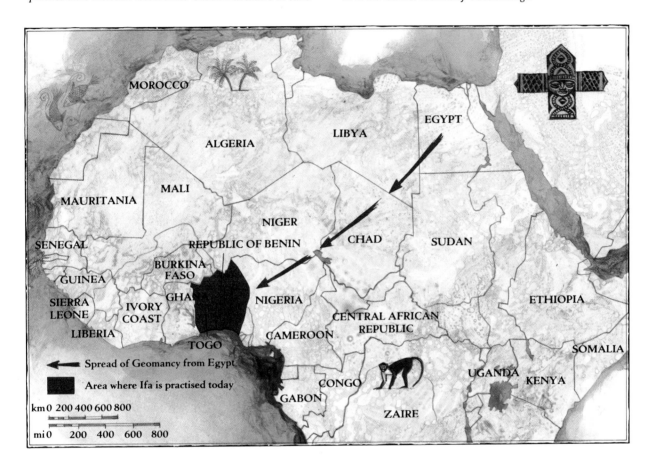

both in Africa and in the new world. The myth of reorganization by imposition from 'above' of an elaborate geomantic system associated with the masculine *logos* may be supplemented by the traditional attribution of cowrie-shell divination to a feminine divinity, Oshun, from whose mediums every Ifa priest is expected to select a wife. From what we know of the migration of the ancient science of geomancy, it seems that 'above' can also be read as north. The random selection of odd or even remainders to generate 16 signs of four dimensions each is as generic to geomancy as is the writing of these signs upon the face (or simulated surface) of the Earth (see Chapter Twenty-three, Ancient Secrets of the Earth).

Even though Ifa's belief system, value system, procedures and literature are entirely its own, some traces of its probable origins as a divinatory technology remain. Orunmila's name may well be a synthesis of the Yoruba word for 'heaven' (*òrun*) and the Arabic word for 'sand' (*ram'l*); and the name Ifa itself may be derived from the Arabic word for 'omen' (*fa'l*). Those most important of omens, bird pressages, are in Arabic called *iyafa*. Here perhaps we have the kernel of Ifa myths about the original Odu, a goddess, arriving on Earth with 'bird power', a euphemism for witchcraft, which may here be defined as the ability to respond intuitively and effectively to whatever a crisis demands.

AN IFA DIVINATION

The manner in which the Ifa oracle is 'opened' may be described as follows. The Ifa priest will seat himself, facing east, on a mat that has been placed on the ground or on the floor. He will then arrange the divinatory artefacts about him. The tray will be placed directly in front of him near a shallow wooden bowl containing the palm nuts. From a small sealed vessel, stored in the commodious covered bowl, he will take wood dust and sprinkle it onto the tray. Using the middle finger of his right hand, the diviner will draw a line from the top of the tray to the bottom and from right to left. Intersecting at the midpoint, these marks form a cross with equidistant branches. A small bowl of cool water will be placed beside the vessel bearing the palm nuts. Then, taking the divining wand in his right hand, while continuously tapping it lightly against the tray, the *Babaláwo* will begin to recite a series of invocations, one of which is as follows:

Olódùmarè
'Unique and permanent container of Being'
Olòjó oni mo júbà
I give deepest respect to the Owner of this day
Ati waiyé ojo, ìbà
And to the worldly forces existing today, my homage
Ati là òrun, ìbà
And to dawning in the heavens, my homage
Ìbà o loni, ìbà o
Praise be to this day, o praise
Ìbà tó tó tó f'onílè àìye
Infinite praise to our great mother, o earth
Onílè mo júbà
Spirit within the earth, my homage . . . .

Further opening incantations are intended to awaken and propitiate the holy spirit of Ifa, the oracle deity Orunmila, the sacred constellation of all divinities and the spirit of the deified ancestors. The priest then takes the bowl of cool water and sprinkles it over the sacred palm nuts. Lifting them from the vessel one at a time, he

CONTINUED ON PAGE 106

SACRED ARTEFACTS IN IFA DIVINATION

1 Sixteen consecrated palm nuts gathered from a special tree (Elaeis guineensis). Palm nuts chosen for divination have four 'eyes' at their base and therefore 'see' in all cardinal directions.

2 A wooden tray upon which the Odu figures are marked. This tray is usually round, but may be rectangular. Carvings along the rim include a schematic central face (facing the diviner across the board), which represents the presence of Elégba, the messenger, guardian of the crossroads and the trickster or 'uncertainty principle' inherent in the workings of fate. Serpentine markings represent the play of fortune.

3 Wood dust from a certain tree (Baphia nitida) which, having been gnawed by termites, dissolves into a beautiful representation of natural entropy. A pinch of the dust, which has been sprinkled on the divining board and had Odu signs marked upon it, and is considered to be imbued with the transformative power of the oracle, is either touched to the client's forehead or given to him sacramentally to swallow.

4 A divining chain containing eight seed halves (Schrebera golungensis). Although the palm-nut procedure is the more sacred and the one used for special consulations, the divining chain, which is said to 'chatter' faster, is in practice the more common vehicle of Ifa divination. The Ifa priest holds it by the centre string or chain, swings it away from himself and towards the client, then lets it fall upon the mat. The two halves of the chain are read from right to left (from the client's perspective). If a seed falls with its convex surface facing up it receives a notation of two marks ($|\;|$), while a concave surface uppermost receives one ($||$). The 'head' of the Odu is that closest to the centre of the connecting chain.

5 A divining wand, carved either from an elephant's tusk or from a piece of wood shaped like one, which is tapped against the divining tray to invoke the spirit of the oracle.

A detail of the divining wand shows the extended body of a chameleon in the position of an ancestor's beard. The chameleon, associated with the divinity of moral purity and exemplary character, travels slowly but arrives with the redemptive message.

6 An assortment of small symbolic objects of vegetable, animal or mineral substance – tokens used in clarifying the intention of Ifa in particular situations. Of these, a bone (signifying 'no' and, depending on the context, ancestors, death, or children) and two cowrie shells tied together (which means 'yes', as well as money or illness, again depending on the context) are the tokens most actively engaged during consultations.

7 and **8** Carved containers (for the palm nuts, divining chain, small objects and certain sacramental ingredients) in the shape of a covered bowl or sculpted cup on a stem.

9 Although it is not used in the divining process itself, no description of the *Babaláwo*'s paraphernalia would be complete without mention of the diviner's bag, often beautifully beaded, which he wears over his shoulder when he walks out of his own residence. Inside the bag are the essential items of his profession, like the palm nuts and the divining chain, ready for a house-call.

All of these artefacts must be consecrated before use as effective transmitters of oracular energy.

This ritual bowl from Ekiti, Nigeria, might contain the palm nuts of Ifa. The cock is considered to be a messenger of spirits. On the lid a forest cat devours a smaller animal.

calls in succession the names of the 16 primary Odu. Holding the palm nuts in his left hand, he takes one from the 16, touches it to the forehead of the client, and while so doing recites a prayer of affirmation and supplication. Replacing this single palm nut, he utters these final invocatory phrases in order to 'open the way' for the oracular spirit:

Emi ọ̀run sọ̀kalè wá
Heaven, descend to us
Wá gbe imu ilè yi
Make this house your home
Sọ̀kalè pèlú agbára
Descend with complete power
Wá mi mímọn wá
Come freshness come!

With his right hand the Ifa priest covers the palm nuts held in his left hand. Now with joined hands containing the palm nuts he touches the four cardinal points of the tray, and subsequently with a circular counter-clockwise motion of

Portrait of Dosso Solo, a hunters' diviner, from Lafiabougou quarter, San, Mali, in March 1983. Solo uses 12 rather than 16 cowries and a geomantic 'sand cutting' method whose markings are allied to those of Ifa.

his right hand effaces the crossed lines he had previously marked in the wood dust. As he does so, the priest chants:

Arére. Atótó. Ifá fẹ́ fọ ohùn. E dáke̩.
Silence. Quiet. Ifa wishes to speak.
Let there be silence.

Immediately, with his right hand, the priest attempts to grasp all of the 16 palm nuts from his left hand. If all are in fact grasped, he will make no mark in the dust on the divination tray. He will transfer the nuts back to the left hand and grasp them again. If only one nut remains in his left hand, he will make a double mark (‖) in the wood dust. If only two remain, he will make a single mark (|). If more than two remain he will begin again. This procedure will continue until a full Odu of eight indices is marked on the tray in the following manner: beginning at the top of the board, the paired markings are made in two columns, first right then left (see diagram on page 102); and as they are written, so they are read – from right to left.

When a person consults Ifa he has a 'presenting problem' which he does not initially tell the diviner, but upon which he focuses by silently declaring its nature to a coin or shell and then placing it on the board. It is a problem – perhaps an important decision to make, or a journey to be embarked upon, perhaps an illness or social maladjustment – which the diviner will assist him in solving in four stages, of which the unfolding of the Odu as described above is the first. By putting the isolated client's case into a generic situational context, the revelation of the appropriate Odu beings preliminary relief, comparable to that felt by a suffering patient experiencing diagnosis of a named and hence intelligible and treatable malady. In effect, Ifa is saying: of the 256 possible windows looking out onto Being, this is the one before which you now stand with a quandary, life crisis, or affliction

The late lamented Araba of Lagos, Chief Fagbemi Ajanaku. Araba means 'Great Spreading Tree' and is the title given to the chief diviner of a city. Ajanaku was also a doctor of traditional medicine. This photograph was taken in 1977.

endemic to this 'place' and under scrutiny of or attack by certain invisible forces, which will have to be placated according to their own individual requirements.

As soon as the Odu is inscribed on the board, its name is pronounced and the Odu is praised in order to activate it. At once the diviner begins to recite texts which are traditionally a part of that particular Odu's canon. These texts include stories in a folkloric vein whose protagonists are always clients (human beings with curious, instructive names; sometimes gods; sometimes animals or natural phenomena, like a pond or a tree; sometimes utensils or other familiar objects) who long ago consulted Ifa for various reasons, and who, depending on whether or not they made the specified sacrifices, were or were not given satisfaction and a bettered or even joyous condition. It is up to the client to identify and listen to the story most pertinent to his own situation.

Having recognized an analogous case, the client then opens his heart to the diviner who now uses the tokens to question Ifa further on the hidden implications of the problem, and thus fine-tune the diagnosis. Conversation with the client also aids in this interpretive phase during which the metaphors of the chosen story-road of the Odu become transparent indications of specific difficulties in the client's attitude and environment.

The *Babaláwo* now specifies the sacrificial ingredients called for by the Odu at hand. Most of these are food substances. Should the client's situation indeed be serious, perhaps more so than he realized, a fowl or four-footed animal might have to lose its life in order to preserve his or that of a family member. Often symbolic items like a cloth of a certain colour are specified. The sooner the offerings are made to the appropriate spiritual forces, the better. Should the client refuse or neglect the obligation, there is nothing more the diviner-priest can do. But as soon as he complies, then a herbal remedy is concocted from leaves or roots associated with the particular Odu and given to the client either to drink or to bathe with.

Thus are resistances clogging the flow between inner self ('head' in Yoruba parlance), behavioural self (social harmony being essential in Yoruba context) and the invisible world temporarily dissipated. The slow-working part of the cure is the paradigmatic story chosen by the client himself from the many recited by the diviner, a story accompanied by a song or chant which enables him to remember and to reflect upon his situation as mirrored in Ifa's indispensable wisdom.

Integral to an understanding of Ifa are the interconnected Yoruba notions of 'head' and destiny. In short, the Yoruba believe that one chooses one's 'head' or inner personality before birth, and this head implies a certain path, including fortune or misfortune, in life. It is possible to consult the oracle and be given an Odu-symbol of one's character and fate combined. By consistent consultation of Ifa and scrupulous observation of obligations to one's 'head-ruling' deity and to one's ancestors, as well as dutiful following of all other truly inspired (as opposed to quack) advice, even a problematic head can get itself together and provide its bodily owner with a satisfactory earthly existence this time around. Consultation on behalf of a new-born baby can get it properly orientated so far as the visible and invisible worlds are concerned. For example, perhaps a certain ancestor has chosen to come back into the world through the medium of this new-born baby, who should be named accordingly. Or perhaps a certain divinity has chosen the child as its putative worshipper. Although various Odu turn up during a life-long series of consultations, one is born under a certain constellation of forces and it is important that this natal Odu be known, and that its idiosyncratic dietary and behavioural prescriptions be observed as soon as possible. Furthermore, certain temperamental characteristics, appropriate to those born under particular Odu-patterns, are better respected, even indulged, at the onset of life rather than retrospectively, after a degree of parental or societal violence may already have been done to the young person's nature.

THE AMERICAS

The difficulties involved in attempting to describe the divinatory methods of the Native Americans are immediately apparent when one considers that there were, until the coming of white people, over 600 separate tribes, each with their own cultural variations. There are still some 487 recognized tribal groups; but among these perhaps only two per cent of the people still carry 'medicine', retaining the old ways which have been stamped out by years of persecution and re-education.

The Native American way of life is based upon a deep relationship to the natural world. As Jamie Sams has remarked, *everything* in the world of the Great Mystery has a story to tell, and it is by observing it that one becomes aware of trends and movements within the pattern of being. Thus the story of divination in North America is at the same time superbly simple and endlessly complex, just as the patterns of the created world are both simple and complex.

Above all, it is the recognition of the interrelatedness of all things and all beings, and of their divine origin, which marks out the Native American tradition and enables those who follow its ways to utilize the signs and languages of the natural world to divine their place in the scheme of the Great Mystery. The beings who inhabit the natural world are themselves sacred, so, in accordance with Native tradition, we have capitalized their names to show that they are Sacred Beings and not simply stones, animals or things.

There are clear echoes here of the old native spiritual traditions of Europe and the Far North, just as there are powerful connections to the traditions of Australia and New Zealand. All these cultural groups share a belief in the sacredness of all things and in the close observation of natural trends as a means of discovering the answers to ages old questions of meaning and progress.

In ancient Mesoamerica (today's Mexico and Central America), a more complex and formalized set of traditions took shape. Careful observations of star patterns and influences by the Mayan, Aztec, Toltec, Zapotec and Mixtec peoples evolved into an intricate astrological and divinatory calendric system that has been kept alive for more than 2,000 years in oral tradition, despite, as in the case of the northern Amerindian world, efforts to suppress or destroy all traces of the native way of life. (In the South, where the great culture was that of the Incas, a more limited form of divination – by animal entrails – flourished, similar to that practised in the classical world – see Chapter Seven).

In the Mesoamerican astro-calendar we may see links with both Tarot (Chapter Five) and astrology (Chapter Six), as well as with the runic alphabets of the Celts and the Norse (Chapters Three and Four). Similarly, in the method of counting out beans or crystals, we are reminded both of the bone oracles of Africa (Chapter Eleven) and of the techniques of geomancy (Chapter Twenty-three).

CHAPTER THIRTEEN

SACRED MEDICINE

Native North-American Divination Systems

Jamie Sams

From the earliest rememberings of our oral traditions until modern times, Native American people have looked to the Earth Mother and Nature for signs, portents, omens and guidance. Our systems of divination have always been more a way of life than a philosophy or religion. The Red Race, which can be defined as the indigenous people of the Americas, has been given the guardianship of Natural Law and the Medicines of Earth, Medicines meaning the strengths, talents and healing ways of being that humankind could find in the natural world. These Medicines would allow the Original People (human beings) to learn how to survive and how to grow spiritually in physical bodies. It was up to our Elders to see that these teachings were passed from generation to generation so that human Two-leggeds would know how to walk on the Earth in beauty and balance, being in harmony with all living things. We have always considered all life-forms on our Mother Planet to be our relatives and our equals. For centuries, we have sought to learn the languages of every life-form in order to know how to live life on Earth with gratitude for all the lessons each teacher in Nature brings.

Native American divination covers the whole of North, Central and South America. The North American continent alone has over 487 recognized Tribes, and although each Tribe has its own separate Tradition, many common practices link each Nation or Tribe with the others. The common threads that are found in every Tribe are the links to the Great Mystery (the Creator), the Earth Mother, Father Sky,

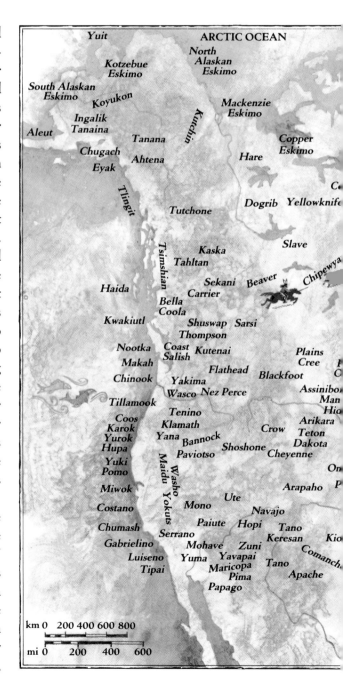

Grandfather Sun, Grandmother Moon and all of Nature. Although some Tribes assign the Sun, Moon and Sky to different identities – early Cherokee teachings spoke of Grandmother Sun and Grandfather Moon – the meaning is the same, and the only thing that is different is the relationship with the human being.

In my training, my Elders have taught me that we are here to walk the Earth in order to bring our spiritual natures into alignment with our physical bodies. We do this by manifesting the Great Mystery's Eternal Flame of Love through our thoughts and actions on the physical plane. This is Divine balance and requires many lessons to be learned. How we learn those lessons depends upon how we see and honour the Sacredness of all life. To accomplish this goal of Sacredness in our lives we must follow a Sacred Path, also called the Beauty Way.

In my Tradition, we believe that sometimes the Great Mystery can be a Divine Trickster and that the joke is how we humans are tricked into growing, learning and evolving. Since Divine and divination have the same root word, it is easy to see how everything the Great Mystery created can be a blueprint or map for human beings to use for growth. We believe that all humans have the same mission in their Earthwalks (physical life). This mission is for each individual to discover his or her gifts, talents and abilities, then to develop those gifts fully and share them with humanity in order to aid the whole of Creation. Our systems of divination are based upon teaching human beings how to understand those lessons of spiritual growth. Unlike many other systems of divination, which point the seeker to romance, success, fame or impending doom, the Native American culture holds a Sacred Point of View, using the signs and languages of Nature to point the way to 'right relationship' with self, family, Nation, Clan, Tribe, Nature and the Great Mystery. Everything else is merely an illusion.

The Dreamtime is the parallel reality or Spirit World where all the tangible, breakable, physical things of life can be stripped away until only the essence remains. We believe that this essence is the Eternal Flame of Love. It is in the Dreamtime that we can see beyond the illusions

TRIBAL LANDS OF THE NATIVE PEOPLE
This map shows the original homelands that were given to the Indian Tribes of North America by the Great Mystery. Each Tribe was given the guardianship of the Earth Mother in their location, in order to preserve the abundance of life for as long as the grass grew, the rivers flowed and the sun shone. Most Tribes were relocated during the Trail of Tears in the 1870s.

and into our essence, which is total connection to all things, bonded with the glue of Great Mystery's fire. To get to the Dreamtime or beyond physical illusion, we use the maps of Nature, the call of our Ancestors' voices, the languages of the trees and stones, and the lessons of the Creature-teachers. We believe that all things that have ever existed in a location are still in that location. The only thing that separates us from those realities is a thin membrane which is composed of our illusory concept of time. In using the lessons of Nature and the guidance provided by those Allies (Allies being any force or living thing in Nature which can teach us), we can come into spiritual balance and bridge the abyss of illusion. When we move into the Oneness of all things, the eternal truths of the world of Spirit and the world of physicality are blended and made known to us.

ANIMAL MEDICINE

Animals are our Creature-teachers and protective spirits. They carry certain strengths which we call Medicines. These Medicines comprise the talents, abilities and instincts that each Totem (Power Animal) embodies. These gifts can assist humans in learning how to live in the physical world. Since Native Americans honour the fact that we are spiritual beings, housed in human bodies, and that we are born into physical life to learn about being human, it is logical that our Creature counterparts should be our teachers. The Totems are a reflection of our animal nature or physicalness, just as the Great Mystery is the Source of our spiritual beings.

In the times of our Ancestors, Native people would walk through the woodlands and observe the Creatures in order to gain the knowledge they needed to survive. If the Birds ate a certain berry, it was okay for human consumption. If the Creatures could drink from a stream, it was pure enough for the Two-leggeds to drink. Sometimes an albino animal would appear in a dream and would be the Spirit Totem for the human Dreamer. Other times, an animal would come to a Two-legged human in a way that was out of

the ordinary, such as an Eagle circling the person five times and then alighting a few feet away without fear and looking into the person's eyes for a moment before flying away. These signs, found through dreams or unusual experiences, were sure messages that the Creature in question was allying itself to a human being in order to teach or to protect that person during his or her Earthwalk (lifetime).

Some examples of the Medicines of the Creature-teachers are: Buffalo – Bringer of abundance; Lynx – Knower of Secrets; Rabbit –

The Rainbow Lizard is the Power Animal who is the Guardian of the Whirling Rainbow Dream Prophecy of the North American Indians. This prophecy came from divining the visions found in the Dreamtime that spoke of the Fifth World of Peace, uniting all races and life-forms on our planet as one.

This standing stone represents the Medicine Woman who is covered in her blanket, looking toward the mountains. The sun shines on the back of her head and shoulders, warming the silent guardian who watches and waits while the women in the Tipi journey into the Dreamtime seeking visions.

Ability to confront fear, bringer of fertility and teacher of how to listen; Deer – Gentleness; and Raven – Teacher of how to use Magic. There are as many Totem Medicines as there species of wildlife on our planet and in our oceans.

Since all life-forms have strengths and challenges, so do the Medicines of animals. For instance, Buffalo is abundance and the challenge is fear of scarcity. There is no bad Medicine, only the challenges which hone the skills each Medicine brings. If we heal our fear of scarcity, we will open to the abundance the Great Mystery brings. The Medicine of each animal therefore has both a dignified and a contrary meaning. Human beings tend to learn through opposites and, since both sides of any question are always present, we have to see the challenges as well as the solutions to learning life's lessons. When, in our human stubbornness, we see life from only one viewpoint, we limit our capacity to find alternatives. Our Creature-teachers have the mission of bringing new and non-threatening viewpoints into our lives in order to enrich our human experience. (See Appendix, Modern Restatements, on pages 211–12, for more information about the Medicine of animals in the *Medicine Cards* and for a full description of the *Sacred Path Cards*.)

THE BEAUTY WAY

The rituals, ceremonies, Traditions and teachings have been gleaned by our Native American Ancestors from centuries of living in harmony with the Earth Mother. All of these Knowing Systems (traditions of wisdom) hold meanings that suggest and instruct, but do not ever force anyone to follow another human being. We use the symbols of Nature in order to enlighten each individual so that each person makes their own decisions. Our understanding is that the Spirit World and the Great Mystery

This Seneca mask is a Traditional Harvest Mask used in ceremony to return thanks to the Creator for the abundance of crops harvested. It is woven of corn husks and sports a corn-cob nose, reminding the Indian People that being grateful for the blessings received is a philosophy that will 'grow corn'.

These typical Indian items include: (top) antique Medicine Bowl used to brew herbal remedies, (bottom right to left) Papago basket filled with Medicine objects (stones and animal hide), Isleta Pueblo pottery vase, Ute Medicine Pouch painted with a Buffalo skull, and a one-sided drum used for healing.

This Sweat Lodge Altar is made of a tree stump with the Sacred Hoop painted around a Turtle, symbolizing the Earth Mother. The Sacred Healing Rattles on the Altar are (right to left): Cherokee Turtle Rattle, Seneca Horn Rattle, Yaqui Gourd Rattle and Lakota Rawhide Buffalo Rattle. The petroglyph stones are copies of the Sacred Petroglyphs found on mountains, containing the picto-history of the Red Race.

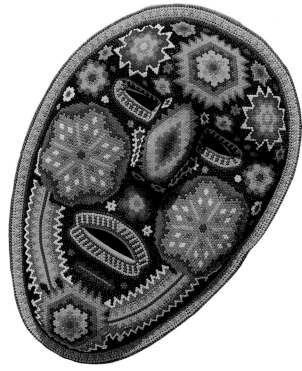

This Huichole Tribal mask is made by pressing each seed bead into the thin coat of beeswax that covers the carved wooden face. The deity, Mescal, is the spirit of the Peyote plant. The Huicholes and their practice of Peyote Ceremonies gave birth to the Native American Church in North America after the Trail of Tears in the 1870s. Peyote is used along with deep prayer to enter the Dreamtime.

work with each person individually, using unique methods of applying spirit to physical life. The decisions made in a person's life are therefore between that person and the Creative Source and bring the rewards as well as the more difficult personal lessons.

If a human being has lost connection to the Great Mystery or the Earth Mother it is a tragic event because that person is no longer connected to the Pathway of Beauty. In this instance it is easy for humans to lose faith, reasoning abilities and intuitive gifts and then to follow a crooked trail. Our Native American way of life not only provides ceremonies that will assist a person in reconnecting with the Creator and All Our Relations, but also gives every person the right to return to the Beauty Way. The Beauty Way is a way of being that never puts anything outside the self. If we are connected to the other members of the Planetary Family such as the Stone People and Plant People, we are never alone. All Native American people see everything as being alive and having spirit and consciousness. Because of this knowing, every living creature in the Planetary Family is a relative of the Original People, the human beings. Our brothers and sisters in the animal kingdom and our relations such as the Cloud People will hear our hearts through *Hail-oh-way-ain*, the language of love, and send us the omens and signs we need in order to reclaim our love of living life and return to the Sacred Path.

Every part of Nature has a language that can point out the signposts which will keep us on a Path of Beauty. The language of the Stones, for example, can be found etched on the faces of the Stone People all over our Earth. Anyone can pick up a Stone and examine the symbols or marks that occur naturally there in order to find what that Stone Person can teach. The markings also show the natural talents of the human who found the Stone Person, even if the seeker has hidden those talents from him or herself.

For instance, a straight vertical line on a Stone means the power of Spirit to conquer all challenges found in the material world. Two arrows crossing and forming an X with the arrowheads pointing up represents the power of mutual respect and friendship. A square represents firm foundations and organizational abilities. A diamond shape represents life, unity and equality for eternity, as well as freedom from fear. The diamond shape also denotes that the seeker has the protection of the Four Winds and is protected in every direction he or she may travel in life. (For more information about the Stone People, see *Other Council Fires Were Here Before Ours* by Jamie Sams and Twylah Nitsch.)

THE MEDICINE WHEEL

All 487 Traditions and Tribes in North America have their own Medicine Wheels and their own significances for the directions, but overall they are very similar. On the Seneca Medicine Wheel (opposite) there are 12 directions laid out like the face of a clock. Each direction has a colour, a Cycle of Truth and a birth month, and represents a pathway any human being may follow to find inner peace, as well as a way to become a peacemaker for the world. This Medicine Wheel can also act as a map or dictionary which will allow a person to understand the languages of the Plant People, the Stone People, the Creature-beings and the elements of Nature, as well as the Medicine objects that Nature gives to each person who asks for assistance.

Each direction has a set of lessons and teaches something about understanding truth more fully. If we draw a line from any position on the wheel to the position directly opposite, we find a Pathway to inner Peace. These Pathways of Peace are the reflections we each receive from life. When we learn any set of lessons represented by one direction on the wheel and then learn the lessons of the opposite direction, we can heal any inner conflict which would keep us from being our personal best. When we find an object in Nature which sends us its message through the colour it carries, we are given the opportunity to find the answer we need for our personal growth.

Each colour on the wheel is a key to the Medicine or gifts, talents and abilities the found

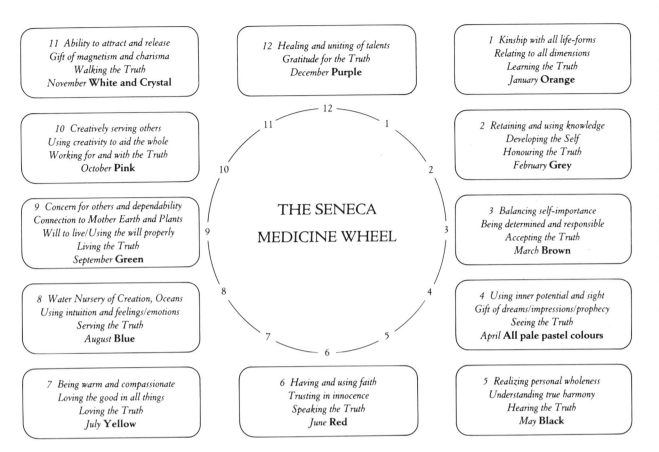

11 *Ability to attract and release*
Gift of magnetism and charisma
Walking the Truth
November **White and Crystal**

12 *Healing and uniting of talents*
Gratitude for the Truth
December **Purple**

1 *Kinship with all life-forms*
Relating to all dimensions
Learning the Truth
January **Orange**

10 *Creatively serving others*
Using creativity to aid the whole
Working for and with the Truth
October **Pink**

2 *Retaining and using knowledge*
Developing the Self
Honouring the Truth
February **Grey**

9 *Concern for others and dependability*
Connection to Mother Earth and Plants
Will to live/Using the will properly
Living the Truth
September **Green**

THE SENECA
MEDICINE WHEEL

3 *Balancing self-importance*
Being determined and responsible
Accepting the Truth
March **Brown**

8 *Water Nursery of Creation, Oceans*
Using intuition and feelings/emotions
Serving the Truth
August **Blue**

4 *Using inner potential and sight*
Gift of dreams/impressions/prophecy
Seeing the Truth
April **All pale pastel colours**

7 *Being warm and compassionate*
Loving the good in all things
Loving the Truth
July **Yellow**

6 *Having and using faith*
Trusting in innocence
Speaking the Truth
June **Red**

5 *Realizing personal wholeness*
Understanding true harmony
Hearing the Truth
May **Black**

object carries. In this manner, anyone can go into Nature and find a feather, a stone, a shell, a leaf, a seed or a piece of bark that could provide an answer or direction to aid that person in making sense of any given situation. Actual in-depth teachings or messages might be felt or heard if the seeker used his or her intuition to sit in silence with the found object and listen. This highly evolved sense of perception is normally developed over many years through specific training as a Seer or Dreamer and is not usually accomplished overnight. The basics of how to interpret the general lessons are, however, easily understood simply by looking at the colours in the found object and then finding the colour on this chart.

If, for instance, a person came upon a stone with a green colour to it (position 9), the stone could teach the proper use of the will and how to increase the life force or will to live. The stone could also teach the person how to Live the Truth, which is that direction's Cycle of Truth. The month is September and so this stone could

be particularly helpful for someone born in that month. The Pathway of Peace that this stone would teach begins at September and goes straight across the wheel to March, which represents Accepting the Truth. Therefore, the Pathway of Peace for the person finding a green stone would be organizing their life so that accepting and living their personal truth can be easily accomplished.

If a person went for a walk by the sea and was looking for some direction or clarity and asked the Allies of nature for assistance, the permission to help the seeker would be given and the door to discovery would be open. In a sacred manner, the asking gives permission to Nature's Allies, whom we know to be the helpers of the Great Mystery and the Earth Mother. Let us imagine that this person then came upon an unusual shell that was on his or her path. The person would then give thanks for the sign and give an offering to the Earth in the place where the shell was found. This offering is traditionally tobacco in our Native teachings, but could be a lock of the seeker's hair, cornmeal, corn pollen, saliva or some other object that was special to the seeker. Before removing the shell, the seeker would ask if the shell wanted to be moved from its Sacred Space on the beach in order to go home with the human being. If the person then felt uncomfortable or ill at ease, the shell has said no. If the answer was yes, the person would feel good about removing the shell.

The colours of the shell could be located on the Seneca Wheel and the general lessons understood. If the shell did not wish to be removed but was willing to give the lessons needed, the person could sit in that location and examine the shell, see its colours and look up the

Jamie Sams' grandmother, Twylah Nitsch, seen here in beaded ceremonial garments, is a Seneca elder of the Wolf Clan Teaching Lodge.

connections and lessons upon arriving home. This simple method of observing the obvious becomes quite easy once a person learns the wheel and applies that wisdom to anything that crosses his or her path. This is one basic form of using the elements of nature as an oracle, which has been used in different forms by my people for centuries.

Our Native American systems of divination are as countless as there are parts to Creation. Each language from some part of our natural world represents a relationship we, Two-legged humans, have to Nature. I cannot be a spokesperson for the whole Red Race, but I can speak from my Sacred Point of View and share the lessons which have been handed down to me. Every Tribe and Nation has its own system of divining or understanding the Creatures and other Relations of our Earth Mother. To cover even one Tradition in depth would overwhelm most non-Native people. Our understandings, our oral traditions and our wisdom of Earth Medicine is 160,000 years older than any written history on this planet and begins approximately 220,000 years before most events recorded in the Old Testament of the Judaeo-Christian religious tradition.

My Elders have taught me that the most Sacred of all our ceremonies is the Give-away. This rite teaches us how to give from the heart with no strings attached. I know from experience that the wisdom is to be shared, to be given away, or those Traditions will die with the last person who was a Guardian of 'the remembering'. It is in this spirit that I share the rich legacy which has been passed to me and I trust that those who learn these languages of our Relations will, in turn, share this wisdom so that all races may learn the Medicines that will heal the hearts of humankind and bring full understanding and peace to our planet.

The understanding of the languages of All Our Relations – animal, plant, stone, shell – or Clan Chiefs of Air, Earth, Water and Fire is no small subject, but I am happy to have been able to share a small part of these Knowing Systems with the readers of *The World Atlas of Divination*.

CHAPTER FOURTEEN

SUN, TIME AND SYMBOLISM

Astrological Divination in Ancient Mesoamerica

Bruce Scofield

Around the time of the early Greeks, and possibly even earlier, an astrological divinatory calendar originated in Mesoamerica, today's Mexico and northern Central America. Later, during the rise and fall of the Maya, the cycle was elaborated upon and perpetuated. When the Spanish arrived in the early sixteenth century, they found a culture that was deeply enmeshed in these same concepts, then perhaps 2,000 or more years old. Today, in the remote Maya villages of rural Guatemala and Mexico, an oral tradition persists in keeping the ancient knowledge alive, albeit in altered and somewhat simplified form. After two and a half millennia, the rise and fall of numerous empires, and constant efforts on the part of Christians to eliminate it, the 260-day astrological divinatory calendar still lives.

TIME: THE BUILDING BLOCK OF REALITY

In Mesoamerica, astrology and divination were linked intimately. At the core of both activities was a cycle of 20 named days. Beginning with a day called Alligator, and ending with one called Flower, the 20 days symbolized various stages of life, much like the 22 Major Arcana cards of the Tarot or the Runes. Because the four directions (north, south, east, west) and their symbolism is so closely woven into the cycle, it might be said that the 20 days are really five cycles of the four directions. Because this cycle was a calendar of sorts, every birth occurs during the influence of one of the days. In this sense, the system is astrological. However, like the Tarot, Runes or

I Ching, the symbolism of the cycle was also utilized as a divinatory system.

An interesting comparison might be made to the Near Eastern seven-day week in use throughout the world today. Our week is actually a remnant of a kind of time-based astrology. The original astrological meanings and usage of the seven-day week have faded during modern times, but the planetary names of the days in the Latin languages points towards an earlier astrological use. During much of Western history, human births and the fate of the new year were judged according to the day of the week they fell on. Today, only a nursery rhyme survives that offers an astrological interpretation for a child born on each day of the week. But the point here is that our seven-day week and the Mesoamerican 20-day count were both attempts to pin symbolic meanings on a cycle of days. In essence both are sets of signs based on time, not space.

The 20 named days are only part of a much bigger picture. A second cycle of 13 days must be added to understand even the rudiments of the system. Just as one day is a sign in the Mesoamerican tradition, so also is a period of 13 days. In fact, the 13-day period or count was probably the most-used astrological framework for interpretation of sky-events, in the same way that the Babylonian zodiac is used by Western astrologers. Now consider the following. Thirteen cycles of 20 days is equal to 20 cycles of 13 days. This permutation takes a total of 260 days and this number is the key to the system. The combined 13- and 20-day cycles are considered

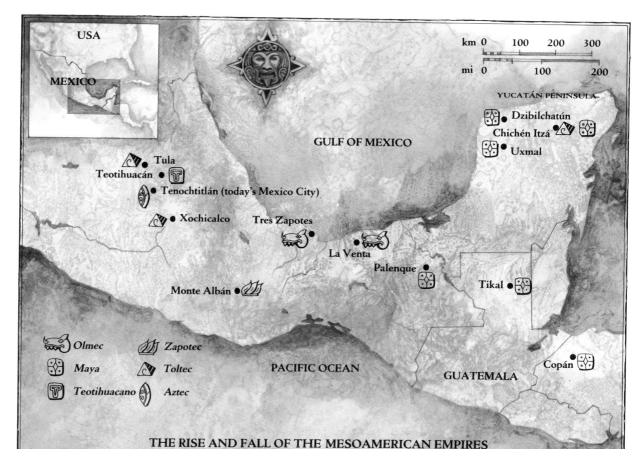

THE RISE AND FALL OF THE MESOAMERICAN EMPIRES

Mesoamerican history has been traditionally divided into three main periods beginning with what is called the Preclassic or Formative Period. Although this period began around 1800 BC, fully fledged civilization made its first appearance about 1,000 years later along the eastern coast of Mexico. A culture later called Olmec thrived during these times and left behind ceremonial centres, pyramids and remarkably sophisticated sculpture. It was from them that the first symbolic writing and the first notions of the 260-day calendar arose.

The Classic Period, dating from roughly 200 BC to AD 900, saw the flowering of Mesoamerican culture in two different areas. In the Guatamalan south and Mexico's Yucatan Peninsula the Maya built dramatic ceremonial centers, many of which stand today and are a mecca for tourists to the region. It was the Maya who developed the 260-day count into a complex astrological-numerological master key to the universe, though only tantalizing fragments of these ideas survived massive book-burnings by Spanish friars.

Approximately contemporary with the Maya was the culture of Teotihuacan. Near present-day Mexico City a gigantic ceremonial centre and city flourished for hundreds of years, leaving behind two huge pyramids and miles of ancient walls, buildings and roadways. Its influence was felt well into the Maya world. Midway between the Maya and the city of Teotihuacan was Monte Alban, the site of Zapotec culture, which in many ways stood on its own terms. Sometime around AD 750 Teotihuacan burned and was abandoned. Not long afterwards the latest Maya centres in Yucatan collapsed. It was during the Classic Period that the worship of the god Quetzalcoatl (feathered serpent), believed to be the creator of the 260-day count, became established.

The Postclassic Period began around AD 900 with a renaissance of both Classic cultures. In the region around Mexico City the Toltecs built a capital at Tula and then began a period of empire building. Their reach extended to the old Maya city of Chichen Itza, stimulating a resurgence of Maya culture. Last came the Aztecs, who built their capital city on the site of today's Mexico City. Like their predecessors, the Toltecs, they were empire builders and carriers, not creators, of a more ancient culture.

the internal parts of the 260-day astrological divinatory calendar of ancient Mesoamerica. But these figures are more than just a count of days, they are also the master numbers for an intellectual and religious tradition that probably saw number as the key to everything.

Four, 13, 20 and 260 – these are the building blocks of reality as it was mapped in Mesoamerica. These ideas appear to be based on both astronomical and biological facts. Four probably comes from the naming of the four directions, and these are defined by the movements of the Sun at the horizon as it is observed throughout the seasonal year. The Sun in its daily movement across the sky creates the day. The day is the corner-stone, or primary measure, of time itself. For the Maya, day, Sun and time were one and the same and one word, *kin*, was used for all three. It is an interesting fact that it takes the Sun about 13 days to cover the same space as the Moon does in one day. A nine-month human gestation is nine cycles of Moon and Sun or about 266 days, a figure very close to 260 days. The planet Venus averages about 263 days for its appearances as morning and evening star. If one uses the fingers and toes for counting, than a count of 20 becomes basic. Other astronomical and numerological explanations have been offered to explain the origination of the key components of the Mesoamerican system, but none has emerged uncontested and universally accepted. Exactly how the 260-day count came to be is still a mystery.

DIVINING BY THE DAY-SIGNS

In ancient times the 260-day astrological calendar was utilized in the timing of political and religious events, and also in the interpretation of one's fate, thought to be sealed at birth. The Maya word for the 260-day count was *tzolkin*, the Aztec *Tonalpouhalli*. Functioning like an ephemeris, a book called *tonalamatl*, or 'book of fate', was referred to by priests and practitioners of astrology and divination. In the case of a birth, parents would take their new-born child to a *tonalpoulque* (reader) to find out what *tonalli* (day-sign) influenced their child. After the

Spanish conquest, the Christian friars strove to destroy this tradition and in order to do so they recorded some details of it so that future friars would know what to look for. Some of this material survives, and although it came to the friars third hand and years after the conquest, it does reveal much about the importance of the 260-day astrological calendar in Aztec society.

The 260-day count was also a master divination device much like the *I Ching*. With its 20 key symbols and 13 variants of each, a total of 260 answers for a question were possible. It is not known exactly how divinations were conducted during pre-Columbian times, but much is known about the tradition as it survives today. The Quiche Maya who live in remote sections of Guatemala have a tradition of shamans or 'day-keepers' who pass on knowledge of the 260-day count orally. They provide a useful service to the community by determining times for rituals and handling personal problems for individuals. Divinations are done with crystals, beans and their memory of the calendar. The procedure is roughly as follows. After the question has been asked, the day-keeper grabs a handful of beans and crystals from a bag and

Discovered in 1790 beneath a street in Mexico City, the Aztec calendar stone has become a symbol of Mexico itself. It is actually a sophisticated cosmogram depicting the cycles of the ages. Five creation cycles occupy the centre, with the fifth and current cycle encompassing the other four. Around this centre is a ring containing the 20 day-signs.

In recent years, scholars have learned to read the complex Mayan hieroglyphs that tell the dynastic histories of ancient empires. This is a detail of a door lintel, part of the 'hieroglyphic stairway' at Naranjo, Guatemala.

lays them on a table. These are sorted into piles of four until they are exhausted. The last pile is critical. If there are two or four beans, then a divination is possible, if one or three, the divination is abandoned. If a reading is possible, then the number of piles are counted and added to the current day-sign in effect. For example, if there are 45 piles, then the day-sign 45 days ahead of the present day is used as the symbol for interpretation. Readings often involve repeating this process several times.

The notions about the 20 day-signs recorded by the Spanish friars leave much to be desired. They are sparse in most cases and extremist in others, a reflection of the Aztec world in shambles after the conquest. The meanings of the day-signs according to contemporary Quiche Maya day-keepers are likewise limited and reflect the realities of their present-day existence. Then there is the problem of correlating the Mesoamerican calendar with the Christian one, a problem that archaeoastronomers and archaeologists have struggled with for decades. I have spent a number of years attempting to put the 20 core symbols on a solid footing without distorting the system. I have taken a pragmatic approach, one that utilizes every available source of information, but emphasizes usefulness, not just idealistic symmetry. A consensus is emerging among a number of astrologers who have examined the results of this reconstruction that supports the definitions and meanings presented.

This corpulent shaman, from Mexico around 200 BC, is apparently reaching into his bag of beans and crystals to do a divination.

THE WHEELS OF TIME

The cycles of 13 and 20 days combined to produce the master unit of 260 days. But the Mesoamerican effort to unify time, number and nature did not end there. Because the 260-day count was symbolic and not tied to the seasons, it could not be used as a civil calendar, so one of 365 days was used for that purpose. However, after 52 years of 365 days, there would be

Teotihuacán covered an area of 8 square miles. Ahead, the 'street of the Dead' extends for 2 miles, passing in front of the 'Pyramid of the Sun', one of several large monuments precisely aligned in both an astronomical and a geomantic sense.

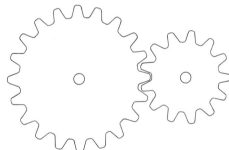

In the Mesoamerican concept of time, 13 cycles of 20 days is equivalent to 20 cycles of 13 days: in 260 days the day-signs coincide and the cycle begins again.

exactly 73 cycles of 260 days and the two counts would combine. This figure, 52 years, was the length of a Mesoamerican 'century' and important renewal rituals were held at the start of each new cycle. The planet Venus has a cycle of 584 days, which happens to dovetail with the 365-day year in the ratio 5:8. After 104 years (2 × 52), the Venus year, the 365-day year and the 260-day year meet precisely. The numerological aspects of these interrelationships are truly astonishing.

The Maya developed a type of mundane astrology that was the 260-day count writ large. A count of 7,200 days called a *katun*, a figure that closely approximates the cycle of Jupiter and Saturn (i.e the time between their conjunctions), was the corner-stone of a creation epoch of 5,125 years. Within this period cycled 20 groups of 13 *katuns* and 13 groups of 20 *katuns* called *baktuns*. Five creation cycles very nearly equals the length of the Earth's precessional cycle, a cycle of approximately 25,700 years that is caused by a wobbling of the Earth's pole which Westerners divide into twelfths and call the astrological ages. Interestingly, the latest creation cycle of the Maya is to end in the year 2012, and in 1993 the 260th and last of the *katuns* will begin.

THE 20 DAY-SIGNS OR *TONALLI*

The astrological attributions of the 20 day-signs below were derived from a sampling of 400 persons and an analysis of the surviving ancient sources. The calendar correlation recommended is that of Goodman–Martinez–Thompson, the most respected among scholars and still in use in remote villages. The day 1–Alligator correlates with 9 August 1992.

In ancient times the 260-day astrological calendar began with the sign 1–Alligator. The next sign was 2–Wind. Then came 3–House, 4–Lizard, 5–Serpent, 6–Death, 7–Deer, 8–Rabbit, 9–Water, 10–Dog, 11–Monkey, 12–Grass and 13–Reed. The next sign, 1–Ocelot, started the 13–day cycle over again and was followed by 2–Eagle, 3–Vulture, 4–Earthquake, 5–Knife, 6–Rain, and 7–Flower, thus completing the 20 named days. It was 8–Alligator, the first of the signs, that came next. In essence then, both the sign Alligator and any sign linked with the number 1 (as in 1–Ocelot, above, for example) function as the head of a sequence. Only once every 260 days does 1–Alligator come up.

Alligator
(Maya = *Imix*, Aztec = *Cipactli*)

Direction: East

Divination: Primitive beginnings, maternal concern
Astrological imprint: Energetic, practical, creative and initiating, but also dominating and parental towards others. Strong nurturing instincts, quite sensitive and private. Experiences or feels rejection from family or parents. Often founders of businesses or associations.

Wind
(Maya = *Ik*, Aztec = *Ehecatl*)

Direction: North

Divination: Diversification, communication
Astrological imprint: Mentally active and communicative, versatile and multi-faceted. Idealistic and romantic, fashion conscious or artistic. Somewhat non-committal or indecisive. Problems with responsibility and obligation.

House
(Maya = *Akbal*, Aztec = *Calli*)

Direction: West

Divination: Strength, resistance to change
Astrological imprint: Powerful, often physically dominating. Organized, patient, with much endurance. Hard worker. Logical approach to problems but also traditional and mentally rigid. Concern for security in home and family. Introspective, needs solitude.

Lizard
(Maya = *Kan*, Aztec = *Cuetzpallin*)

Direction: South

Divination: Procreation and dispersion
Astrological imprint: Interest in leadership and performance. Self-esteem an important issue. Influential, with reputation for being different. Fanatical interests and high standards. Strongly influenced by sexual matters.

Serpent
(Maya = *Chicchan*, Aztec = *Coatl*)

Direction: East

Divination: Changes and transformations
Astrological imprint: Strong-willed, high-powered, extremist. Mysterious, charismatic, dramatic, with 'sex appeal'. Strong emotional reactions cause great upheavals in relationships. Intelligent, well-informed, fanatical and obsessive.

Death
(Maya = *Cimi*, Aztec = *Miquitztli*)

Direction: North

Divination: Belief and sacrifice
Astrological imprint: A sign of politics, obligations, sacrifice and faith. Involved or interested in civic affairs. Not natural leaders and will accept secondary roles or positions. Traditional in faith or religion. Materialistic, concerned with domestic security and real estate. Close experiences with death.

Deer
(Maya = *Manik*, Aztec = *Mazatl*)

Direction: West

Divination: Meetings and joinings
Astrological imprint: Peaceful, inspiring and generous, but also outspoken, deviant and dominating. Not overly interested in leadership. Strong feelings for family and friends. Needs companionship. Interests or abilities in the arts. Sensual, sexual, intuitive and sensitive to the concerns of others.

Rabbit
(Maya = *Lamat*, Aztec = *Tochtli*)

Direction: South

Divination: Conflict, advantage
Astrological imprint: Energetic, busy, nervous. Contrary. A fighter and joker. Needs physical activity and exercise. Often extremely intelligent, but also paranoid and wild. Liking for performance, games and risk-taking. Appreciates music and humour, sometimes self-destructive.

Water
(Maya=*Muluc*, Aztec=*Atl*)

Direction: East

Divination: Compulsive actions

Astrological imprint: Strong emotions. Powerful imagination and psychic. Romantic and performance conscious. Dominates others with emotions. Struggles with responsibility and self-control. Sexual.

Dog
(Maya=*Oc*, Aztec=*Itzcuintli*)

Direction: North

Divination: Guidance and movement

Astrological imprint: Loyal and consistent. Good team player. Needs variety. Likes leadership, but will wait for turn. Thoughtful, political and artistic. Struggles with emotional maturity.

Monkey
(Maya=*Chuen*, Aztec=*Ozomatli*)

Direction: West

Divination: Ego, performance

Astrological imprint: Needs attention. Likes centre stage, performing, artistry, etc. Multiple interests, curious, communicative. Quick learner. Emotionally distant but sexually active. Seeks leadership positions.

Grass
(Maya=*Eb*, Aztec=*Malinalli*)

Direction: South

Divination: Crisis and healing

Astrological imprint: Calm on the surface. Slow to anger, courteous and kind. Sensitive, touchy, easily hurt. Represses bad feelings. Hard worker, ambitious.

Reed
(Maya=*Ben*, Aztec=*Acatl*)

Direction: East

Divination: Power and authority

Astrological imprint: Popular, accomplished and generally competent. Will fight for principles and take on challenges. Capable of intense work but knows how to relax. Concerned with human nature.

Ocelot
(Maya=*Ix*, Aztec=*Ocelotl*)

Direction: North

Divination: Secrecy and entanglement

Astrological imprint: Private, sensitive and psychic. Aggressive streak but avoids confrontations. Becomes deeply involved in relationships. Good counsellor. Often concerned with religion or spirituality.

Eagle
(Maya=*Men*, Aztec=*Cuauhtli*)

Direction: West

Divination: Perspective

Astrological imprint: Independent with own ideas about life. Scientific and exacting mind. Perfectionist yet open to ideas. Ambitious and escapist. Popular.

Vulture
(Maya=*Cib*, Aztec=*Cozcacuauhtli*)

Direction: South

Divination: Rejection

Astrological imprint: Serious, realistic and pragmatic. Hardened to life, callous at times. Status-conscious, authoritative, although sometimes dominated by others. Has high standards. Competent and critical.

Earthquake
(Maya=*Caban*, Aztec=*Ollin*)

Direction: East

Divination: Balance

Astrological imprint: Mentally active, rationalizing and clever. Usually liberal and progressive. Sense of humour. Seeks leadership but is usually controversial.

Knife
(Maya=*Etz'nab*, Aztec=*Tecpatl*)

Direction: North

Divination: Choice

Astrological imprint: Practical, with good co-ordination. Extremely social but struggles in close relationships. Polite and often indecisive.

Rain
(Maya=*Cauac*, Aztec=*Quiahuitl*)

Direction: West

Divination: Purification

Astrological imprint: Youthful, restless, mentally active and friendly. Imitates rather than initiates. Multi-faceted. Over-compensates for insecurities. Drawn to religion or philosophy. Concern for others. Concerned with healing.

Flower
(Maya=*Ahau*, Aztec=*Xochitl*)

Direction: South

Divination: Perfection

Astrological imprint: A resistant idealist. Socially awkward, but well intentioned. Interests in art and beauty. Difficulties in close relationships due to expectations. Stubborn, but devoted to friends and lovers. Easily hurt.

This 'cosmogram' (right) shows the 20 day-signs as they cycle through the four directions. The symbolism is that of the Mixtec calendar from the Codex Fejervary-Mayer. The border is marked with 260 small circles at intervals of 13, marked by each of the 20 signs. This progression begins within the upper right-hand corner and moves counter clockwise. Year bearers prominently occupy the four corners of the design. The signs are Alligator, Jaguar, Deer, Flower, Reed, Death, Rain, Grass, Serpent, Knife, Monkey, Lizard, Earthquake, Dog, House, Vulture, Water, Wind, Eagle, Rabbit. This is the order of the 13-day periods. The four arms of the cross and the centre symbolize the five regions of the world. East is at the top, south to the right, west at the bottom and north on the left. The Sun is located in the east. Xiuhtecuhtli, the lord of central fire, is in the centre being fed blood from the rest of the diagram. He is the first of the Nine Lords of the Night. The other eight are (clockwise from east in order) Pilcintecuhtli, Iztli, Mictlantecuhtli, Cinteotl, Tlazolteotl, Chalchiuhtilicue, Tlaloc, Tlazolteotl.

The Caracol at Chichén Itzá (above) is believed to have been an observatory. The circular tower at the top of the structure has sightlines to significant rising and setting positions of the Sun and Venus. In the background is 'El Castillo', the pyramid.

THE EASTERN WORLD

India, China, Japan and Tibet – the oldest civilizations anywhere in the world – possess a proliferation of divinatory systems, many of which were established while the rest of the world was still in a primitive state. In almost every case these systems derive from ancient oral tradition and consist of layers and accretions from different periods of the culture.

In the West when a sign or premonition of the future is sought by divinatory methods, it is by no means a foregone conclusion that such an answer will be forthcoming. In the East, and particularly in China, heaven is expected to make its will known in any one of a bewildering number of ways. This reflects a degree of fatalism, apparent particularly in the kinds of divination practised in the Far East. The future is a course laid down for each and every person; he, or she, must follow the way, and though an individual may obtain glimpses of future events, these often cannot be changed.

Several of the systems discussed here deal with energies that have been polarized into complementary opposites (the yin and yang which form the basis of the Chinese system of I Ching, Chapter Sixteen). These energies are seen as representing the natural law of the universe and the changing patterns of existence.

In almost all of the traditions in this book we have seen that natural law is an important element of divination. In Feng Shui, for example, the right relationship of everything to everything is of paramount importance in achieving a harmonious environment. In Indian astrology the human form is seen as a microcosm of the universe, and the stars which influence parts of the body are thus a divine reflection. The 'benific' and 'malific' planets in Indian astrology are polarized in the same way as the yin and yang energies in the I Ching. In both the I Ching and Feng Shui we encounter the observation of animals, birds and nature in general and the understanding that the patterns inherent within them are meaningful to the reading of future events. The same may be said of Mah Jongg, which is related to bone oracles, to Tarot and to the I Ching, all of which represent the significance of 'random' or 'chance' events.

Tibetan divination, with its emphasis on the reading of omens in the flight and cries of birds and in the actions of animals, shares this connection with the natural world, which is full of intimations of the divine. Tibet both influenced and was influenced by the culture and belief systems of India and China, and so the teachings of Buddhism, which contain many of the beliefs described in this section, may be seen to underlie the divinatory techniques in these countries. The fact that religious belief still occupies a central place goes a long way towards explaining why there is a deeper sense of the efficacy of divination in the East than in most other parts of the world today.

CHAPTER FIFTEEN

THE WAY OF THE EMPEROR

The Oracle and Game of Mah Jongg

Derek Walters

Take a stroll through a city's Chinatown one hot summer's afternoon and you may be puzzled by a strange clattering noise, seeming to come from every direction. Look up, beyond the shops and restaurants, to the open windows above, and you might spot the source of the curious sound. What might have been mistaken for the shuttling of a very old loom, or the clicking of a dozen antique typewriters, will be the sound of Chinese workers at their favourite pastime: the game of Mah Jongg. Hundreds of the bamboo and bone tiles, sliding and colliding over the polished surface of every available table, are producing the intriguing and distinctive rattle that the Chinese call 'the Twittering of the Sparrows'.

Almost exclusively known as a gambling game today, Mah Jongg is the modern descendant of one of the world's most ancient forms of divination, with a history full of astonishing twists, turns and side-roads. The Chinese equivalent of playing cards and the Tarot, Mah Jongg's antecedents are several centuries older than its Western cousins and, incredible though it may seem, its evolution is related to such widely different concepts as the game of chess, the navigator's compass and paper currency.

THE MAH JONGG TILES

The standard set consists of 144 pieces, about the size of a finger joint. Westerners call the pieces 'tiles', although the Chinese word for them is the same as the word for cards or dominoes – *pai*. Today, the tiles are usually made of plastic, but they may be made from wood, bamboo, cardboard, bone or any convenient material. Antique sets are usually handmade, with a bone or ivory face jointed into a polished bamboo back, which gives them a distinctive curved shape, missing from the more convenient, but soulless, modern plastic ones.

The face of the tile is carved or embossed with a name or value. Sometimes this will be a Chinese character, or a symbol, while a few of the tiles will have a simple picture of a flower or other figure, the quality varying considerably from one set to another. Although the number of unfamiliar signs may be intimidating to the uninitiated, the tiles' names are actually much more straightforward than they might appear at first glance.

The traditional game of Mah Jongg has not been eradicated in communist China, despite it being frowned upon by the authorities. Although these players in Kunming, Yunnan province, may be oblivious to the game's mystic origins, they will be familiar with its ancient symbolism.

To begin with, apart from eight tiles called the Flowers or Guardians, which are distinctly different from the others, each of the tiles is replicated four times, forming four 'packs' of 34 tiles. Each of the four packs comprises three suits (bamboos, circles or discs, and characters) of nine tiles each, 27 in all; four directions (often called the 'four winds'); and three colours (called 'dragons' by western players).

To summarize, the complete set consists of:

One of each of the eight Guardians or Flowers

Four of each of the following:

Bamboo suit (1 to 9)

Circles suit (1 to 9)

Characters suit (1 to 9)

Directions (East, South, West, North)

Colours (Green, Red, White)

The suits are marked along similar lines to ordinary playing cards or Tarot cards, but instead of hearts, spades, diamonds and clubs, the tiles show bamboo stalks, circles, and, in the case of the 'characters', a Chinese number, followed by the symbol *Wan*, meaning 10,000. Uniquely, the 1 Bamboo tile shows a bird of uncertain species. There is, however, an interesting difference between the design of playing cards and Mah Jongg suit tiles. Although the Mah Jongg tiles are engraved in red, green and black, these colours are not associated with any particular suit in the same way that hearts and diamonds are always red, or spades and clubs black.

The four direction tiles are marked, in black, with the Chinese characters for East, South, West and North, while some sets, made for export, also have E, S, W, or N marked in one corner of each tile.

The three remaining tiles, the colours, are shown by the Chinese character *Fa*, meaning 'Commence', engraved in green (and therefore called the 'Green Dragon' by western players); the character for 'Centre' in red; and a tile which is either completely black or with just an empty frame (sometimes referred to as the 'White Dragon').

THE EIGHT GUARDIANS

The remaining eight tiles form two sets representing the four seasons, Spring, Summer, Autumn and Winter. These may be shown symbolically by flowers appropriate to the season – usually plum blossom for Spring, orchid for Summer, chrysanthemum for Autumn and evergreen bamboo for Winter – while the other four guardians may be shown by seasonal occupations, such as the Fisherman, Woodcutter, Farmer and Scholar. But there are many regional variations in these 'flower' tiles. Their inclusion is almost an anomaly and some players discard them as being superfluous. But in some parts of the Far East, particularly in Japan, there are sets of cards used for fortune-telling and leisure games which are composed exclusively of flower cards.

THE SYMBOLISM OF MAH JONGG

Even in the heat of a gambling session for high stakes, the mystical origins of Mah Jongg are never forgotten. The four players sit in positions known as East, South, West and North, but because the four directions are meant to represent the four quarters of the heavens (a mirror image of the Earth), East and West are reversed in relation to North and South. In Chinese philosophy, the four directions are related to the four seasons, shown by the Guardian tiles, while the four directions plus the Centre relate to the five elements of Chinese philosophy: Wood (Spring or East), Fire (Summer or South), Metal (Autumn or West), Water (Winter or North), with the remaining element, Earth, being represented both by the Centre tile and by the playing area itself. Even the colours used for the tiles are symbolic: the colours green, red, black and white are the colours associated with the elements, seasons and directions: green for East, Wood, and the Spring; red for South, Fire and the Summer; black for North, Water and Winter; and White for West, Metal and Autumn. Furthermore, just as the four directions represent the four seasons, so the number of tiles in a player's hand – 13 – represents the number of lunar months in a year.

The fact that there are nine tiles in each suit is highly significant. For the Chinese nine is a mystic number. An arrangement of the numbers one to nine was said to have appeared on the back of a tortoise – which emerged from the River Lo, and inspired China's first philosopher, Fu Hsi, with the understanding of the Cosmos. Today, just as over 2,000 years ago, Chinese mystics practise a system of nine-house numerology according to precepts traditionally ascribed to the great sage.

THE HISTORY OF MAH JONGG

Games of chance were known in ancient China, but their origins are inseparable from methods of divination. In Tibet, for example, as recently as the last century, dice and counters were used exclusively for foretelling future events, and not for gambling (see Chapter Nineteen, Mirrors of the Sky). In Chinese religions the purpose of divination was, and still remains, a method of obtaining an answer from the gods. This reveals a fundamental difference between Western and Eastern attitudes to the celestial world. When the Westerner offers a prayer, publicly it may be a form of thanksgiving for favours received, or privately a petition to ask for further favours. Very infrequently, in cases of dire distress, the petitioner may ask for a 'sign' to indicate a course of action, although usually the form and meaning of the sign is left for the heavenly authorities to decide. But for the Chinese worshipper, such signs are expected as a matter of course, and prayer is presumed to be a two-way form of communication. Through some form of sortilege, or the casting of lots, heaven is able to reveal its will, and consequently the course that destiny must take.

Although today the concept that a petition may achieve a response through lots is absent from Western religious practice, it was not always so. In the Bible, Aaron is said to have carried 'Urim and Thummim' in his breastplate, and we are told that the Urim and Thummim were used for judgement before the Lord (Exodus 28:30 and Leviticus 8:8). Their use must have been so familiar that the patriarchs

did not bother to record a description of them, nor the way that they were used, and it was only when the Urim and Thummim failed to respond that the demented Saul was constrained to visit the Witch of Endor (I Samuel 28:6–7). What the Urim and Thummim were can only be guessed at, but it is entirely probable that they were similar to the two ancient traditional methods that are still found being used in Chinese temples today. These are the two blocks of wood called *chiao pai* and the bundle of sticks known as *chim*.

The *chiao pai* are two comma-shaped blocks, one side curved and the other flat, which are thrown on to the ground. Whether the blocks both fall curved sides up (yin), flat sides up (yang), or with one curved and one flat uppermost is regarded as a positive, negative or neutral response, although interpretation does vary from one part of China to another.

A yes-no answer, albeit frank and concise, does not give detailed advice in difficult situations. In such cases, petitioners use the *chim* for more sophisticated responses. *Chim* consist of bundles of sticks or bamboo slips, which are shaken in a horizontally held cylinder until one of the slips falls out. The slip bears a number or sign similar to domino spots, the number being a reference to a verse in a mystic book which can be interpreted in the light of the question put to the oracle. Modern versions of the oracle often use up to 100 sticks, and the mystic responses may be from texts that are only a few centuries old; but the original form of the sticks were marked with only one of four signs, even though there may have been as many as 64 sticks in a bundle.

In another method of consulting the oracle, the signs were marked on special divining dice. At some very early date, some bored bystander must have conceived the notion of debasing the divining dice into a game of chance, and the popularity of the invention is self-evident. But once the dice had lost their spiritual values, they soon became the source of contention. Dice are too easily prone to manipulation, and an accidental – or purposeful – jolt at a critical

*Divining sticks (*chim*) and divining blocks (*chiao pai*) at the Lung Shan (Dragon Mountain) temple, near Taipei. Unlike most divining sticks, the ones used at this temple are about a metre long. The rods are shuffled about, one is selected, and the* chiao pai *are then cast to see if the correct one has been chosen.*

moment could dispose of a fortune. To avoid this problem, the gaming signs were transferred back to slips of wood, like *chim*, or on to more substantial blocks of clay, the precursor of dominoes. But before we see what became of the dominoes, we find another intriguing thread woven into the tapestry of Mah Jongg's history.

Several centuries before the building of the Great Wall of China, and before the separation of astronomy and astrology, astronomers were busy recording the movements of the planets, and cataloguing the positions of the stars. To this end, a simple form of planisphere was invented to show the daily movement of the celestial sphere in relation to its annual rotation. Because the Earth is symbolically square, and the heavens circular, the planisphere took the form of a disc rotating on a square base. The edge of the square was marked with the names of the 28 Chinese constellations through which the Sun, Moon and planets passed, while at the centre of the disc a pointer was formed from the seven stars of the Great Bear, known to the Chinese as the Ladle. This constellation was regarded as supremely important by Chinese astronomers; its handle pointed to the first of the Chinese constellations, and its edge pointed to celestial north, while the entire constellation sweeps round the heavens like the hands of a cosmic clock. By placing counters to represent the planets at appropriate positions on the planisphere, early astronomers were able to plot their courses and calculate their future positions. This act of moving pieces about on a board was the inspiration for board games such as Chinese chess and another ancient Chinese game called *Liu Po*. Although the rules of *Liu Po* have now been lost, in its heyday, 2,000 years ago, it was a very popular pastime, and models that have been discovered at archaeological sites reveal it to be an ancestor of Mah Jongg.

The elegance of the planisphere led to its

The more usual way of consulting the oracle is shown by this worshipper at a temple in Hong Kong. He first casts the chiao pai *and, on receiving a favourable answer, shakes the box of* chim *until one of the bamboo slips falls out.*

The game of Liu Po is portrayed in a clay funerary model discovered in a tomb of the Han dynasty (second to first centuries BC). This ancient pastime is the forerunner of cards, dominoes, and even chess.

being used as a model for several other contrivances. When the magnetic power of lodestone was discovered, it seemed to be perfectly valid to cast the lodestone in the shape of the Ladle, since this constellation always pointed to the north. And the compass plate, instead of being marked simply by the cardinal points, was marked with the same mystic astronomical signs as were found on the planisphere. Thus it is that, even today, Chinese junks plying their courses through the South Pacific navigate with the aid of an instrument originally designed for the use of astrologers, sages and magicians.

The advance of Chinese technology was to produce yet another surprise. Perhaps the most influential discovery of all time was the invention of printing. But its impact was not confined to the publication of books and writings on an undreamt-of scale: it also revolutionized commerce through the introduction of paper currency, and balanced that with the more frivolous creation of playing cards, several centuries

before the Tarot was devised in the West. The ease of printing meant that designers had ample scope to modify existing games, and today several varieties of playing cards are to be found, including Mah Jongg itself. Yet the Chinese never relinquished their fondness for the solid, tactile quality of the domino-like pieces of the Mah Jongg. And, as noted earlier, although the Chinese word for playing cards (*pai*) is the same as the word for Mah Jongg pieces, playing cards are often more disparagingly referred to as 'portable cards'.

Alas, however, today the ancient oracular function of Mah Jongg has all but been over-shadowed by the gambler, and it is now only at the end of a gaming session that the matriarch of the family might gather the pieces together to divine what the future may hold. Yet

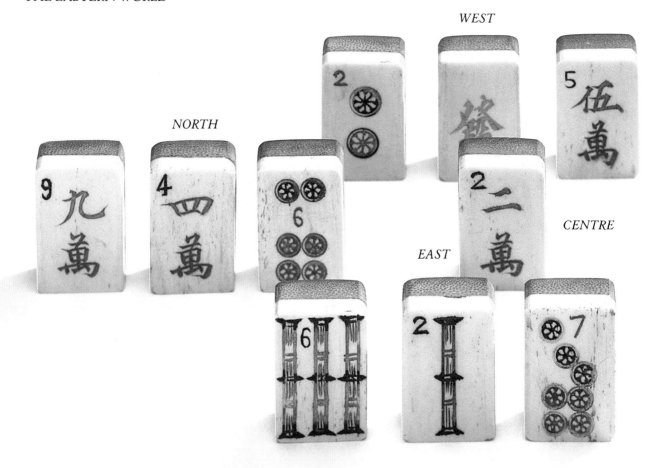

WEST

NORTH

CENTRE

EAST

These tiles were selected by a lady planning to travel. The central tile, 2 Wan (Sword), shows a choice to be made. The three tiles in the foreground, 6, 2 and 7 Bamboo, are all 'watery tiles', relating directly to the question. To the right, the tiles in the 'south' represent the immediate future, and the red 'Centre' tile reveals that immediate objectives will be attained, confirmed by the Door (1 Wan) opening to the favourable

South tile. Problems are shown by the distant tiles, particularly the Pine (2 Circles), representing a younger male, and the House (5 Wan). The final tiles, on the left, show a change in circumstances: 9 Wan represents the end of an episode, 4 Wan rest or retirement, and the Peach (6 Circles) extravagance. The lady was a travel courier, worried about leaving her son at home while she went to the Bahamas for the winter!

SYMBOLISM OF THE MAH JONGG TILES

BAMBOO TILES

1 **Peacock** Self, pride, success.
2 **Duck** Devotion, partnership.
3 **Toad** Recovery from sickness.
4 **Carp** Determination. Long life.
5 **Lotus** New life, vision. A baby.
6 **Water** Travel, correspondence.
7 **Tortoise** Learning. Illegitimacy.
8 **Fungus** Virtue. Eccentricity.
9 **Willow** Tact. Resilience.

CIRCLE TILES

1 **Pearl** Honour, refinement. An older woman.
2 **Pine** Strength, literature. A young man.

3 **Phoenix** Good news.
4 **Jade** Worth, good deeds.
5 **Dragon** Good fortune.
6 **Peach** Fine arts. A young lady.
7 **Insect** Craft, skill, manual work.
8 **Tiger** Authority. An older man.
9 **Unicorn** Ability to see ahead.

WAN (CHINESE NUMERALS)

1 **Open door** New opportunities.
2 **Sword** A choice, a decision. Twins.
3 **Earth** Land, the countryside. Relocation.
4 **Lute** Music, leisure.
5 **House** A building, real estate, the home.
6 **Fire** Loss, danger.

7 **Stars** Dreams, ambitions, imagination.
8 **Knot** Tying or untying.
9 **Heaven** Spiritual matters. A ceremony.

DIRECTIONS

East The Self.
South Good fortune, growth, progress.
West The objective or partner.
North Difficulties. Shortage.

COLOURS

Green (Go) Go ahead, don't delay.
Red (Centre) Achievement of ambition.
White Documents. Ghosts.

the inseparable tie between games of chance and the oracle of lot-casting leaves no doubt as to the reason why the Chinese are notorious for being such inveterate gamblers. Nowhere else does chance play such a large part in both religious and social life.

READING MAH JONGG TILES

Many people who have used Mah Jongg find that it has a specific advantage over the Tarot. Although the variety of Mah Jongg tiles is more limited, since for the most part each tile is repeated four times, it is this very repetition which intensifies the message delivered by the oracle. If a tile appears at the beginning of a reading and then reappears later, its significance is heightened and this directs the reader to examine such factors as the tiles that are close by and the time-scale involved.

When setting the tiles out for a reading, 13 tiles are taken, as in the game of Mah Jongg, and set out in sets of fours, representing the four seasons, with one central tile representing the question of the moment. The three tiles nearest the reader represent the present situation, those to the right the immediate future, those furthest away the objective and the hazards which have to be faced, while the four at the left refer to the more distant future, or the situation as it will be in a year's time. Should one of the eight Guardian tiles be selected, another tile is drawn and placed beside it. The Guardian reveals the existence of a difficulty, and its solution.

SOUTH

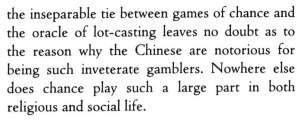

CHAPTER SIXTEEN

THE CHINESE BOOK OF CHANGES

Ancient Wisdom from the *I Ching*

Nigel Pennick

The *I Ching* is the ancient Chinese Book of Changes. It is a text that gives the user an insight into the forces, literally the 'changes', operating at any particular moment in time. The *I Ching* is the crystallization into writing in antiquity of the even more ancient oral tradition of divination. In traditional divination, patterns seen in natural things were used as indicators of immediate conditions in the eternal flow of events in time. In China, the patterns that diviners saw in Nature were standardized and related to a book of readings – the *I Ching* – thereby putting these patterns into a formal framework which is still useful today.

YANG AND YIN: THE ORIGIN OF THE *I CHING*

According to the Confucian and Taoist religions, when the *Great Extreme* (*Tai Ji*) came into being at the beginning of all existence it produced the two complementary opposites, yang and yin. These represent odd and even, plus and minus, male and female, light and darkness, day and night, and so on. Literally, the ancient meaning of yin was 'the shaded, north side of a hill', when yang meant 'the sunny, south side of a hill'. Yang controls heaven and all things positive, active, masculine, hard, moving and living. Yin controls the Earth and all things

The Former Heaven Sequence of trigrams on a nineteenth-century luck-bringing talisman was used in Feng Shui to ward off evil influences. The Former Heaven Sequence is the cosmic ideal, while the Later Heaven Sequence is its earthly application. The tiger symbolizes the west. Its corresponding trigram is K'an.

negative, passive, dark, soft, still and non-living. Traditionally, yang is shown as a solid, single continuous line, and yin as a broken line, in two distinct pieces.

yang   yin

In this belief-system, the eternal changes of existence are ascribed to the waxing and waning of the relative qualities of yang and yin. Any particular circumstance contains a specific balance of these qualities, and they can be determined by consulting the *I Ching*.

The four seasons clearly demonstrate the working of this yang-yin principle: in winter, yin is at its maximum and yang at its minimum. Then in springtime, yang and yin are equal, with yang waxing and yin waning. Summertime has the maximum yang; then autumn has again a balance of yang and yin, with yang waning and yin waxing. Finally, in the next winter, yin is

Chinese sages interpret the yang-yin symbol. This painting is on a Chinese ceramic dish, bearing the identification mark of K'ang Hai (1661–1722).

THE EIGHT TRIGRAMS: THEIR NAMES, MEANINGS AND CORRESPONDENCES

Ch'ien represents heaven, creative originality in all things. It signifies a change for the better, substitution or variation to achieve harmony. Its three unbroken lines represent vitality, strength and good fortune.

K'un represents the Earth and feminine things. Its three broken lines signify the ultimate in yin qualities. It is the complementary opposite of *Ch'ien*.

Chen represents thunder, the movement and development of things. Its two broken lines and one solid one signify apprehension and alterations in the status quo.

Sun denotes penetration (wind and wood). It represents pliability and influence, and the growth of vegetation.

K'an, which means 'pit', signifies danger, and also flowing water. It is connected with the mind, thought and concentration. The unbroken line at the centre represents inner strength, but this is countered by the broken outer lines.

Li denotes separation (fire and lightning), but in divination it signifies beauty and firmness. Its form, two solid lines enclosing a broken line, represents adherence.

Ken, meaning 'mountain', represents stopped action, either a blockage to progress, or a well-earned rest during some process.

Tui represents happiness, joy and satisfaction, manifested as achievement and progress. Its weak yin line is compensated for by two strong, unbroken yang lines.

again at its maximum. This general principle applies to all things. The Chinese symbol of existence, the yin-yang, shows this essential unity. The dark yin has within it a 'seed' of light yang, whilst the light yang has its complementary 'seed' of dark yin.

During the creation process, yang and yin gave birth to four primary symbols. These are each represented by two lines:

To these primary symbols were added a further line, of either yin or yang, creating the eight trigrams. These trigrams have names and specific relations to one another: they are related to the eight directions of space; they determine the divination of fortune in the *I Ching* and the orientation of buildings in the Chinese art of placement, Feng Shui (see Chapter Seventeen).

According to legend, the diagrams of the *I Ching* were invented by an inspired man. This parallels exactly the legendary origin of the Ogam script with Ogma and geomancy with Idris (see Chapters Three and Twenty-three). In the case of the *I Ching*, its originator was Fu Hsi, fabled first emperor of China, who also invented weaving and fishing nets. He devised the trigrams after examining the basic patterns underlying all things in the world. One of the *I Ching* commentaries, *The Great Appendix*, describes this revelation:

In ancient times, when Fu Hsi ruled all things under heaven, he looked up to contemplate the bright forms in the sky, then looked down to contemplate the patterns forming on the earth. He contemplated the patterns of birds and animals and the properties of their habitats. Near at hand, he found in his own body things for consideration, and also observed distant things in general. Thus he devised the eight trigrams, in order to clarify the

heavenly processes in Nature, and to understand the relations of all things.

A related story tells how Fu Hsi discovered the first eight trigrams by studying the patterns on a tortoise shell. In the archaic Lungshan period in China, tortoise shells were used in divination. A tortoise shell was heated in a fire until it cracked and the pattern of cracks was then interpreted by a trained diviner. In creating the trigrams, Fu Hsi made some order of these random patterns according to Chinese cosmic theory.

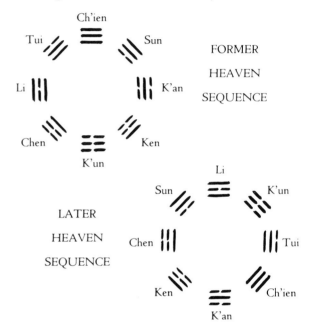

Customarily, the basic eight trigrams are laid out in the form of an octagon. Two layouts are used: the older is the Former Heaven Sequence, which is attributed to Fu Hsi, and the subsequent one is the Later Heaven Sequence, which is attributed to King Wen, first ruler of the Chou dynasty.

According to tradition, the full development of the *I Ching* took place in 1143 BC, when a feudal lord named Wen (who subsequently became King Wen) was imprisoned by the emperor and threatened with death. During his time in prison, he used his enforced solitude to expand and refine the *Book of Changes*, relating divined patterns to specific texts. He did this by doubling up the trigrams to make six-line hexagrams, and allotting each one to a corresponding text. Each hexagram combined the meanings of two trigrams, and thus described a specific interaction of qualities. The 64 hexagrams of the *I Ching* comprise all the possible combinations of paired trigrams.

Later, Wen's son, the Duke of Chou, added further material to the book. Chou's addition of 384 commentaries became an integral part of the divinatory text. They allowed more detailed readings, using a divination starting with the four primary symbols.

The oracle then took on its present form, where the divination results in the creation of a hexagram containing certain elements that refer to a unique 'energy' or quality of existence. In total, the *I Ching* permits 11,520 possible situations to be described. These are said to express every possible physical, social and psychological condition. They are explained in the corresponding text in the *Book of Changes*.

The final form of the *I Ching* consists of King Wen's 64 hexagrams and their accompanying descriptions; the Duke of Chou's further interpretations of the lines; and additional Confucian commentaries. Fortunately, it escaped the wholesale burning of books ordered by Emperor Ch'in Shih Huang Ti in 213 BC. In the year AD 175, the texts of the *Five Confucian Classics*, including the *I Ching*, were engraved on stone. It was revised during the Sung dynasty (960–1279), when a commentary by the philosopher Chu Hsi (1130–1200) was added. The present standard edition, on which Western translations are based, is the K'ang Hsi edition, which was published in 1715.

THE *I CHING* THROUGH THE AGES

Legends apart, it is likely that the text of the *I Ching* dates from the Chou dynasty (*c*. 1000 BC). It developed greatly during the Han dynasty (202 BC–AD 220), when the diagrams were classified systematically according to cosmological-religious principles. This is a direct parallel of what happened in other parts of the world, where early spontaneous techniques were the basis for later formal systems. But in contrast to the West, where divination is not considered a legitimate part of the culture, the *I Ching* became an integral part of traditional Chinese life

The eight trigrams are often used together in a charm called Pak Kua (*both trigrams and hexagrams are called* Kua)*, which is often used as a talisman in Feng Shui to ward off harm. Surrounding the Yang and Yin motif, the trigrams appear on flags and plaques and also form the surrounding for geomantic mirrors set up at bad places to reflect away harmful spirits or energies. As in the* Vintana *of Madagascar, which links the oracle of geomancy (for prediction) with locational geomancy (for good and bad places in the landscape), the* Pak Kua *links the trigrams with Feng Shui. The form of the eight trigrams makes them a relative of the 16 tetragrams of Western geomancy, as both have a combination of odd and even.*

and thought, and remains so today. Once based solely in China, it has since spread to all parts of the globe.

Throughout history, the *I Ching* has been used by Chinese generals in the conduct of war. In the twentieth century, the Chinese Nationalist leader Chiang Kai-Shek praised the value of the *I Ching* as both an oracle and a record of the ultimate values of Chinese life. The *I Ching* was also used in warfare by his opponent, the Communist leader Mao Zedong, whose forces eventually overcame those of the Nationalists in the Chinese Civil War. Although most 'esoteric' belief-systems were rejected by Maoism, the *I Ching* seems to have been exempt from suppression because it works.

Western interest in the *I Ching* began in the

This Neolithic oracle bone bears inscriptions in early Chinese characters. The I Ching *was developed from earlier divination techniques that used bones or tortoise shells. The patterns on the shells or bones were formalized into the trigrams and hexagrams used today.*

nineteenth century. In 1834, *Y-King, antiquissimus Sinarum Liber*, by P. Regis, was published at Paris. This was the first translation of the *I Ching*, by Jesuit missionaries, into a Western language. In 1889, C. de Harlez published a French translation at Brussels: *Le Yih-King, Texte Primitif: Rétabli, Traduit et Commenté*. An English edition was published by James Legge at Oxford in 1899. But the most influential work in the West was the edition translated by Richard Wilhelm, *I Ging: das Buch der Wandlungen*, published in German at Jena in 1924. Wilhelm's translation had a seminal foreword by psychologist C.G. Jung, whose insights into the *I Ching* transformed Western awareness of its nature and use. Jung was the first Westerner to recognize its universal relevance. When he used it, he found 'undeniably remarkable results',

inexplicable yet meaningful connections with his own thought patterns. Since Jung's day, the *I Ching* has taken its place in the West alongside other ancient traditional means of self-knowledge. Today, it is used in occultism, mathematics, psychology, and business studies.

CASTING THE HEXAGRAMS

The traditional way to generate the hexagrams uses stalks of the yarrow plant (*Achillea millefolium*). The divination begins with 50 long stalks of yarrow. First, the diviner takes one of them away, leaving 49 (7 × 7, an important 'square number' in divination). This is put on one side. Then the remaining 49 are divided into two random piles. Once this is done, four stalks are removed from one pile, then the other, in turn, until three, two, one or no stalks are left in each pile. The diviner then counts the stalks remaining. From this, he or she obtains various numbers which are interpreted as the four primary symbols: old yang (─⊖─), old yin (─x─), young yang (───) and young yin (─ ─). The whole procedure is done a further five times, producing six lines – the hexagram – which can be either old lines, young lines, or a mixture of both. The hexagram is looked up in the book, and the answer to the question is read.

Confucian and Taoist teachings tell that when a power reaches its apex or culmination, becoming 'old', it is then transformed into its opposite. Thus an 'old yang' line is in the process of moving from yang to yin. When an 'old' line appears in a hexagram, it creates a second hexagram as the line moves from, for example, yang to yin. The second hexagram must be taken into account when consulting the text, and the 'moving' lines are particularly important for the reading.

Another way of generating hexagrams uses coins. Many *I Ching* users like to use old Chinese cash coins. These round coins with square central holes were originally ordinary currency, but nowadays they are sold for oracular use. The side of the coin with four characters is the yang side and has a value of three. The reverse has a value of two. The three coins are cast six times, producing a value of six, seven, eight or nine at each throw. Each number corresponds to a quality of yang or yin: a six is old yin, seven is young yang, eight is young yin and nine old yang. It is equally valid to use Western-style coins in *I Ching* divination. Here, the 'head' side is taken as positive (yang, value 3) and the 'tail' as negative (yin, value 2).

	Trigram	Family	Part of body	Compass direction	Element	Season	Natural feature
☰	Ch'ien	father	head	NW	metal	late autumn/ early winter	heaven
☷	K'un	mother	belly	SW	earth	late summer/ early autumn	earth
☳	Chen	eldest son	foot	E	wood	spring	thunder
☴	Sun	eldest daughter	thighs	SE	wood	late spring/ early summer	wind
☵	K'an	middle son	ear	N	water	winter	moon
☲	Li	middle daughter	eye	S	fire	summer	sun
☶	Ken	youngest son	hand	NE	wood	late winter/ early spring	mountain
☱	Tui	youngest daughter	mouth	W	water/ metal	autumn	lake

The trigrams have many correspondences: they express family relationships, natural features, parts of the human body, directions, seasons and elements. The two sequences have their own connections, too. The Former Heaven Sequence is used to express the seasons (the passing of time), while orientation and location are expressed through the Later Heaven Sequence. This table shows the correspondences of the trigrams according to these sequences.

A simpler method of making hexagrams uses the Six Wands Method. This uses six special wands, painted black with a white bar across one side. They are thrown onto the ground or a table-top, then are picked up beginning with the rod nearest to the caster. Those that show the white bar are yin, and those that do not are yang. The drawback of this method is that only one hexagram is produced. There can be no moving lines, so the Duke of Chou's commentary is not available for use.

The *I Ching* also lends itself to modern computer technology. There are even hand-held, battery-powered *I Ching* computers which give instant readings anywhere.

However they are generated, the hexagrams are accumulated from the bottom upwards, as in the traditional way of writing Chinese characters. This is in accord with Nature, because all things grow from the ground upwards. The first line generated is thus the lower line, and the sixth, final one, the upper line. Like the trigrams, each hexagram has a name and a basic meaning.

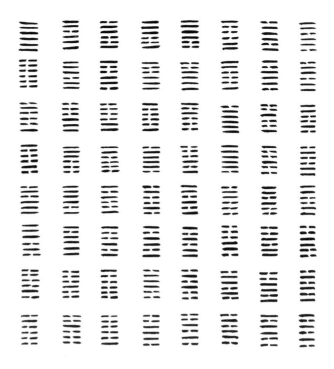

The 64 hexagrams are laid out here in sequence, with the first at the top left. Each column is read from the top downwards, so hexagram 8 is at the bottom of the left-hand column, hexagram 9 is at the top of the next column to the right, and so on.

1 *Ch'ien*, creativity.
2 *K'un*, quiescence.
3 *Chun*, difficulties at the beginning (birth pangs).
4 *Meng*, youth (inexperience).
5 *Hsu*, nourishment (contemplation).
6 *Sung*, conflict.
7 *Shih*, the army.
8 *Pi*, unity.
9 *Hsiao Ch'u*, restraint (by the weak).
10 *Lu*, treading.
11 *T'ai*, peace.
12 *P'i*, disharmony (stagnation).
13 *T'ung Jen*, social harmony.
14 *Ta Yu*, wealth.
15 *Ch'ien*, modesty.
16 *Yu*, enthusiasm (calm confidence).
17 *Sui*, adaptive following.
18 *Ku*, reparation (decay).
19 *Lin*, conduct (getting ahead).
20 *Kuan*, consolidation (contemplation).
21 *Shih Ho*, biting through.
22 *Pi*, gracefulness (adornment).

23 *Po*, breaking-down (shedding).
24 *Fu*, return.
25 *Wu Wang*, simplicity (simple integrity).
26 *Ta Ch'u*, restrained power.
27 *I*, nourishment.
28 *Ta Kuo*, excess.
29 *K'an*, the deep (the perilous chasm).
30 *Li*, fire (brilliant beauty).
31 *Hsien*, stimulus (mutual attraction).
32 *Heng*, continuance.
33 *Tun*, retreat.
34 *Ta Chuang*, great power (vigorous strength).
35 *Chin*, progress.
36 *Min I*, advancing darkness.
37 *Chia Jen*, family.
38 *K'uei*, disunity (opposites).
39 *Chien*, obstruction.
40 *Hsieh*, liberation.
41 *Sun*, decrease.
42 *I*, increase.
43 *Kuai*, determination (renewed advance).
44 *Kou*, temptation (sudden

encounters).
45 *Ts'ui*, harmoniousness (collecting together).
46 *Sheng*, pushing upwards (ascending).
47 *K'un*, oppression (exhausting restriction).
48 *Ching*, the well.
49 *Ko*, revolution.
50 *Ting*, the cauldron.
51 *Chen*, thunderclap.
52 *Ken*, keeping still.
53 *Chien*, progressive development (gradual advance).
54 *Kuei Mei*, the marrying maiden.
55 *Feng*, fullness (abundant prosperity).
56 *Lu*, the travelling stranger.
57 *Sun*, the penetrating wind.
58 *Tui*, joyousness.
59 *Huan*, dispersion.
60 *Chieh*, limitation.
61 *Chung Fu*, truth.
62 *Hsiao Kua*, small successes.
63 *Chi Chi*, completion achieved.
64 *Wei Chi*, before completion.

DRAGON LINES IN THE LAND

Feng Shui

Derek Walters

Feng Shui is the name of an ancient Chinese philosophy which relates every aspect of our lives to our surroundings. Literally, Feng Shui translates as 'wind and water', but there is no exact Western equivalent for the expression. The Chinese understand it to mean an environment that brings peace of mind, good health, long life, happiness and, ultimately, prosperity. Whether it is the geographical location, or the man-made buildings around us, the position of the furniture, or even a carefully posed single flower in a vase, all these produce or affect the prevailing Feng Shui, for good or for harm, as the following story shows.

The seven newly-built houses tucked away in a quiet corner of a private housing estate had every amenity that a young married couple could want. Modern, comfortable and within easy reach of the city, they would have been the pride of their eager new owners when they first crossed the threshold. Yet within months of the seven houses being occupied, five of the couples who had such golden hopes for their future lives had parted and gone their separate ways. It was as if this one enclave, unlike the other streets and roads of the neighbourhood, held some grim and sombre secret that blighted the happiness of those who had unwittingly made their homes there. But why?

This sad series of events took place in a residential suburb of England's second largest city. There seemed no rational explanation. Yet if it had happened anywhere in the Chinese-speaking world, the reason would have been evident, and uncontested. The location's Feng Shui was bad. But what may be apparent to the Chinese eye may not be so easy for the Western mind to comprehend. Explain Feng Shui in rational terms, and the Western sceptic dismisses it as plain common sense. Explain it in terms of Chinese philosophical belief, and the sceptic dismisses it as superstition.

When a Feng Shui expert was asked to inspect the area, he asserted that because the road at the back of the estate ran into a wider one, which in turn ran into a major trunk road, all the *ch'i*, or positive force, was being drained away. Next he looked at the homes themselves, and was disturbed to find that the stairs faced

A woodcut illustration from the Yellow Emperor Classic, perhaps the oldest extant Feng Shui text, shows a house facing north-east, with a side entrance north-west, producing the favourable Ch'i locations 'Generating Breath' and 'Lengthened Years' respectively.

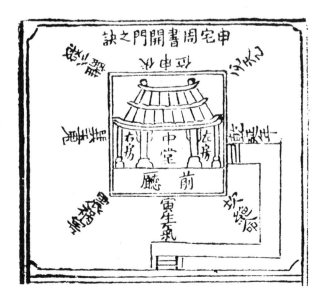

the main entrance – again causing the homes' own energy to cascade out of the house. But standing by the window, it was possible to indentify another, subtly psychological reason for the 'weak energy' in the house. Anyone staying in the house for any length of time could not fail to be aware of the constant flow of traffic – moving always away from the house. Subconsciously, a feeling of unease and restlessness would be generated, leading to a desire to get away, perhaps from the house, perhaps from everything that it represented: marriage, family, even the home.

But, the remarkable thing about this example is that, while the rational, psychological explanation applied only to this particular case, the elementary precepts advanced by the Feng Shui expert would apply in a much wider variety of situations. It is a guiding principle of conventional scientific research that when there are several possible theories to account for a particular phenomenon, the simpler and more universal theory is the one most likely to be true.

Feng Shui is a complex subject, with as many facets as, say, music – something which is partly an art and partly a science, but mostly an intrinsic quality that is beyond definition. If the scenery surrounding a village has rolling hills, trickling streams, a waterfall and naturally sculpted rocks, the environment may be said to have good Feng Shui. If, then, electricity pylons are erected in front of the house, or a new motorway cuts a gash through a wooded valley, the Feng Shui is likely to be destroyed – but not just because the landscape is now less pleasing to the eye. The principles of Feng Shui reveal the consequences that follow its destruction: fire, accident, illness, misfortune or separation may pursue those obliged to live in the regions where the Feng Shui has been toppled. Fortunately, Feng Shui techniques not only reveal what kind of locations are beneficial, but also how it is possible to rectify or at least improve a situation that lacks the essential qualities to produce a harmonious environment.

Until a few years ago, it might have been supposed that Feng Shui practices were confined to the Chinese-speaking world, but the impact is much more widespread. It comes as no surprise that Feng Shui principles are respected from Bangkok to Tokyo and from Ulan Bator to Jakarta, given the unifying factor of Buddhist influence in the nations adjoining China; but perhaps less predictable is its appearance in Madagascar and East Africa, where even the most primitive dwellings are constructed according to Feng Shui principles, even to the point of having the Eight Diagrams, an ancient secret talisman, carved on the lintel (see Chapter Twenty-three, Ancient Secrets of the Earth).

Now, with the growth of interest in philosophies beyond our own, interest in Feng Shui is world-wide, and Western-based businesses in Europe and America frequently find it prudent to call in the services of a consultant versed in the practice and mysteries of Feng Shui.

THE HISTORY OF FENG SHUI

The first known textbook on Feng Shui was compiled in the ninth century AD by the sage Yang Yun-sung, but he wrote principally about the Feng Shui produced by the fantastically vivid landscapes of the Kuei-lin region. His precepts are therefore known as the 'form school' of Feng Shui. Not long afterwards, other scholars, surrounded by less visually arresting scenery, compiled manuals of Feng Shui which were based on the ritual significance of the compass points: ideas which had been enshrined a thousand or more years before in the sacred Book of Rites. This aspect of Feng Shui was consequently known as the 'compass school'.

Until recent years, commentators on Chinese traditional customs had assumed that Feng Shui was – in terms of China's history – a comparatively recent innovation. But archaeological excavations have recently unearthed compass plates dating from the first century BC which are identical in detail to illustrations in books written a thousand years later. This reveals that although Yang Yun-sung might have been the first known author of a book expounding the principles of Feng Shui, the practice and oral traditions were already extremely ancient.

The Form and Compass schools are mutually dependent, and though there is a mystical side to Feng Shui, its foundation being based on the Chinese scriptures, at the core lies a good deal of common sense. The earliest Feng Shui consultants were in fact the equivalent of today's surveyors and valuers.

Thus, the ideal site for a farmstead would be on the slope of a hill, neither at the peak, where there would be a shortage of water, nor at its foot, which would make it difficult to defend. It would be close to running water, and face south for the sunshine while being protected from the wind from the north. But although not every house could be aligned north-south in a perfect environment, it was presumed that such a setting would ensure security, prosperity and so, ultimately, happiness.

There is, however, in addition to the Form and Compass schools, another canon of traditions, which sceptical Western observers scathingly regard as a collection of superstitions. These precepts have no classical foundation and

The prosperity of Hong Kong is said to be due to the favourable Feng Shui produced by the twin influences of the Dragon Mountains of Kowloon and the surrounding ocean. But overdevelopment has sapped the strength of the Dragon influences, leaving the future of Hong Kong in peril.

defy objective explanation; neither do they have any common thread relating them together. Yet these *ad hoc* prescriptions are widely known among the Chinese and universally accepted. So whereas the Feng Shui master might give a scholarly analysis of the surroundings, and carefully plot the location and orientation according to precise Feng Shui laws, the client could feel very disappointed if the consultant did not also leave behind a sealed packet of mystic ingredients, a talisman or two, and burn a few obligatory sticks of incense to placate the wayward spirits.

YANG AND YIN FENG SHUI

The study of buildings in relation to their environment is known as yang or positive Feng Shui. Although this is the more obvious aspect of Feng Shui, for the Chinese there is another, vitally important aspect of Feng Shui: yin or negative Feng Shui, which applies, not to houses for the living, but to the dwellings of the dead. This aspect of Feng Shui is a study in itself, covering funeral rites and ceremonies, the correct alignment of tombs, and the selection of dates for burial. Closely related is a whole genre of magical myths and legends woven round the abilities of the yin Feng Shui master to summon the corpses of the newly deceased in order that, zombie-like, they could perform his bidding. Although this is the material from which countless Chinese horror movies are built, the source of the belief is surprisingly benign. If an elder relative had died in a far-off city, poor families may not have been able to afford the cost of transporting the deceased for interment in the ancestral grave. The family would therefore call on the services of a skilled Taoist master of yin Feng Shui, and, provided that the animating force had not yet completely left the corpse, the sorceror could command the corpse's physical body to make its own way to the desirable tomb which had been prepared for it.

THE LOCATION

When a site is being assessed to find its potential Feng Shui qualities, the first step is to look at the surrounding landscape. In the ideal situation, there would be an open space in front of the building, with rolling hills behind. The main feature of the landscape would be the Dragon, a prominent hill or mountain, and various features of the hill would be identified by the Feng Shui consultant as the Dragon's head, body, and limbs, while streams and rivulets would be regarded as its veins. The community that lived in the benign gaze of the Dragon would be certain to become wealthy. Indeed, if it were not for the presence of the Nine Dragons (in Cantonese, *Kowloon*) to the north of Hong Kong, that city would never have achieved its present prosperity.

There are many places where the terrain is flat and featureless, yet there is still good fortune inherent in the patterns of rivers, lakes and waterways that surround the area. In cities, the meanderings of watercourses may be imitated by the flow of traffic through busy thoroughfares. Similarly, the silhouettes of the roofs of buildings on the skyline will have as much significance in an urban landscape as the shapes of hills in a rural setting.

THE INFLUENCE OF FIVE

To understand more fully the significance of the shapes on the skyline, whether natural or man-made, it is important to be familiar with the underlying philosophy of the Five Elements. ('Elements' may not be an accurate translation of the Chinese technical term, but it has been sanctioned by long usage.)

The five elements, or forces, are called Wood, Fire, Earth, Metal and Water. Four of these five elements are related to the four cardinal points, with Earth being at the centre. The Four Cardinal points are in turn related to four seasons, each of which has its own symbolic colour and shape. Thus wood, which encompasses all growing vegetative life, is the element related to the Spring, the beginning of the year, the sunrise and the eastern direction. The appropriate colour is bluish-green, like the green of plants, or the Great Sea to the east of China, while the associated shape is tall and narrow, like the trunk of a tree.

Fire, shown by the heat of the sun, is the element of midday, the Summer, the South, animal life and the colour red. Its symbolic shape is triangular, the sharp points of the triangle being likened to flames.

Earth, at the centre, is not associated with any direction or season, but is symbolized by flat shapes and the colour ochre, like the earth of central China. It represents stability and all earthenware materials.

Metal is the element of Autumn, signifying either swords or agricultural implements. The appropriate colour is silvery white, like the element itself, but also like the snows of the Himalayan mountains to the west of China. Metal is represented by circular shapes, perhaps in allusion to metal coins.

The astonishing scenery of Kuei-lin has inspired Chinese poets and painters for centuries. It was here that Yang Yun-sung first outlined the principles of 'form school' Feng Shui, equating the shapes of the hills to the astrological Dragon and Tiger.

Finally, the element Water represents Winter, night and the colour black, and symbolizes all fluid situations, including speech and communication. Because Water lacks form, irregular shapes denote the Water element.

If a particular shape dominates the location, the related element influences both natural and human events. For example, acutely angled triangles would put the affected area in danger of accident through fire, unless there were other, balancing features. To this end, it is important to realize that each element is able to 'produce', or reinforce, the next in the sequence: Wood – Fire – Earth – Metal – Water – Wood. Conversely, each element destroys and neutralizes the effect of the next but one in the series; thus Wood destroys Earth, but is itself destroyed by Metal.

WOOD
burns,
producing
FIRE
produces ash or
EARTH
from which is mined
METAL
which melts, like
WATER
which nourishes
WOOD

WOOD
takes away the
nourishment from
EARTH
muddies and pollutes
WATER
which extinguishes
FIRE
which melts
METAL
which chops down
WOOD

Thus a building with a sharply pointed roof, representing the element Fire, in an environment mainly surrounded by tall trees, or buildings with columns and pillars, would be in a Wood environment. As Wood 'produces' Fire, the situation is stimulating. Feng Shui scholars aver that this type of location produces very intelligent children, while several manufacturing and commercial enterprises also benefit from this combination of elements.

A professional geomancer uses the Lo P'an *to ascertain the orientation of a tomb, at Ping Tung in southern Taiwan. If the tomb has good Feng Shui this will ensure that the ancestors will be content, and this in turn will bring merit and good fortune to their descendants.*

FLOW GENTLE *CH'I*

Having taken into account the surrounding environment, the orientation of the building and various other features, the consultant will then enter the building to advise on the interior. At some point the Feng Shui master is bound to consult the *LoP'an*, through which it is possible to locate the ideal positions for various functions such as the study, the bedroom, or the correct siting of doors and windows.

The *LoP'an* is a specially designed compass. It is to the Feng Shui master what the stethoscope is to the doctor, the virtual insignia of his calling. The face of the compass dial is divided into several circles, each sub-divided into numerous further divisions representing, not only different compass points, but lucky and unlucky directions, the hours, months and days associated with each compass point, and even the constellation exerting the greatest influence at that moment and in that direction.

The web-like arrangement of divisions resembled a net to the Chinese, who thus called it the 'net plate' – in Chinese, *LoP'an*. The saucer-shaped 'net plate' sits in a square base which has two cross-threads running over the pivot of the compass needle. When a site is under inspection, the sides of the square base are aligned with the walls of the room or building. The circular plate housing the compass needle is then turned until the south point on the dial lines up with the compass needle (Chinese compasses point to the south, not the north). The cross-threads on the base then indicate the various favourable or unfavourable times associated with the orientation of the building, enabling the consultant to suggest the correct positioning of the entrance, or the ideal moment for the building's inauguration.

There must, for example, be a good flow of *Ch'i*. This is something peculiar to Chinese philosophy and consequently defies adequate translation. Loosely speaking, *Ch'i* is a current of good, healthy energy through the building.

Ch'i meanders and flows in curves: it should bubble effortlessly through the building, without ending in enclosed areas, where it stifles and consequently exerts a bad influence. While it may be likened to the flow of fresh air through a house, *Ch'i* is not just fresh air, for it can be deflected from, or along, its course by the means of suitably positioned mirrors. It is unwise for *Ch'i* to flow straight through a house without being able to pass on its revitalizing forces: a corridor or hallway which runs straight to the rear from the front entrance is such a case, as the *Ch'i* fails to permeate the rooms.

Similarly, reception rooms which have windows at both ends lose their *Ch'i*. In effect, there is no comfortable focal point where it is possible to sit without having a window at one's back – subconsciously creating a feeling of unease. The solution is simple: blinds should be drawn over one of the windows during the day, so that light enters from only one direction. Alternatively, the room should be partitioned or otherwise divided into two smaller areas.

In China, a garden provides the ideal opportunity to balance the Feng Shui of the locality with its surrounding scenery. For this reason, the English landscaped garden has a much more favourable Feng Shui than the formal, continental style.

SECRET ARROWS

The converse of *Ch'i* currents, which flow in undulating lines, are *Sha*, which shoot along straight lines like an arrow. The Chinese aversion to straight lines was one of the reasons why railways were slow to develop in China. If straight *Sha*-transporting lines, such as are produced by roads, paths and telegraph wires, are unavoidable, they must approach the house obliquely, in order for the *Sha* to be deflected.

Sha can also be produced by angles pointing at the house: these might be found in the sharp corners of other buildings, or roads which suddenly turn, forming a bend which is like an arrowhead. Such secret arrows are sure portents of impending accident.

A path that curves towards a house is preferred to one that runs straight up to the entrance. Winding or zig-zag paths are able to deflect the adverse influences of harmful Sha, *which always travels in straight lines.*

MIRROR ON THE WALL

Mirrors are often used to encourage the flow of *Ch'i* and to dissipate harmful *Sha*. Mirrors have always fascinated the Chinese, and were regarded as a door to the world beyond. Indeed, it was customary for the backs of mirrors to be decorated with cosmic symbols, so much so that the designs on the backs of Chinese mirrors are an authentic chronicle of the history of Chinese cosmological thought.

The mirror most often employed today for Feng Shui purposes is in an octagonal frame, on which are depicted the Eight Trigrams – a powerful demonifuge and talisman. The actual mirror is often concave or convex, the better to dissipate harmful *Sha*. Mirrors, however, are not favoured in bedrooms, because they stimulate the *Ch'i*, thus provoking a restless sleep. It is also regarded as dangerous for the dreamer's soul to catch its reflection in a mirror, lest it take fright and leave the body.

THE EIGHT TRIGRAMS AND THEIR SYMBOLISM

The Eight Trigrams, found among the religious symbolism of nations from East Africa to Japan, are simply the eight possible arrangements of three lines, whole or broken (see Chapter Sixteen, The Chinese Book of Changes). They have been recorded in inscriptions which are several thousand years old.

Li	South. Fire and heat. Middle daughter. Heating; the kitchen; furnaces and ovens.
K'un	South-west. Nourishment. Mother. Medical centres, welfare, children's rooms.
Tui	West. Joy, laughter. Youngest daughter. Recreation, entertainment.
Ch'ien	North-west. Heaven. Authority. Father. Strength. Management, design, training.
K'an	North. Wheels, rotation, danger. Middle son. Workshops, garages, machinery.
Ken	North-east. Obstacles. Mountains. Youngest son. Entrances, security, barriers.
Chen	East. Thunder. Movement, speed. Eldest son. Transport, roads, distribution.
Sun	South-east. Trade, growth. Eldest daughter. Continuous operation: assembly lines and routine.

STAR LORE IN THE EAST

Sidereal Astrology

Valerie J. Roebuck

Sidereal astrology, an astrology based on the fixed stars which is widely practised today in the countries of South and Southeast Asia, developed in the Indian subcontinent as part of the world-picture shared by Hindus, Buddhists and Jains. It owed its origin to two main sources, one of them indigenous, the other derived from cultures to the West.

The earliest Indian star-lore is to be found in the Vedas, four collections of hymns and prayers, composed from about 1500 BC on. The Vedas, written in often mysterious and riddling language, are full of awe and wonder at the power of the gods, combined with a strong sense of questioning of the meaning of things. In both respects they contain the seeds of later Hinduism. Many of the gods and goddesses of the Vedas are connected with the phenomena of Nature: earth and sky, fire and wind, dawn and night. The people of India 3,000 years ago, living in small settlements in a vast land, were acutely aware of how fully they depended on these powers for their survival.

They relied on the Sun for heat, and the light by which they worked, though in the Indian climate its power could also be destructive. The Moon was the measurer of time, its cool light a welcome sight after the heat of the day. The fixed stars too were revered: some of them were regarded as holy men and women, once mortal, but now living in the sky. Notable among them were Dhruva, 'the Fixed' or Pole Star, and the Seven Sages of the Great Bear. Agastya, a sage who took Vedic teachings to South India, was identified with the southern star Canopus. (The

planets, it appears, had not yet acquired any special significance: perhaps they were thought of as bright, moving stars.)

Most important among the stars were the lunar mansions, the constellations among which the Moon appeared to move in the course of its monthly journey. Originally the mansions varied in size according to their actual appearance in the sky, but by about 400 BC they had been systematized into a lunar Zodiac of 27 equal mansions, which could be used for making accurate measurements of celestial positions. Although the Indians may have learned some of their science from the Babylonians, the lunar mansion system seems to be purely Indian in origin.

Through centuries of observation, the Vedic star-lore developed into *jyotiṣa*, the study of the heavenly bodies. The early *jyotiṣins* (practitioners of *jyotiṣa*) combined the functions of astronomers, astrologers, mathematicians and meteorologists. They had not only to create a reliable calendar, based on the movements of the Sun and Moon, but also to watch for omens in the sky, and forecast the weather and outbreaks of disease. Their work was concerned with matters that affected the community as a whole, it was not yet with drawing up individual horoscopes.

The change from the Vedic star-lore to a developed system of astrology was largely inspired by the Greeks, whom the Indians called 'Yavanas' or Ionians. In the early centuries of the Christian era there were a number of Greek settlements in India. Best known now are probably those of Gandhāra, which covered parts of the present-day Afghanistan, Pakistan and north-west India, but there were others in the west coast areas of Gujarat and Maharashtra, important ports for the sea-trade between the Indian and Graeco-Roman cultural spheres.

The earliest Greek influence on Indian *jyotiṣa* seems to have come to western India from Alexandria, which was the main centre of science for late Greek civilization. Around AD 140, Yavaneśvara, 'Lord of the Greeks', translated a Greek astrological text into Sanskrit. This is now lost, but its influence can be traced in surviving works by Sphujidhvaja, in the mid-third century, and Mīnarāja, in the fourth. All these men seem to have been rulers among the Greek communities of western India. Sphujidhvaja's astrology is very close to that of the Alexandrian Greeks, though it already includes a certain amount that is purely Indian, such as references to the lunar mansions. Mīnarāja's, though it uses the Greek structure, is recognizably Indian astrology as it is known today.

For in taking over the Greek system, the Indian astrologers did not keep it unchanged, but adapted it to their own cosmology. Although they adopted the 12-sign Zodiac, they did not abandon their own system of lunar mansions, but found a way of reconciling the two. Previously they had counted the mansions from Kṛttikā, the Pleiades, but they now made Aśvinī (the two stars β and γ Arietis) the first mansion, so that both signs and mansions were measured from the same point.

THE DEVELOPMENT AND INFLUENCE OF INDIAN ASTROLOGY

The Indian Subcontinent, also known as South Asia, has been a centre of civilization since at least 3000 BC. It is similar in size to Europe (excluding Russia), and has a comparable variety of terrain, climate, language and people. Despite this variety, the area possesses a strong cultural unity, which has persisted throughout recorded history. An outstanding feature of South Asian civilization is its ability to absorb ideas from other cultures, but in doing so to develop them and give them a character of its own. Best known among its gifts to the world are its distinctive achievements in religion, philosophy and the arts. Less appreciated, perhaps, are its discoveries in mathematics and the sciences, including the 'Arabic' – really Indian – system of numbers which, by superseding the unwieldy Roman system, made modern mathematics possible.

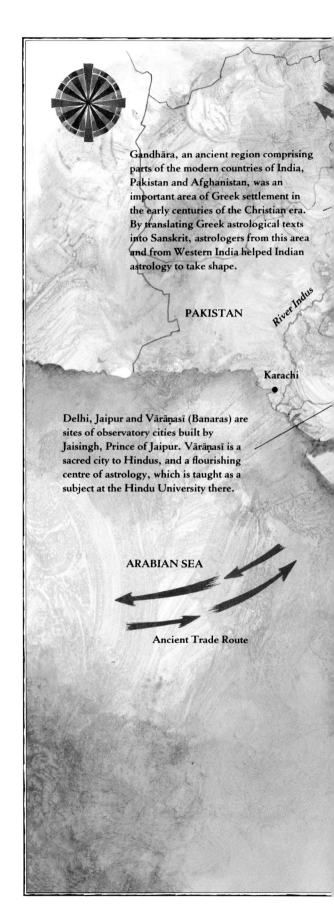

Gandhāra, an ancient region comprising parts of the modern countries of India, Pakistan and Afghanistan, was an important area of Greek settlement in the early centuries of the Christian era. By translating Greek astrological texts into Sanskrit, astrologers from this area and from Western India helped Indian astrology to take shape.

PAKISTAN

River Indus

Karachi

Delhi, Jaipur and Vārāṇasī (Banaras) are sites of observatory cities built by Jaisingh, Prince of Jaipur. Vārāṇasī is a sacred city to Hindus, and a flourishing centre of astrology, which is taught as a subject at the Hindu University there.

ARABIAN SEA

Ancient Trade Route

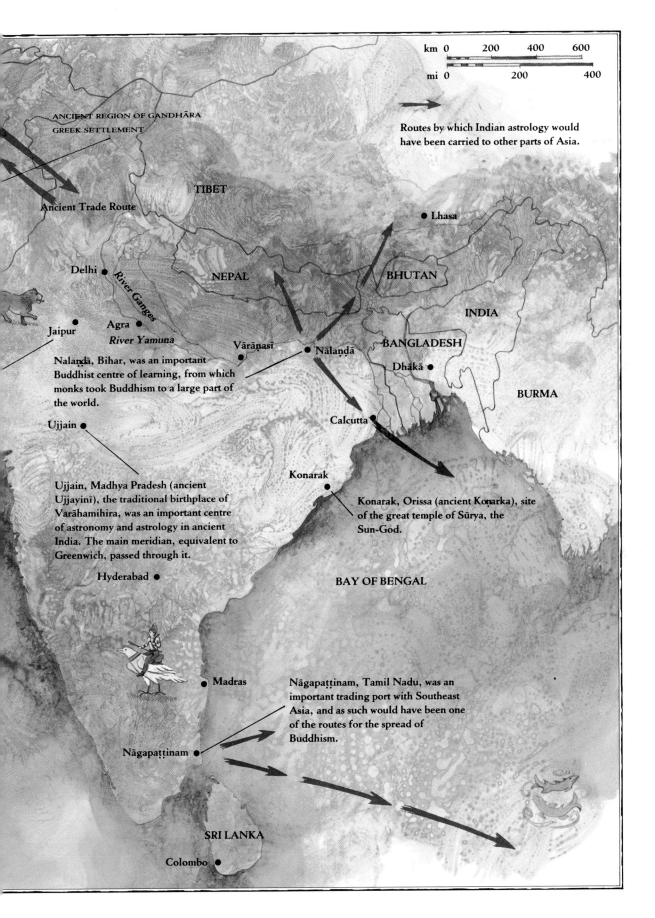

ANCIENT REGION OF GANDHĀRA
GREEK SETTLEMENT

Routes by which Indian astrology would
have been carried to other parts of Asia.

Ancient Trade Route

• Lhasa

TIBET

• Delhi

River Ganges

NEPAL

BHUTAN

INDIA

Jaipur •   Agra •

• Jaipur   *River Yamuna*

Vārānasī •   • Nālandā

BANGLADESH

Nālandā, Bihar, was an important
Buddhist centre of learning, from which
monks took Buddhism to a large part of
the world.

Dhākā •

BURMA

Ujjain •

Calcutta •

Konarak •

Ujjain, Madhya Pradesh (ancient
Ujjayinī), the traditional birthplace of
Varāhamihira, was an important centre
of astronomy and astrology in ancient
India. The main meridian, equivalent to
Greenwich, passed through it.

Konarak, Orissa (ancient Konarka), site
of the great temple of Sūrya, the
Sun-God.

Hyderabad •

BAY OF BENGAL

• Madras

Nāgapattinam, Tamil Nadu, was an
important trading port with Southeast
Asia, and as such would have been one
of the routes for the spread of
Buddhism.

Nāgapattinam •

SRI LANKA

Colombo •

A more fundamental adaptation was the use of a different Zodiac system. Although Greek astrologers were by now using the tropical Zodiac (see Chapter Six, Shapes in the Stars), the Indians soon returned to the more ancient sidereal Zodiac, in keeping with the greater importance they gave to the fixed stars.

Later Indian astrologers used a system of sidereal astrology into which both Greek and Vedic elements had been fully assimilated. By common consent, the greatest of them all was Varāhamihira, believed to have been court astrologer to one of the Gupta emperors around the middle of the sixth century. Varāhamihira wrote on every aspect of *jyotiṣa*, effectively giving Indian astrology the form in which it has been practised ever since. His works are still studied by Indian astrologers today.

The main development since Varāhamihira's time has been the growth in importance of the lunar nodes, Rāhu and Ketu. These are the points at which the apparent paths of the Sun and Moon intersect, and eclipses can occur. By about the ninth century they had come to be treated as dark planets on a par with the seven visible ones.

This change seems to have been influenced by the spiritual movement known as Tantra, which found astrology congenial to its view of each human being as a microcosm, reflecting the greater universe or macrocosm. The Tantric cult of the Nine Planets, visualized as gods, seems to have reached its height in the mid-thirteenth century with the building of the Sun Temple at Konarak, Orissa. It was conceived as a colossal chariot of the Sun, and adorned with magnificent sculptures, including figures of the Sun-God and the planetary deities.

Indian astrology has both influenced and been influenced by the thought of many other civilizations. It spread to the Buddhist cultures of Tibet and Southeast Asia, where it combined with local traditions to appear in new and distinctive forms. It affected the astrology of the Islamic world, and was influenced by it in turn, though mainly in matters of detail; the basic structure had by now become fixed.

Through the Islamic world, a few of the ideas of Indian astrology reached medieval and Renaissance Europe, but the main influence in that direction began much later, when, from the nineteenth century on, Western thinkers became interested in Eastern philosophy. In recent times, in the hands of Western astrologers, Indian astrology has helped to generate new forms of sidereal and harmonic astrology.

THE SIDEREAL ZODIAC

Both Indian and Western astrology chart the movements of the planets in relation to the ecliptic, the apparent path of the Sun through the sky, which they divide up into a Zodiac of

Key

1 Aries
2 Taurus
3 Gemini
4 Cancer
5 Leo
6 Virgo
7 Libra
8 Scorpio
9 Sagittarius
10 Capricorn
11 Aquarius
12 Pisces

This Lotus and Zodiac, c. twelfth century, is from Pattancheruvu, Andhra Pradesh. The stone cylinder is topped by a lotus surrounded by the signs of the Zodiac. The signs run clockwise, beginning with the Ram at the bottom (see key).

The temple of Sūrya, the Sun-God, at Konarak, Orissa, was built in the reign of King Narasimhadeva (1238–64). Even in ruins, it stands over 30 metres high, and was originally twice that height.

twelve equal signs. However, they begin their Zodiacs from two different points.

The Western system uses a tropical Zodiac, based on the seasons of the solar year, while the Indian system uses a sidereal Zodiac, based on the fixed stars. 0° Aries in the tropical Zodiac corresponds to the position of the Sun at the spring equinox (the 'vernal point'). 0° Aries in the sidereal Zodiac is the point among the fixed stars at which the Sun is thought to enter the constellation of the Ram. The Western signs,

unlike the Indian ones, have long ceased to coincide with the constellations from which they take their names.

The Zodiac and the Planets: *an engraving based on an eighteenth-century Indian painting. In the centre Sūrya, the Sun-God, rides a chariot drawn by seven horses (the days of the week). Surrounding him are the deities of the Moon (no. 5 on the diagram), Mars (6), Mercury (7), Jupiter (8), Venus (9), Saturn (2), Rāhu (3) and Ketu (4). The outer ring shows the signs of the Zodiac. From* The Hindu Pantheon *(1810) by Edward Moor, a pioneer of Indian studies in the West.*

The discrepancy is caused by the *precession of the equinoxes* (see Chapter Six, Shapes in the Stars). Not only does the Earth turn on its own axis, but, because of the gravitational pull of the Sun and Moon on its bulging equator, the axis itself revolves, like that of a spinning top which is slowing down. As a result, each of the Earth's Poles is turning in relations to the stars, completing a full circle every 25,800 years. As the Poles turn, the positions of the equinoxes move too, in the opposite direction to the movement of the Sun and planets, at the rate of 50" of arc per year, or a degree every 72 years.

The difference between the tropical and sidereal systems at any given time is called the *ayanāṃśa*, a Sanskrit term that has been adopted by Western astrologers. When calculating an Indian-style chart, the astrologer should work out the positions of the planets, the Ascendant, etc., from the ephemeris in the usual way, but complete the calculation by subtracting the appropriate *ayanāṃśa* (generally considered to be in the region of 24°) from each.

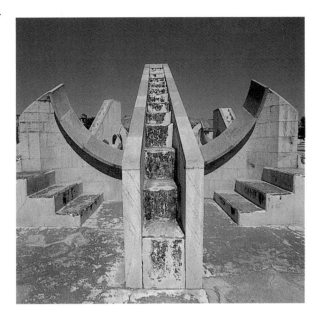

Even without the telescope, Indian jyotiṣins of former times made observations of remarkable accuracy, using measuring instruments of great size. The Jaipur Observatory is one of three built in the late-seventeenth century for the astrologer-prince Jaisingh. The Rāśivalaya Yantra (above) was used to calculate the position of the Sun. The view of the Observatory (below) is from the top of the tallest instrument.

THE SIGNS OF THE ZODIAC (RĀŚI):

Indian names and symbols, with Western equivalents.

1   *Meṣa*, the Ram: Aries
2   *Vṛṣabha*, the Bull: Taurus
3   *Mithuna*, the Couple, the woman holding a *Vīnā* (stringed instrument) and the man a mace: Gemini
4   *Karkaṭa*, the Crab: Cancer
5   *Siṃha*, the Lion: Leo
6   *Kanyā*, the Maiden, often depicted in a boat, and holding a lamp and grain: *Virgo*
7   *Tulā*, the Scales, often shown as a merchant weighing his goods in the market-place: Libra
8   *Vṛścika*, the Scorpion: Scorpio
9   *Dhanus*, the Bow, often, as in the West, a centaur archer: Sagittarius
10 *Makara*, the Sea-monster, a mythical aquatic beast, typically resembling an ornate crocodile with an elephant's trunk, although the astrological version is often shown as a deer with a fish's tail: Capricorn
11 *Kumbha*, the Water-pot, sometimes, as in the West, shown as a man emptying a water-pot carried on his shoulder: Aquarius
12 *Mīna*, the Fishes: Pisces.

In texts in English, the Indian signs are generally called by the names of their Western equivalents: a convenient custom so long as it is remembered that it is the sidereal, not the tropical, Aries or Taurus that is meant.

THE HOUSES (*BHĀVA*)
The houses are reckoned from the Ascendant, the point of the ecliptic rising at the time of the birth or event. The method most commonly used is a form of the Equal House system, in which each house is an exact 30° portion of the Ecliptic;

however, the Ascendant marks the centre of the first house, not, as in Western astrology, its cusp. The areas of life covered by the houses are similar, but not identical, in the two systems:

1   Ascendant: the body, appearance and personality
2   Wealth: property, family, speech
3   Brothers: brothers and sisters, courage, food
4   Kin: the early life, roots, and above all the mother
5   Sons: offspring, intelligence, actions done in past lives
6   Enemies, or Wounds: ill health and other obstacles
7   Wife: the marriage-partner, love, respect
8   Death: the life-span, death, and future rebirth
9   Religion: the spiritual teacher, the father and the proper way of life
10 Work: career, status, knowledge
11 Gain: income, prosperity, success
12 Loss: expenditure, misfortune, travel.

THE PLANETS (*GRAHA*)
The planets are named in the order of their days of the week, an ancient Babylonian sequence preserved in both European and Indian languages. All have masculine names, and are pictured in art as male gods. For astrological purposes, however, the Moon, Venus and Rāhu are regarded as feminine planets, and Mercury, Saturn and Ketu as neuter.

Sūrya or *Ravi*: the Sun
Candra or *Soma*: the Moon
Maṅgala 'Auspicious', or *Aṅgāraka*, 'Burning Charcoal': Mars
Budha, 'Knower': Mercury
Bṛhaspati, 'Lord of Sacred Speech', or *Guru*, 'Spiritual Teacher': Jupiter

Śukra, 'White' or 'Sperm': Venus
Śani, 'Slow', or *Śanaiścara*, 'Slow-goer': Saturn.
The list of nine planets is completed by the two lunar nodes, pictured in myth as Eclipse Demons pursuing the Sun and Moon: *Rāhu*, 'Seizer': the North Node *Ketu*, 'Banner', 'Sign': the South Node.

The planets discovered in historical times, Uranus, Neptune and Pluto, have not yet acquired a settled place in Indian astrology.

Planets are said to be strong in their signs of rulership, which are the same as in the Western system: the Sun rules Leo, the Moon rules Cancer, Mercury rules Gemini and Virgo, Venus rules Taurus and Libra, Mars rules Aries and Scorpio, Jupiter rules Pisces and Sagittarius, and Saturn rules Aquarius and Capricorn. But they are stronger still in their signs of exaltation, in which their energy is most harmoniously expressed: the Sun in Aries, the Moon in Taurus, Mars in Capricorn, Mercury in Virgo, Jupiter in Cancer, Venus in Pisces, and Saturn in Libra.

For the purpose of prediction, some planets are said to be 'benefic' or 'lucky', and others 'malefic' or 'unlucky'. Jupiter and Venus are benefic, the Sun, Mars, Saturn, Rāhu and Ketu malefic. The Moon is benefic when waxing or full, malefic when waning or new. Mercury is benefic in conjunction with benefic planets, and malefic with malefics: on its own it is slightly benefic. Strong planets are well disposed, and when in exaltation, even malefics are benign.

Aspects and conjunctions are always measured sign-to-sign, so that any planet in Aries is in opposition to any planet in Libra. Rāhu and Ketu do not form aspects, only conjunctions. No account is taken of 'easy' and 'difficult' aspects, only of the nature and compatibility of the aspecting planets.

THE LUNAR MANSIONS
(NAKṢATRA)

Just as a sign of the Zodiac represents the Sun's movement in a month, a lunar mansion corresponds to the Moon's movement in a day. The Moon takes about 27.3 days to circle the ecliptic, and Indian astrology generally divides the ecliptic into 27 equal mansions, though for certain purposes a 28-fold system may be used, an extra mansion being inserted between numbers 21 and 22. In myth and iconography, the mansions are visualized as the wives of the Moon-God, whom he visits night by night. In a birth-chart, the mansion occupied by the Moon is particularly significant, especially if it is full, waxing, or strongly placed.

1 0° Aries: *Aśvinī*, 'Possessing Horses', 'the Horsewoman': a horse's head
2 13° 20' Aries: *Bharaṇī*, 'Bearing': female sexual organ
3 26° 40' Aries: *Kṛttikā*, 'the Cutters': a weapon or a flame
4 10° Taurus: *Rohiṇī*, 'the Growing (or Red) One': a temple, an ox-cart, or a cow's head
5 23°20' Taurus: *Mṛgaśiras*, 'the Deer's Head': a deer's head
6 6° 40' Gemini: *Ārdrā*, 'the Moist One': a tear-drop
7 20° Gemini: *Punarvasū*, 'the Two Good-Again': a quiver of arrows
8 3° 20' Cancer: *Puṣya*, 'Nourishing': a cow's udder
9 16° 40' Cancer: *Āśleṣa*, 'the Clinging': a coiled snake
10 0° Leo: *Maghā*, 'the Great', 'the Bountiful': a royal throne-room
11 13° 20' Leo: *Pūrvaphalgunī*, 'the Former Reddish (or Small) One': a swinging hammock
12 26° 40' Leo: *Uttaraphalgunī*, 'the Latter Reddish (or Small) One': a bed or couch
13 10° Virgo: *Hasta*, 'the Hand': a hand
14 23° 20' Virgo: *Citrā*, 'Bright', 'Many-coloured', 'Wonderful': a bright jewel
15 6° 40' Libra: *Svāti*, 'Self-going': a young shoot blown by the wind
16 20° Libra: *Viśākhā*, the 'Forked' or 'Two-branched' (or *Rādhā* 'Delightful'): a gateway decorated with leaves
17 3° 20' Scorpio: *Anurādhā*, 'Additional Rādhā', 'After-Rādhā': a staff, or a row of offerings to the gods
18 16° 40' Scorpio: *Jyeṣṭhā*, 'the Eldest': a circular talisman
19 0° Sagittarius: *Mūla*, 'the Root': a tied bunch of roots
20 13° 20' Sagittarius: *Pūrvāṣāḍhā*, 'the Former Unconquered': a winnowing basket or fan
21 26° 40' Sagittarius: *Uttarāṣāḍhā*, 'the Latter Unconquered': an elephant's tusk
Intercalary Mansion. Abhijit, 'the Victorious': a triangle or three-cornered nut
22 10° Capricorn: *Śravaṇa*, 'Hearing' or 'Limping': three footprints side by side
23 23° 20' Capricorn: *Śraviṣṭhā*, 'the Most Famous' (or *Dhaniṣṭhā*, 'the Wealthiest'): a musical drum
24 6° 40' Aquarius: *Śatabhiṣaj*, 'The Hundred Physicians': a circle enclosing a space
25 20° Aquarius: *Pūrvabhadrapadā*, 'the Former Lucky Feet': the first end of a bed (the head?)
26 3° 20' Pisces: *Uttarabhadrapadā*, 'the Latter Lucky Feet': the other end of the bed
27 16° 40' Pisces: *Revatī*, 'Wealthy': a drum.

The lunar mansion and Zodiac systems are reconciled by dividing the ecliptic into 108 *navāṃśas* or ninth-signs, each of which is also a quarter of a mansion. The *navāṃśas* are allotted in order to the rulers of the 12 signs of the Zodiac, nine times repeated, and are often used for drawing subsidiary charts. The use of *navāṃśas* and other subdivisions of signs by Indian astrologers helped to inspire the recent development of harmonic astrology, in which additional charts are calculated from the main one.

Rāhu and Ketu, the Lunar Nodes, are pictured as eclipse demons who seek to devour the Sun and Moon. Here Rāhu, fanged and ferocious, grasps two slices of Moon, while a serpent-tailed Ketu holds a sword and (in the missing hand) a bowl of fire. These are part of a set of Nine Planets from the Sūrya Temple, Konarak, now in the British Museum.

INDIAN ASTROLOGY TODAY

Because they have part of their heritage in common, there is much in the Indian system that a Western astrologer will find familiar: far more so than in the case of, say, the Chinese system. However, the ways in which it is used reflect differences in the nature of Indian and Western society. Whereas modern Western astrology has to a great extent rejected prediction, and concentrated on individual psychology, Asian astrologers are still prepared to talk about benefic and malefic planets, and to forecast the events of the client's life. In this respect, their way is closer to the Western astrology of earlier times.

Unlike their Western counterparts, Indian astrologers may even attempt to forecast the time of a client's death. For Asian people, death is not the taboo subject it may be elsewhere; indeed it is important to prepare for it properly in order to face it in a calm state of mind. The truth of reincarnation is taken for granted, and some Indian astrology books give rules for working out from the birth-chart where we spent our last life and, from the chart of the time of death, in what kind of realm we are likely to be born in the next one. This approach is not as fatalistic as it may appear, since in the South Asian religions the events that happen to us are believed to be the result of our past actions, either in this life or a previous one. By living well in the present life, whatever the circumstances, we can build up a store of merit which will bring about happier rebirths in the future.

People in India or Southeast Asia might go to an astrologer for advice over any kind of problem. An entrepreneur might ask about the prospects for an investment, a farmer might want to know where to look for a missing animal, and of course anyone might want help in resolving difficulties in the family. Some would go to an astrologer in the market-place, but others would have a personal astrologer whom they consulted regularly, just as they might have a personal physician.

Both men and women practise as astrologers. The knowledge is handed down in certain families of the Brahmin (priestly) class, but it is also possible to study it at university. Some priests or monks are learned in astrology, and may use it in giving advice to their followers.

As well as dealing with mundane problems, Indian astrology provides a framework for relating the human body and mind to the Cosmos as a whole. The universe is pictured as *Kālapuruṣa*, the Time Man, who symbolizes both the Creator and every human being. His body is composed of the signs of the Zodiac: Aries is his head, Taurus his face and neck, Gemini his shoulders and arms, Cancer his chest, Leo his heart, Virgo his belly, Libra his hips and navel, Scorpio his sexual and excretory organs, Sagittarius his thighs, Capricorn his knees, Aquarius his lower legs, and Pisces his feet.

The planets represent his inner qualities. The Sun is his true self, the Moon his mind, Mars his courage, Mercury his speech, Jupiter his knowledge and happiness, Venus his desire, and Saturn his sorrow. The strength of the planets within the birth-chart is said to show the strength of those qualities within the individual, with the exception of Saturn: a strong Saturn means *less* sorrow, because it brings understanding. Viewed on this level, all the signs and all the planets are equally 'benefic' and equally holy.

Some Indian astrologers combine their art with other methods of divination. This one, working in a street in Calcutta, seeks omens in the behaviour of the birds, seen in a cage beside him.

CHAPTER NINETEEN

MIRRORS IN THE SKY

Tibetan Methods of Divination

Jay L. Goldberg

Clouds drift among high mountain peaks, silence spreads across vast plateaus, and the ear strains at the sound of ethereal winds. This is the kingdom of Tibet, the Roof of the World, the Land of Snows, long known to the world only through a veil of mystical obscurity. This once-forgotten land has been a place of interest for the spiritually minded for many years, held in high regard as a place of mystery and wonder. This is not just the outsider's point of view, but in many ways is held by the Tibetan people. For them, the world truly is a place of awe, in both a terrifying and a bewildering sense. To make some order of it, or at least to obtain a feeling of security, Tibetans have always sought the aid and reassurance of divination.

There are a large variety of divinatory systems in Tibet: astrology, mediumship, reading omens in bodies of water, viewing images reflected in mirrors or on thumb-nails, tying knotted cords, calling forth visions in dreams, casting dice, and interpreting naturally occurring phenomena such as the colour and placement of rainbows, the direction or type of thunderous sounds, or the direction and time of calls of black birds. This does not exhaust the list, but it does give an idea of the extent to which Tibetans sought divinatory knowledge.

Some of these forms of divination are indigenous to Tibet itself, but a great influence was also exerted by both India and China. The indigenous religion of Bon was the sole belief system in Tibet for centuries, and it had a number of its own divinatory systems. However, with the arising of Buddhism in Tibet, this entire belief system underwent a drastic change.

It was under the leadership of King Srongtsan Gampo (AD 617–650) that Buddhism was introduced into Tibet. He had two wives, one from Nepal and one from China, each of whom influenced him to such an extent that he converted to Buddhism. He sent translators to India to obtain Buddhist texts and teachings. This started a flow of cultural interchanges that eventually revolutionized the religious beliefs and outlooks of Tibet.

A century later, under the rulership of Tri Srong Detsen, a large cultural exchange of Tibetans going to India and Indian teachers coming to Tibet occurred. During this period, the vast collection of Indian Buddhist scriptures were translated into Tibetan, and many Tibetans travelled to India to obtain the knowledge of Buddhism first hand. However, it was not only from India that the religious beliefs of Tibet were influenced, but from China as well. Chan (Zen) monks wandered through Tibet spreading their own form of Buddhism. Finally, according to Tibetan historical chronicles, King Tri Srong Detsen wanted to settle the question of which form of Buddhism should be embraced by the Tibetans. For this purpose he ordered a grand debate to be held. Accordingly, in about AD 750, a debate between the Indian Master Kamalashila and the Chinese Master Hwa Shan was held for several days. The debate ended in favour of Kamalashila and Indian Buddhism was decreed the official religion of Tibet. This did not mean, though, that the Chinese religious beliefs were obliterated in Tibet. Their influence continued

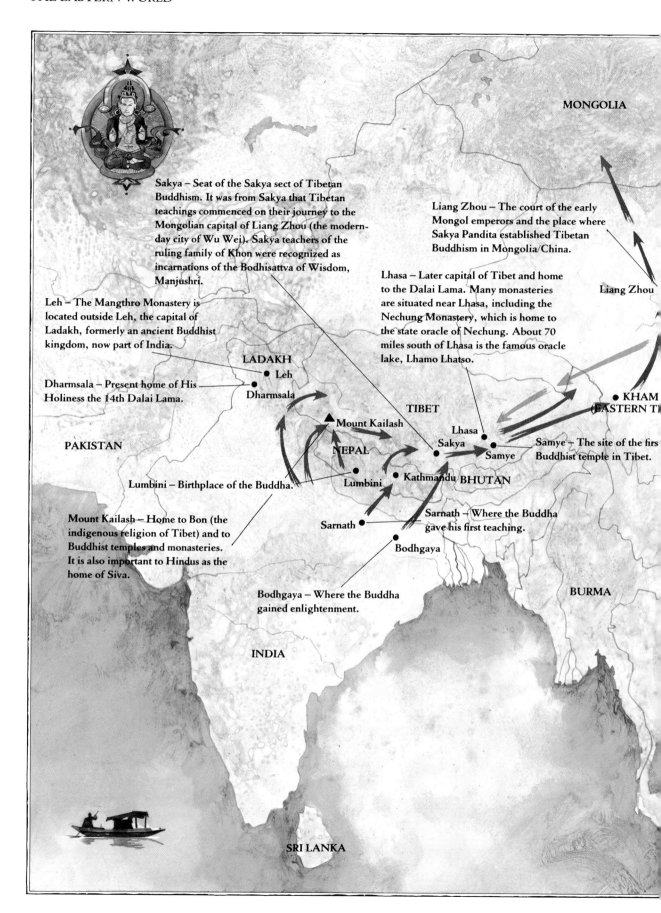

Sakya – Seat of the Sakya sect of Tibetan Buddhism. It was from Sakya that Tibetan teachings commenced on their journey to the Mongolian capital of Liang Zhou (the modern-day city of Wu Wei). Sakya teachers of the ruling family of Khon were recognized as incarnations of the Bodhisattva of Wisdom, Manjushri.

Liang Zhou – The court of the early Mongol emperors and the place where Sakya Pandita established Tibetan Buddhism in Mongolia/China.

Lhasa – Later capital of Tibet and home to the Dalai Lama. Many monasteries are situated near Lhasa, including the Nechung Monastery, which is home to the state oracle of Nechung. About 70 miles south of Lhasa is the famous oracle lake, Lhamo Lhatso.

Leh – The Mangthro Monastery is located outside Leh, the capital of Ladakh, formerly an ancient Buddhist kingdom, now part of India.

Dharmsala – Present home of His Holiness the 14th Dalai Lama.

Samye – The site of the first Buddhist temple in Tibet.

Lumbini – Birthplace of the Buddha.

Sarnath – Where the Buddha gave his first teaching.

Mount Kailash – Home to Bon (the indigenous religion of Tibet) and to Buddhist temples and monasteries. It is also important to Hindus as the home of Siva.

Bodhgaya – Where the Buddha gained enlightenment.

MONGOLIA

Liang Zhou

LADAKH

Leh

Dharmsala

TIBET

Lhasa

Sakya

Samye

KHAM
(EASTERN TI

PAKISTAN

Mount Kailash

NEPAL

Kathmandu BHUTAN

Lumbini

Sarnath

Bodhgaya

BURMA

INDIA

SRI LANKA

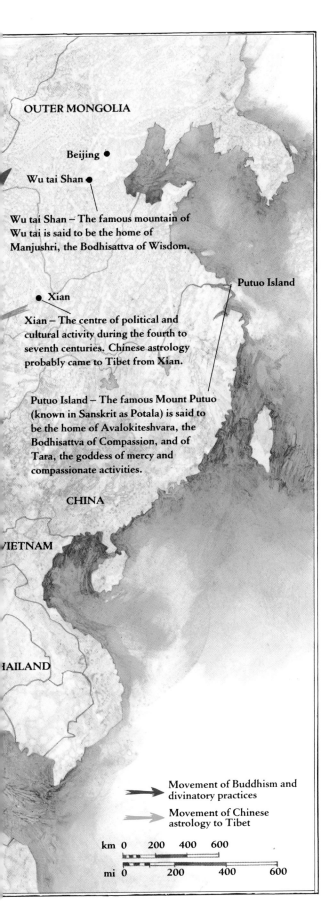

OUTER MONGOLIA

Beijing ●

Wu tai Shan ● ●

Wu tai Shan – The famous mountain of
Wu tai is said to be the home of
Manjushri, the Bodhisattva of Wisdom.

Putuo Island

● Xian

Xian – The centre of political and
cultural activity during the fourth to
seventh centuries. Chinese astrology
probably came to Tibet from Xian.

Putuo Island – The famous Mount Putuo
(known in Sanskrit as Potala) is said to
be the home of Avalokiteshvara, the
Bodhisattva of Compassion, and of
Tara, the goddess of mercy and
compassionate activities.

CHINA

VIETNAM

THAILAND

→ Movement of Buddhism and
divinatory practices

→ Movement of Chinese
astrology to Tibet

km 0   200   400   600

mi 0   200   400   600

to be felt in subsequent years (this being
symbolically represented by the story of Hwa
Shan leaving one of his shoes behind when he
departed for China).

The new religion did not become fully
entrenched until the arrival of the Indian
Tantric Master, Guru Padma Sambhava, around
775. Through his mystical power and acumen,
he demonstrated the Vajrayana school which
was the most esoteric form of Buddhism
promulgated in India. Its use of deity worship,
meditative visualizations of Buddhas and other
supramundane beings, yoga and elaborate ritual-
ism appealed to the Tibetan mentality.

One of the main goals of the Vajrayana is
compassion. This is the belief that the practitioner must work to allay the sufferings of
others. Although this was primarily accomplished through acts of charity, morality,
meditation and wisdom, other techniques that
might benefit others were also taught. And
among these teachings are found many different
forms of divination.

By the eleventh and twelfth centuries, Buddhism had become the religion of the masses as
well as of the royalty. At this same time China
and large portions of central Asia were ruled by
the Mongols. In the middle of the twelfth
century, the Mongols, wishing to consolidate
power over Tibet and to bring a cultural and
religious veneer to their empire, invited the

WHERE SHAMANISM AND BUDDHISM MEET
*Tibet lies between the two great civilizations of India and
China. Although Tibet possessed its own shamanistic system,
called Bon, it was greatly influenced by the Buddhist beliefs of
India and China. As early as the seventh century, Buddhist
monks travelled to Tibet to spread their religious ideas and to
meditate in the solitude of the vast mountain ranges of this
Himalayan kingdom. Royal patronage encouraged Tibetans to
travel to India for the purpose of translating and studying
Buddhist scriptures. Other forms of knowledge, such as poetry,
logic and astrology, were also learned and brought back to
Tibet. Along the way, various divinatory systems were acquired
and passed from one culture to another. Several of these forms
of divination were integrated into the Tibetan belief-system and
were later transmitted to Mongolia and parts of China.
Throughout Tibet, India, Nepal and Bhutan there are
hundreds of Tibetan Buddhist temples and monasteries.*

grand Lama of the Sakya Sect, Sakya Pandita, to their capital of Liang Zhou (in the north central part of modern China). However, it was the priest-king relationship between Sakya Pandita's nephew, Chogyal Phagpa, and the Mongolian emperor Kublai Khan that confirmed the conversion of the Mongolian empire to Buddhism. During the next 50 years or so, all the Buddhist scriptures that had been translated into Tibetan from Indian Sanskrit were now translated into Mongolian, and the Vajrayana school of Buddhism spread north and east from Tibet.

DIVINATORY SYSTEMS IN TIBET

It is not possible to explain here all the different types of divinatory systems in Tibet. However, I would like to make mention of a few, show a common basis for many of them, and elaborate on a specific system. As mentioned earlier, divinatory systems in Tibet had three sources: their own indigenous forms, those from India, and those from China. Some of these systems incorporated from outside Tibet did not, however, retain their 'pure' form since they were sifted through Tibetan beliefs and ultimately came out with a Tibetan flavour.

ASTROLOGY

Astrology has been popular through the centuries in Tibet and two distinct systems were practiced, one originating in India and the other in China. The Indian form was known as 'white astrology' and the Chinese as 'black astrology'. These terms came from the Tibetan names for the two countries, India being known as the 'vast white continent' because the majority of people there wear white clothes and China being the 'vast black continent' because the majority of its people wear dark clothes.

The Indian form of astrology was learned by fewer people and was considered to be a more complicated system than the Chinese. Unlike the Chinese, which relies primarily on the elements and animal symbols, Indian astrology deals with more detailed calculations of planet positions within a complex constellatory matrix (see Chapter Eighteen, Star Lore in the East).

The Chinese system used in Tibet is very similar to that found in China. It was commonly utilized in Tibetan almanacs and was very popular among the monastic community (who were the main interpreters for the lay community).

This system uses animals to represent years, months and days (which are divided into 12 two-hour periods). The 12 animals are: rat, ox, tiger, hare, dragon, snake, horse, sheep, monkey, bird, dog and pig. In addition to these, the five elements of wood, fire, earth, iron and water are also considered. The Tibetan calendar is divided into 60-year cycles; this is accomplished by combining an animal and an element together to represent one year. For example, the year

beginning in February 1991 was known as the Iron Sheep Year, while 1992 is the Water Monkey Year, and 1993 the Water Bird Year.

When astrological calculations are sought, it is the interplay between different animals and elements in one's life that determines the types of results one encounters. Births, marriages, annual readings, life readings and especially death are the most important occasions for the use of astrology. No Tibetan funeral is carried out without first seeking the advice of an astrologer in matters such as how to dispose of the body, rituals to be conducted on behalf of the departed so that they will obtain a good rebirth, and rituals or prayers to be conducted on behalf of the surviving relatives. Yearly almanacs are published with general astrological readings that indicate the type of year it will be for a person's life force, physical body, power, luck and intelligence.

DIVINING OMENS

Tibetans look upon the world around them, both the mental and the physical world, for signs to divine the fortunes of their lives or specific

One of the methods for seeking omens was to invoke the guardian spirit of a lake and request that it bring forth visions on the lake's surface. Information about the rebirth of the Dalai Lamas was sought in this manner. This lake is in central Tibet.

occasions. Whenever someone leaves on a long journey, signs are always sought. For example, upon embarking on a trip, if a person or vehicle laden with goods is seen, this is considered a good sign, while seeing an empty vehicle is considered unfortunate. The following are previously unpublished excerpts I translated from a Tibetan text, known as *The Illuminating Mirror*, edited by Lang Dor Lama Rinpoche. Some of these texts come from Tibetan writings, while some are Tibetan translations of Sanskrit texts.

OMENS IN DREAMS

Dreams that appear in the pre-dawn part of the night should be considered important for determining the occurrence of good or bad results.

Dreaming of climbing to the top of a high mountain means one will obtain a high rank or position. Dreaming of the sun shining without any clouds means the arising of bliss and happiness. Dreaming of vast crops, grains, honey or ripened fruit, obtaining food and clothes or using a treasure indicates that one will gain wealth. Dreaming of donning good clothes means one will receive praise and respect from others. Dreaming of donning armour means one will not be harmed by disease or evil spirits. If one dreams of sitting in a nice house then good fortune and good luck will occur. Dreaming of carrying a weapon in one's hand means that one's opposing enemies will not harm one. If one dreams of being adorned with ornaments then one will become famous. Dreaming of happily arriving at the other side of a river means one will accomplish whatever one wishes. Blowing or playing musical instruments such as cymbals, drums and conch shells means the arising of fame in the world for oneself. In brief, if one dreams of beautiful forms and feels happy and joyful at the time of awakening, then these indicate the certain obtainment of joyful results.

Dreams of blizzards and crossing a swamp which one falls into, going into a filthy place, wearing clothes stained by excrement, wearing filthy clothes, filth falling from the sky or finding filthy things indicates some type of obscuration for oneself. Making use of gold dust, riding a saddleless horse or donkey and being naked indicate one's own death. Seeing one's reflection in a mirror crying, wearing clothes with no collar or no hat or going on a vacation indicates the arising of suffering. Wearing tattered clothes or rags, eating and drinking filthy substances, insects sticking to one's body and being held by creatures such as wolves is explained to be the arising of an illness. Collections of barley, parched barley, beans or many empty containers, or dreams of pieces of bows and arrows indicate being gossiped about or that people sing your praises, which causes you to become puffed up about yourself and so turn into a bad person. Being pierced by a weapon, being pursued by soldiers, floods, fire or lightning, seeing hail storms, or falling into a pit indicates being harmed by others. Having one's body bound, going beneath the ground, being held in prison or cutting one's head or body portends harm by curses or black magic. Dreaming of being naked and riding on a donkey in a southern direction or dreaming solely of red flowers indicates an obstacle to one's life (i.e. a sudden death). If on awakening one feels unhappy, this shows that the dream is a sign of an unhappy occurrence.

OMENS IN APPEARANCES

If ravens or stinging insects make a nest or hive in one's house, then it is explained that a sudden fright or death will occur. If meat falls from the mouth of a flesh-eating bird, the place where the meat fell will experience some form of punishment. If branches and leaves grow on a dried-up tree, it is said to mean that fighting among the inhabitants of that area will occur. If one sees bent weapons and bright rays from a fire, or if the times for cold and hot weather are reversed, then many harmful events will occur that year. If in the womb a child is heard to talk, cry or laugh then destruction for that area will occur.

OMENS IN THE CRIES OF RAVENS

The sounds of ravens are examined in relation to the time of day and the direction from which the sound comes. For example, if we consider the period from noon to 3.00 p.m., then we would see: if a raven makes a noise in the east wealth will be gained; if the noise comes from the south-east a quarrel will ensue; if noise is made in the south a great wind will be coming; if the noise comes from the south-west an enemy will be coming; if the noise comes from a western direction a woman will be coming; if from the north-west someone close to you will come; if made in the north a good friend will be coming; if the noise is made in the north-east there will

This is a holy image of Guru Padmasambhava, the great Indian Buddhist master. It was through his efforts that the Vajrayana form of Buddhism was established in Tibet during the eighth century. A master of meditation and of Tantric practices, he built the first Buddhist temple in Tibet at Samye.

be a fire that causes damage; if the noise is from above the ruler of the land will grant you something near to your heart.

ENLIGHTENED BEINGS, DEITIES AND SPIRITS

Within the Vajrayana school of Buddhism, distinctions are made among the many classes of enlightened beings, deities, spirits and worldly sentient beings. The most important and holy of these are the Buddhas (such as the Buddha Shakyamuni who gained enlightenment under the Bodhi tree in India more than 2,500 years ago) and the Bodhisattvas (those training to become fully enlightened Buddhas and who have already gained some of the stages leading to that final stage of perfect Buddhahood). Some examples of these Bodhisattvas are Manjushri, Avalokiteshvara, Vajrapani and Tara.

Another class of beings, known as Protectors of the Religion, are deities with a very fierce appearance. These deities have promised to aid and protect from obstacles those practising the spiritual path. Some of the Protectors are wrathful manifestations of enlightened beings. Others were malevolent spirits who have been converted to the Buddha's teaching and have assumed the role of Protectors. For example, when Guru Padma Sambhava built the first Buddhist temple in Tibet at Samye, he encountered great interference from the local spirits who resided there. They were displeased with this new religion and caused great obstacles to the temple being built. To overcome this, Guru Padma Sambhava subdued the spirits of that locale through his spiritual and magical powers, converted them to the Buddhist faith and established them as Protectors of the Religion. The Protectors are worshipped at the temple and special offerings are made to them daily.

In the worldly realms, besides sentient beings of the celestial, human, animal and nether worlds, there are also spirits of the earth, of bodies of water, of mountains and other locations that receive offerings to appease them. Although these are not looked upon as gods or supramundane beings, they are viewed as having power to harm or benefit others.

From the point of view of divination, some of these beings from the various classes are linked to divinatory systems. For example, the Bodhisattva of Wisdom, Manjushri, is the patron saint of astrology. Below, we examine his relationship to a system of divination that uses dice. The female Bodhisattva of Transcendental Activities, Tara, is sought for divination through dreams. Palden Lhamo, a Protectress, is associated with a number of divinatory systems.

DREAM DIVINATION

A person usually goes into a week-long meditation retreat to invoke the blessings of Tara. During this week the meditator visualizes a form of Tara and recites a special mantra of hers thousands of times. Then he or she receives a sign during the retreat that Tara's gift of dream divination has been granted. Endowed with that attainment, when that person wishes to seek the answer to some problem, he will briefly meditate upon Tara just before going to sleep and will clearly think of the question at that time. During his sleep, Tara will provide him with a dream vision to answer the question he had in mind. I personally know a Tibetan nun presently living in Nepal who has great proficiency in this dream divination method. Many times she has been approached by others seeking solutions to their problems, and who have testified to receiving accurate and beneficial advice.

MEDIUMSHIP

The Protectors of the Religion are a very common source of aid for divinations. Their assistance comes in a variety of ways, but the two most renowned are mediumship and dice divination. Each monastery in Tibet has its own special Protector. At some of these monasteries, the Protector takes possession of a chosen monk (who is usually trained for the position) and, speaking through that monk, gives predictions for the year for that monastery and its monks. The Protector also entertains specific questions that anyone wishes to bring forth. The most famous 'oracle protector' of Tibet is the state

oracle who is commonly called the Nechung Oracle. Prior to the Chinese Communist takeover of Tibet in 1959, this oracle was located in the Nechung Monastery near Lhasa, the capital of Tibet. On a regular basis, the Nechung Oracle prognosticated the future events of the country, and was always consulted on matters of state. He was also consulted for very special occasions, such as locating the reincarnation of the Dalai Lama, the spiritual and temporal ruler of Tibet, upon his passing away. The present Nechung Oracle lives in Dharmsala, India, near the residence of His Holiness the 14th Dalai Lama, who is living in exile. (For an excellent presentation of the history and rituals surrounding the Nechung Oracle, see John F. Avedon's *In Exile From The Land of Snows*.)

Another instance of this type of mediumship is presently found in Mangthro Monastery in Ladakh, India. A Tibetan monk by the name of Trungpa Dorje Palsang left his homeland in eastern Tibet during the fifteenth century and travelled through western Tibet, finally settling in Ladakh, which is now part of the Northern Indian province of Kashmir. A local spirit from his hometown attached itself to him and begged to tag along no matter where he went. He was a well-accomplished monk, and when he finally settled in Ladakh a number of monks approached him and became his followers. Finally, a monastery was established there under his leadership. He decided to establish the spirit that followed him as 'Protector of the Religion' for that monastery, and so the monks offered it special rituals on a daily basis. As an aid to the monastery, the 'Protector', known as Rongtsen Kawa Karpo, takes possession of a monk in order to give advice. A system was established for a monk to act as a medium for the spirit for a five-year period. The monk must first go into a meditation retreat for a year. Then, during part of the new year celebration, which lasts for the first 15 days of the first month of the Tibetan lunar calendar (usually around middle to late February), the Protector takes possession of the monk's body. During the first part of this, he performs harrowing feats, such as slashing his tongue with a knife and running quickly on the edge of the monastery's outer wall, which drops, sheer down the side of a mountain. Then he gives his annual predictions for the monastery. Both monks and laypeople seek his advice.

VISIONS ARISING IN BODIES OF WATER

Another form of divination in Tibet utilizes lakes or other bodies of water. In parts of central Tibet, there are famous lakes where visions are seen. The practice is to make offerings to the Protector or spirit of that locale and request their assistance in granting a vision. The most famous of these lakes is Lhamo Lhatso. Here, officials of the government have come to find help to locate the reincarnation of the Dalai Lama. John F. Avedon describes one such event:

In the spring of 1935, Tibet's newly appointed Regent, Reting Rinpoche, joined by a senior minister of the old ruler's cabinet, journeyed to the sacred lake of Lhamo Lhatso, seeking a vision. . . . The Thirteenth Dalai Lama himself had been discovered by means of a dramatic vision of his birthplace, seen by hundreds and lasting for a week, in the centre of its waters.

After spending some days in prayer at nearby Chokhorgyal Monastery, the Regent's party rode their ponies to the base of the rocky slope overlooking the lake. Proceeding upward on foot, they reached the top of a sheer ridge, whereupon they dispersed in different directions, each to seek his own vision. Alone among them, Reting Rinpoche witnessed a remarkable sight. On staring at the clear alpine waters, he discerned three letters from the Tibetan alphabet float into view: Ah, Ka and Ma. The image of a great three-storied monastery, capped by gold and jade rooftops, followed. A white road led east from the monastery to a house before a small hill, its roof strikingly fringed in turqoise-coloured tiles, a brown and white spotted dog in the courtyard. (In Exile From The Land of Snows, pp.4–5).

Besides extracting visions from bodies of water,

there is also a practice of seeking for them on mirrors or even on one's thumb-nail. Having first recited a special Sanskrit mantra, which has been passed down from teacher to disciple for centuries, the practitioner will blow upon a mirror or his thumb-nail, causing a vision to appear. The problem with this method, according to a number of Tibetan lamas, is that though they have the power of the mantra which causes the vision to appear, they don't have the ability to see the vision. They must rely upon others who have the capability of seeing the vision (in many instances, young children are found to have this ability). Due to this, they find the method unreliable.

THE CASTING OF DICE

Probably the most popular and relied upon method of divination used today among Tibetans is the casting of dice. Lamas from all the traditions of Tibetan Buddhism engage in this practice. Since the teachers are always striving to help others, they cast the dice for the faithful in order to advise them on how to deal with the problems which they face. I have seen lines of people waiting before a lama's residence solely for the purpose of having a dice divination performed. Concerning the purpose of dice divination, His Holiness Sakya Trizin, the spiritual head of the Sakya sect of Tibetan Buddhism, wrote in his introduction to MO: *Tibetan Divination System,*

There are two primary functions of the MO [dice divination]. First of all, it is a system that allows us to help ourselves to see a situation or event clearly. Secondly, if we use it for others with the proper motivation of performing a selfless act of giving – as has been extensively done by many of the great teachers of Tibet – it is a system that enhances our practice of Bodhisattva's path. There is also a secondary function of the MO. The central, most profound teaching of the Buddha is Pratitya Samutpada, which may be translated as interdependent origination or codependent arising. This teaching simultaneously explains the essence of the interplay of causes and conditions on the relative, worldly level of reality and the essence of emptiness or selflessness on the ultimate level of reality. Although diligent efforts are needed in concentration and insight to attain a realization of interdependent origination, a system such as MO reveals a glimpse of the interdependence and casual play of the world in which we live and may hopefully induce one to investigate it on a deeper level.

There are several different systems of this form of divination, but the one that relies upon the Protectress Palden Lhamo and the one that relies upon the Buddhist saint of wisdom, Manjushri, are preferred. The system that invokes Palden Lhamo uses three dice with the usual dots running from one through six on them. There are 15 possible answers, and each answer is divided into different categories, such as one's life forces, wealth, illness, etc.

The one that invokes the Bodhisattva Manjushri uses one dice upon which the last six of the seven syllables of Manjushri's mantra, OM AH RA PA TSA NA DHIH, are written. About this form of dice divination His Holiness Sakya Trizin had this to say:

Many methodologies of MO have been utilized in Tibet. The system here, compiled by the great master Jamgon Mipham from the sacred Tantras expounded by the Buddha, obtains its authority from the spiritual power and wisdom of Manjushri – the Bodhisattva who embodies the transcendental knowledge of all the Buddhas. It is Manjushri's speech as epitomized in his holy mantra, OM AH RA PA TSA NA DHIH, and the sanctity of his all-pervasive wisdom that empower one to obtain an accurate answer that reflects the interplay of conditions concerning the situation and its outcome. In the Manjushri Nama Samgiti (Chanting the Names of Manjushri), *the Buddha himself extolled the great qualities of Manjushri and stated that the mantra of Manjushri, OM AH RA PA TSA NA DHIH, is an expression of the wisdom experienced by all enlightened beings. Therefore, by relying upon the compassionate blessings of Manjushri and the power of his*

Manjushri is considered the embodiment of the wisdom of all the Buddhas. His knowledge and wisdom are all-pervasive, and so his blessings are sought by all alike. Whether for an insight into the Buddha's wisdom or a glimpse into the inner workings of this world, prayers are made to him.

mantra, you should have no doubt that the wisdom of all enlightened beings is manifesting itself in the throw of the dice.

For a further description of MO: Tibetan Divination System *and its method of use, see* Appendix: Modern Restatements, on page 211.

The scope and variety of divinatory systems in Tibet is truly vast, and a few of these have been covered in scant detail. Tibet's unique forms of divination grew to evolve into a potent force that affected its entire population. From Tibet it travelled to Mongolia and China, and today in many countries of the world, both East and West, you can find Tibetans and others utilizing these notable, rich and ancient forms of divination.

AUSTRALIA AND NEW ZEALAND

The Australian continent contains the oldest surviving cultural link with the Stone Age, and in the Aboriginal people we see a primal race still practising the earliest form of spiritual activity, a totally shamanistic world-view that parallels that of some of the other cultures we have seen, such as the Norse, Celtic, Lapp and Amerindian traditions.

As in many other cultures, the professional services of an augur, called a *mekigar*, are required to invoke the oracular elements in creation. Change is enacted through ritual, and once again, as so often before, we see that it is the *land* itself that supplies the necessary ingredient for divinatory practice. It is the intimate relationship of the *mekigar* with the elements, animal life and creation that enables him to penetrate the spirit world and to return with answers to his questions. Indeed, as James Cowan indicates, it seems that the augurs are in almost constant dialogue with the inner world, which in Australian tradition is embodied in the Dreamtime, the time of the ancestors, mighty individuals who have attained mythical, even divine status, and who make their continued presence felt in the shape of the landscape itself.

Among the Maori of New Zealand the same holds true. As in the case of the Australian Aborigines, the Maori originated in Asia, and brought with them something of the racial memory of that land. Between them they give a picture containing some of the most ancient cultural references we possess, one of which, divination, is shown to be of central importance to both peoples.

The parallels between Maori and Celtic traditions have been noticed before. Both were a warrior race, who sought to propitiate the gods before battle and used prognostication to foretell the outcome. The remarkable similarities between certain of the Maori divination methods mentioned here and those of the Celts discussed in Chapter Two cannot go unnoticed: both peoples believed in the second sight, in the signs provided by animals and birds, and in the throwing of marked sticks to foretell the future. As far as we know the Maori are unique in using kites to divine events to come, while the complicated *niu* rite is, so far as we are aware, unlike anything practised elsewhere in the world.

The common links between these antipodean cultures, as between so many of those we have discussed, therefore lie in the importance of communication with the ancestors and gods, and in an understanding of the significance of the patterns supplied by nature.

CHAPTER TWENTY

WILD STONES

Aboriginal Sorcery in Divination

James G. Cowan

The Aboriginal tradition of Australia is the oldest unbroken contact we have with our Stone Age forebears. For over 50,000 years the Aborigines have been living on the Australian continent, practising a semi-nomadic existence over a period spanning at least two Ice Ages. Many of their myths and stories tell of two major migrations from the Asian mainland, before such journeys were curtailed by rising sea levels. Arriving in Australia by way of island-hopping and short canoe voyages, the original settlers came into contact with a lonely landscape populated by large animals, some of which are still with us today, such as the kangaroo and duck-billed platypus.

Their early culture and belief-systems were coloured by the philosophic concepts they brought from Asia. But the landscape they encountered would have been vastly different from any previously experienced; it is so powerful that these settlers would have spent many generations coming to terms with its spiritual dimension. Eventually, all divinatory activity was necessarily conditioned by the land, its earth-centred power (*djang*) and the mythology surrounding it.

THE DREAMING

Central to the Aboriginal belief-system is the Dreaming. The Dreaming means 'the time of the ancestors'. It is a primordial condition that transcends time and represents a body of spiritual lore pertaining to the creation of the world. The principle of manifestation is governed by Sky Heroes, those mythical beings who made the landscape, who passed on custom and law to the Aborigines, and who live on as visible icons in tribal territory in the form of 'frozen' motifs made up of unusual landforms, sacred water-holes and trees, which themselves embody a metaphysical or Dreaming presence.

The Aborigine's relationship with the Dreaming is the centre of his life. No other reality holds so much significance, not even his tribal or family relationships. His totemic being – his sense of ancestry – is derived from the Dreaming, his kinship ties find their origins there, and his ultimate destination at death is his return to it as his primordial source. He does not worship the Dreaming so much as acknowledge his inseparability from it as the basis of his spiritual essence.

Much of the Aborigine's ritual life revolves around making contact with the Dreaming and the Dreaming ancestors. Although a deeply spiritual being, he acknowledges the demands of this world. Indeed, one is struck by the relationship between all the elements in this cosmic drama: man, animals, birds, insects, flora, and the wide land which both possesses and is possessed by an Aborigine while he is alive. An Aborigine acknowledges that he 'belongs' to a stretch of country because of his dream affiliations: his father may have dreamed

A tribal custodian guards the sacred churinga *boards at a cave dedicated to the Great Snake in Central Australia. These boards are used in all ritual activity as invocational devices. The cave symbolizes the vulva of a Maletji woman. On the far right we see the Great Snake's penis about to fertilize the Dog-woman.*

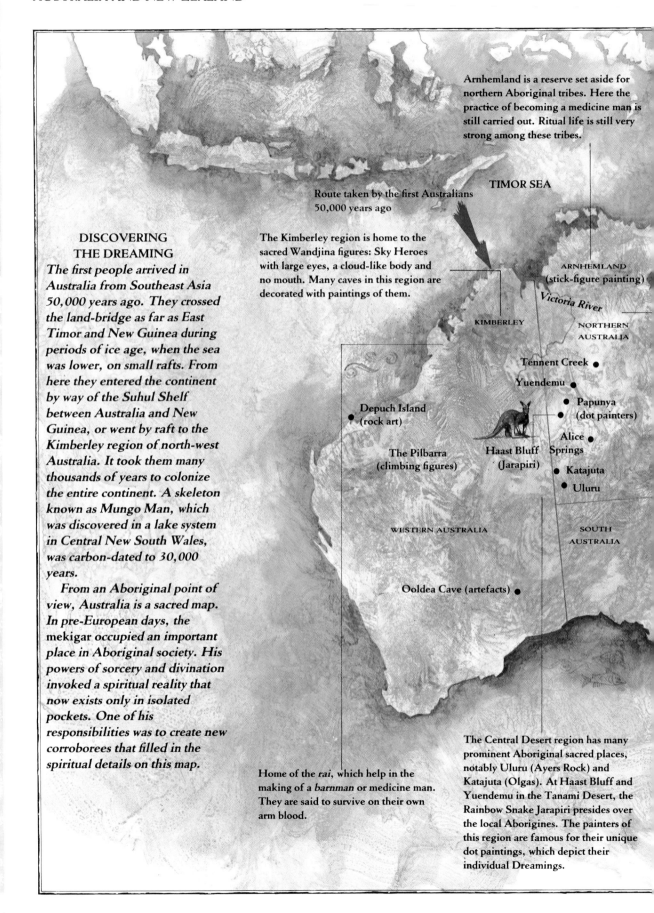

Arnhemland is a reserve set aside for northern Aboriginal tribes. Here the practice of becoming a medicine man is still carried out. Ritual life is still very strong among these tribes.

TIMOR SEA

Route taken by the first Australians 50,000 years ago

The Kimberley region is home to the sacred Wandjina figures: Sky Heroes with large eyes, a cloud-like body and no mouth. Many caves in this region are decorated with paintings of them.

ARNHEMLAND
(stick-figure painting)

Victoria River

KIMBERLEY

NORTHERN
AUSTRALIA

Tennent Creek •

Yuendemu •

• Papunya
(dot painters)

Depuch Island •
(rock art)

Alice •
Springs

The Pilbarra
(climbing figures)

Haast Bluff
(Jarapiri)

• Katajuta
• Uluru

WESTERN AUSTRALIA

SOUTH
AUSTRALIA

Ooldea Cave (artefacts) •

DISCOVERING
THE DREAMING

The first people arrived in Australia from Southeast Asia 50,000 years ago. They crossed the land-bridge as far as East Timor and New Guinea during periods of ice age, when the sea was lower, on small rafts. From here they entered the continent by way of the Suhul Shelf between Australia and New Guinea, or went by raft to the Kimberley region of north-west Australia. It took them many thousands of years to colonize the entire continent. A skeleton known as Mungo Man, which was discovered in a lake system in Central New South Wales, was carbon-dated to 30,000 years.

From an Aboriginal point of view, Australia is a sacred map. In pre-European days, the mekigar occupied an important place in Aboriginal society. His powers of sorcery and divination invoked a spiritual reality that now exists only in isolated pockets. One of his responsibilities was to create new corroborees that filled in the spiritual details on this map.

Home of the *rai*, which help in the making of a *barnman* or medicine man. They are said to survive on their own arm blood.

The Central Desert region has many prominent Aboriginal sacred places, notably Uluru (Ayers Rock) and Katajuta (Olgas). At Haast Bluff and Yuendemu in the Tanami Desert, the Rainbow Snake Jarapiri presides over the local Aborigines. The painters of this region are famous for their unique dot paintings, which depict their individual Dreamings.

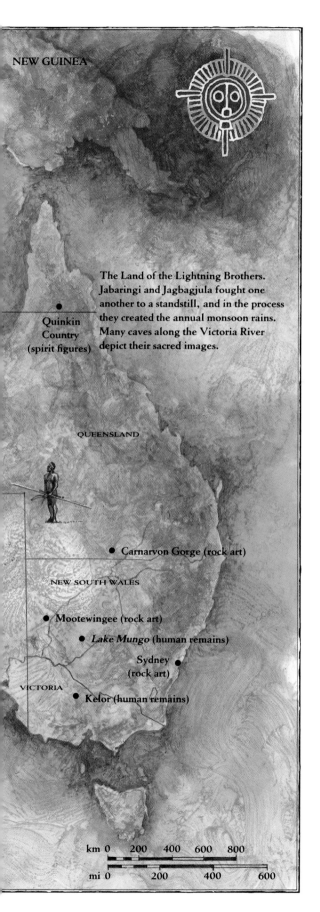

The Land of the Lightning Brothers. Jabaringi and Jagbagjula fought one another to a standstill, and in the process they created the annual monsoon rains. Many caves along the Victoria River depict their sacred images.

NEW GUINEA

Quinkin Country (spirit figures)

QUEENSLAND

Carnarvon Gorge (rock art)

NEW SOUTH WALES

Mootewingee (rock art)

Lake Mungo (human remains)

Sydney (rock art)

VICTORIA

Kelor (human remains)

km 0   200   400   600   800

mi 0   200   400   600

of his conception in this territory, or his spirit-child (*muri*) may have entered his mother's womb there. Later, his totemic origin will also bind him to his country in such a way that he becomes the hereditary custodian of it until his death. These key-men become responsible for retaining the sacred lore, the dance and songs relating to their region, as well as the mythic background inherent in the land itself. Without their knowledge, no landscape, whether actual or Dreaming, can be evoked by others. It follows that if a hereditary line dies out, as it has done in many parts of Australia today, the Dreaming of that particular region dies with it. As a result the land dies to the world of men and becomes 'rubbish country', an object of scorn and derision, finally a desanctified landscape.

A Binbinga medicine man or karadji *from the MacArthur River region in Central Australia, at around the turn of the century, carries on his back a bark-wrapped bundle containing items for ritual use. This man acknowledged encountering spirits that killed him and then finally restored him to life during his period of initiation.*

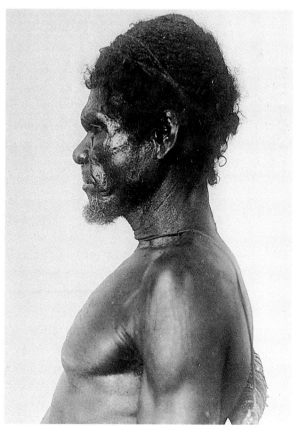

THE *MEKIGAR:* MAN OF MAGIC

A core belief in Aboriginal spirituality is that one can cross over into the Otherworld through ritual action. Divinatory activity is therefore of great importance in the ritual life of the individual and the tribe, and a central figure in this activity is the *mekigar*. The *mekigar* or *karadji* (his name varies depending on his tribe) is a man who is set apart from his contemporaries by the nature of his vocation, his intelligence and his special powers. As a young boy he is often physically different and may be recognized 'by the light radiating from his eyes', as one commentator observed. By and large, his office is inherited from his father, although it is acknowledged that the powers of a *mekigar* cannot be handed on by a father, but rather acquired only from the great Baiami (All-father) himself. While a father or practising *mekigar* may have the authority to initiate a postulant into the secrets of his craft, he can only do so on the understanding that the candidate has already been made aware of his vocation by way of visionary contact with his Dreaming ancestors.

Circumstantial and oral testimony suggests that a would-be *mekigar* undergoes a form of initiation that consists of ritual death at the hands of *Oruncha* spirits, accompanied by prolonged bouts of meditation in the wilderness. Ritual killing involves the use of quartz crystals which are pressed into the postulant's legs and breastbone. He then lies down on the ground while the officiants jerk their hands towards him, all the while holding other crystals which are later rubbed into his scalp. Meanwhile a hole is cut under his forefinger, into which crystals are inserted. Finally the postulant is asked to eat meat and drink water that has been impregnated with crystals. Sometimes a crystal is inserted in a hole in his tongue. Grease is rubbed all over his body and a sacred representation of the *Oruncha* painted on his chest and forehead. He is told to remain in the men's camp until his wounds have healed. He also has to observe certain food taboos, sleep with a fire between himself and his wife, and hold himself aloof from everyone, otherwise the power that has entered him on

This cave painting at a Wardaman cave in Northern Australia shows copulating spirit-figures. Such caves are ritual centres that the tribes visit on their annual wanderings. The paintings are often extremely old, although retouched as a part of ritual. Sacred sex is an important ritual activity among northern tribes, who worship Kunapipi, a female Great Snake.

initiation might leave him altogether.

The first phase of his initiation now over, a *mekigar* continues his education under the guidance of his mentor. Finer details in the arts of bone-pointing (the act of condemning a man to death), sorcery and diagnostic techniques in the cure of illness and psychic disorder are all taught to him. These are the more practical aspects of his craft and underlie the important social contribution the man makes to his community in the role of doctor. They do not, however, convey fully the spiritual metamorphosis he has undergone in his pursuit of the power associated with the ritual insertion of quartz crystals. These artefacts, along with australite rocks and unusual stones and bones, are regarded as power-bearers of rich symbolic significance. Among the eastern tribes these are known as 'wild stones' and are said to embody the Great Spirit himself. The quartz crystal owes its extraordinary prestige to its celestial origin, as originally Baiami's throne was said to be made of crystal. Quartz crystals are, in a sense, a form of 'solidified light'.

Accompanying his transition, a *mekigar* was often said to grow feathers on his arms which, after a few days, developed into wings. The growing of feathers as an expression of spiritual transformation lends credence to the idea that the *mekigar* is more than a medicine man; he is a keeper of sacred lore by the nature of his spiritual attainments.

A great deal of emphasis is placed upon

Aranda tribesmen perform a corroboree in April 1901. Deeply committed to ritual life, Aborigines regularly come together to perform sacred dances in accordance with their totemic origins. The dancers' bodies are decorated with patterns denoting the symbolic presence of the Sky Hero to whom the dance belongs. Ritual activity is focused on necessities such as rain increase or ensuring a plentiful supply of animals in a region.

Jagbagjula and Jabaringi, the two sacred Lightning Brothers of Wardaman spirit lore, are responsible for making rain each season and are therefore at the centre of extensive ritual practices. Their ferocious battle over the wife of one brother brings on lightning and rain, so important for the land's renewal. This is one of many cave paintings in Northern Australia that represent these sacred beings.

breathing techniques among *mekigar*. One report suggests that a *mekigar* used to sit on the bottom of the river for days at a time, talking with the spirits. He was able to hold his breath for the entire period of his immersion, returning to the surface with bloodshot eyes and covered in mud. Such accounts may not be factual in a physiological sense (although it would be risky to discount them entirely), but they do indicate a preoccupation with breathing techniques similar to those practised in other spiritual disciplines.

DEVELOPING THE INNER EYE

In his role as doctor, a *mekigar* is often called upon to use his 'inner eye' to diagnose ailments. One *mekigar*, Mowaldjali, gives us a clear outline of the functional use of the 'inner eye'.

> *The diagnostician's eye, that is a magic eye, is the one with which he checks the liver, urine, the gall bladder, the heart and the intestines. He checks these completely. 'Ah yes,' he says. 'The trouble is in the back of the neck!' He sees perfectly . . . they call him the expert. He is trained by the* rai *[spirits]. In the beginning he is unable to see very far. His sight is still dim. As yet he does not know [understand]. So the* rai, *they send a spirit-animal or insect out to him. Then his eyes begin to open and he is astonished. That's the way he begins to see further and further. He has become an expert.*

This 'third eye' indicates spiritual rather than physical vision. A *mekigar* is capable of discerning illness by way of an interior power not available to others.

A *mekigar* develops this power during meditation. It is during contemplative phases that he is able to enter the spirit world and converse with the Sky Heroes. One text details the importance of meditation among these men:

> *When you see an old man sitting by himself over there, do not disturb him for he will growl at you. Do not play near him, because he is sitting down with his thoughts in order to see. He is gathering his thoughts so that he can feel and hear. Perhaps he then lies down, getting into a special posture so*

> *that he can see while sleeping [i.e. meditating]. He sees indistinct visions and hears persons [the* rai*] talk in them. He gets up and looks for those he has seen; but not seeing them, he sits down again in the prescribed manner so as to see what he has seen before.*

Here we have a vividly descriptive account of a *mekigar's* encounter with visionary experience. In the act of meditation he leaves himself, and is able to enter the imaginal realm where divination can occur.

A DIVINE LANGUAGE

The contact Aborigines make with the Otherworld, the Dreaming, is carefully choreographed. A man cannot converse with Sky Heroes except by way of ritual activity. He is not free to engage in exclusive dialogue with the spirits, since they belong to all men and in themselves are immune from any form of singular discourse. The 'other language' he learns to speak when conversing with the Sky Heroes is more often than not a priestly language quite distinct from the one he might use on an everyday basis. Language is a vital part of invocation, of divination, and a man who has reached an advanced initiatory phase in his life is entitled to speak this 'language of the gods'. Others defer to him in these matters, knowing that he alone has attained a 'third eye', the gift of the *rai*. Such men are known as 'men of high degree', partaking of a special spiritual quality which we might associate with sainthood.

DIVINATION AS A TRIBAL ACTIVITY

Since Aborigines do not believe they can influence the future except through ritual activity, there is little call for the *mekigar* to foretell the future. Influencing the future is largely a collective activity participated in by the elders of the tribe, involving complex rituals which may span many months. The mythic life surrounding the landscape is so important that, to the outsider at least, Aborigines appear to be constantly engaged in a Dreaming dialogue with the Sky Heroes. The dances and songs, the incantations and body-paintings, even the ritual ground where such events take place, all are made a part of the symbolic essence of sacred expression. Divination *per se* becomes a collective act of all elders who desire to ensure that the cosmic flow is maintained.

The divinatory act for Aborigines is therefore much more than an isolated event. An Aborigine's whole life is an act of divination since he rarely acknowledges any separation between himself and the Dreaming. Although the *mekigar* may be a man of visionary experience *par excellence*, it does not mean that his talents are allowed to obscure the role played by his fellow tribesmen in any rite of passage. Each body of knowledge complements the other. Mediumistic lore, the lore of the shaman, may be in the hands of the *mekigar*, but ritual lore, the lore of the prescribed manifestation of Sky Heroes in this world, is in the hands of every dancer, songster and story-teller who is able to enact their appearance during important ceremonies pertaining to his totemic existence. It is this complementary relationship between the individual and the tribe that makes divination among the Aborigines such an all-embracing affair. All men have the right to experience the reality of the Dreaming, and sharing this imaginal realm becomes an act of brotherliness, a demonstration of congeniality among men.

The Aborigine was – and to a certain extent still is – loathe to see himself as passive in his relationship with the Sky Heroes. Although they are world-creators and objects of veneration, their activity did not cease at the time of the Dreaming; their role as materializers still continues. Aborigines see themselves as participants in this primordial event, and so have the power to initiate change through ritual action. It is this form of divination that an Aborigine adheres to: to augment a fruitful landscape, whether as a food source or as the principal theatre of cosmic drama, delineates his importance both as a part of Nature and as a man, for he knows that it is his concern which makes the land fruitful. It is his songs and his ceremonies

This Gagadju tribesman is in his totemic country near Kakadu, Northern Australia. His country is determined by his conception, and remains his throughout his life. It is then passed on to a new custodian in the same way.

that contribute to the land's spiritual power. As one old tribesman remarked, 'When we sing the sacred songs, the animals listen and are happy. When we don't sing them they go away and the land becomes barren.'

For the Aborigine, ritual action makes the difference between a world that is continually revitalized – and a world that is spiritually dead.

ANCESTORS, GODS AND MEN

Maori Methods of Divination

David Simmons

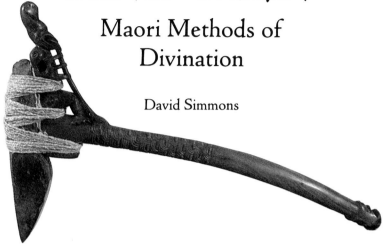

In order to understand ancient and modern Maori divination it is necessary to have some understanding of the way Maori view the world. While most Maori are now members of Christian or Christian-derived churches and other world religions, ancient beliefs remain part of their world-view. The place of the ancestors, who may influence and direct the actions of their descendants, is just one example of ancient belief which continues to be relevant today.

THE MAORI WORLD

The world of the Maori consists of three realms. The original realm is *Te Kore* (the Nothingness), in which all is in potential and from which come the *wai ora*, the waters of life, here undivided. In this realm were created the primal parents, Rangi the Sky Father and Papa the Earth Mother. They copulated and the birth of their first child ushered in the next realm, *Te Po* (The Night), in which their children, the gods, live. The children separated their parents, whose tight embrace did not allow them room to live.

Above the Sky Father are 10 or 12 heavens in which the gods live. Beneath the Earth Mother is the Underworld, also said by some to

be divided into levels in which live the descendants of the gods, including man after death. The creation of man by the god Tiki, or Tane according to some tribes, involved adding the life force of man to the already existing life force of the gods. When man dies he can enter the realm of the gods either proceeding by the entrance under Cape Reinga in the far north to Rarohenga, the Underworld; or, if he is a high chief or first-born of the senior genealogical line, he is taken by spirit canoe to the heavens where his eyes become stars.

The realm in which humankind lives is *Te Ao Marama* (this world), the world of light, which lies between Earth and Sky. The waters of life flow into this world and are part of all things, down to the rocks of the earth and the crystals in them. Here those waters are divided into the dark waters of the sky and the clear waters of the great deep. It was on the great waters of the

Iripeti, a sacred ancestral adze (above), has a genealogy going back to its maker 25 generations ago. The adze was rehafted when a new high chief was installed to succeed to his grandfather. The old handle was taken off and buried with the previous holder. The adze is a fearful thing if used in divination because its mere presence may kill the wrongdoer.

THE COMING OF THE MAORI

Maui, the demigod, sailed on the waters of the deep. With a hook made from his grandmother's jawbone, he fished up the island known as Te Ika a Maui, the Fish of Maui – the North Island of New Zealand. Then came Kupe, who found the fish still alive. He killed it and made it suitable for men to live on. He named it Aotearoa, Land of the Long White Cloud. From the other islands in the Pacific came the ancestors sailing in their great canoes. They settled the land, and here they completed the migration that had taken their ancestors from east to west, from the Solomons to Easter Island, Hawaii, Tahiti and the Cook Islands. Here they became Maori.

Hikurangi Mountain, on which Maui's canoe is said to rest, is itself an ancient name, for it is the mountain on which the first light fell at the separation of Earth and Sky. For the thousand years that men have lived here, so have these stories been told.

Tauwhare Mountain

Tahuhunui's house

Hikurangi Mountain

Auckland

Thames

TE TAI TAPOKOPOKO A TAWHAKI
(The Billowing Sea of Tawhaki)
THE TASMAN SEA

Mokoia Island

Waihou River

Lake Rotorua

Urewera

TE IKA A MAUI
(The Fish of Maui)
THE NORTH ISLAND

TE MATAU A MAUI
(Maui's Fish Hook)
HAWKES BAY

Wellington

TE MOANANUI A KIWA
(The Great Sea of Kiwa)
THE PACIFIC OCEAN

Christchurch

Aoraki (Mount Cook)

*First came the Turehu (fairies),
Then came the Polynesians,
They fought and married,
Maori is their name.
Then came the Europeans,
They fought and married,
New Zealander is their name,
But still Turehu are heard,
And Maori stand tall.*

TE WAKA A MAUI
(The Canoe of Maui)
THE SOUTH ISLAND

TE PUNGA A MAUI
(Maui's Anchor)
STEWART ISLAND

km 0 50 100 200 300

mi 0 50 100 200

deep that the demigod Maui sailed to fish up these islands: Te Ika a Maui, the Fish of Maui, is the fish which is the North Island of New Zealand. (From above, the North Island looks like a sting-ray.) His canoe remains on a mountain, Hikurangi, on which the first light fell when Earth and Sky were separated.

Today a chief standing on the tribal meeting place, the *marae*, will pay homage to Earth, Sky. the gods, the ancestors and the sacred tribal mountains and rivers as part of the ritual of greeting visitors. The ancestors, who are present with the visitors on the *marae* to protect their descendants, and the newly dead, who are with them, are greeted by the home people. The visitors also greet the ancestors and newly dead of the *marae*, and the ancestors of both sides are farewelled and asked to return to the other world. The living are greeted and the final expression of grief for the dead, the *hongi* or touching noses, completes the ritual.

THE GUARDIAN ANCESTORS

Communication between the three realms and between the gods, the demigods, the ancestors and their descendants is a normal occurrence. The ancestors guard and guide their descendants quite directly by personal intervention and sometimes by personal appearances. For example a great priest, a *tohunga*, was eating with friends when his nose twitched violently. He stopped eating and over the next three days prepared himself for death, for this was a sign from his ancestors. On the third evening the sun lay a golden path over the sea and his spirit followed to the homeland.

Tohunga means expert. In this context it could be defined as spiritual expert, or more pejoratively as witch-doctor – but that is a speciality of certain *tohunga makutu*, i.e. black magic experts. *Tohunga matakite* were and are seers. A graduate of the college of learning, the son or in some instances the daughter (i.e. the eldest born) of a chief was taught spiritual matters in order to ask for the goodwill of the gods and ancestors. As a direct descendant of the gods that person had *mana*, or spiritual power, and was in conse-

quence *tapu*, or sacred. Such people are seen as having a special relationship with the ancestors and gods, and can interpret the omens and signs that are directed towards them.

A person may also be a seer because he shows that he is able to find lost treasures or put right transgressions of *tapu*. These people may be male or female and are also often healers. There is also the *tohunga rongoa*, the expert in Maori medicines and massage, who learns the craft from grandparents. Ordinary people are also aware of omens and portents, and there are often knowledgeable 'aunties' who will be rung up. Children are still being trained in the arts of the *tohunga*.

DREAMS

The ancestors, and perhaps the gods, also send dreams in which great faith is placed. The *kuia*, or elderly women, are often those consulted when a particularly troubling dream is experienced. There are on record a number of instances where an expedition was abandoned because of dreams. A chief called Tahuhunui was so named because the land and the house his father was building were abandoned because of a dream, leaving only the *tahuhu*, or ridge pole, to be seen as the canoe sailed away. Some ladies today are also particularly good at dreaming of winners in horse races.

BODY TWITCHES

Twitches and starts while sleeping can be sure signs of evil things to come, although precise interpretations may vary. Both arms thrown across the chest and gurgling could each foretell killing, the first in war, the second as murder. For some people, signs in the body on the left side are lucky, for others the right side is lucky. In most tribes the left side is the female side, the spiritual side, but in some it is the reverse, and the left side is that of the male line. More usually, the right side is the male side, the side of the human life force, of war and warriors. Most genealogical lines have more *mana* (prestige) on the male line, but again this may not be true of certain tribes or individuals.

SPIRIT GUARDIANS

Chiefs' families, small tribal units or often whole tribes have ancestral or spirit guardians. Certain birds are thought of as descending into the Otherworld at night, returning in the morning. Some are messengers from the heavens, like the Hokioi, a great bird which never lands, and whose cry is heard in the sky when a high chief is about to die. The bush falcon is a messenger from earth to the heavens and was used in ritual: the bird was imprisoned by its flight feathers when the ridge pole was placed on the front post in a new ceremonial house; if it freed itself it was good news that it carried to the gods; if not, the house was abandoned.

A fantail laughed when Maui the demigod attempted to ensure the retention of immortality, so the appearance of a fantail is considered to be a sign that death is to occur, that a relative has died, or that the ancestors are present and must be recognized lest misfortune befall. For war parties in the old days, hearing an owl was a sign that the hearer would die. Many people still regard the cry of the owl as a sign of death to come. The guardian spirit of one chiefly family of Te Ati Awa is a peculiar white owl that

Matuatonga, a tribal fertility symbol, stands among the gardens on the island of Mokoia in Lake Rotorua. This ancestral image of great mana *is said to have been brought to New Zealand by the ancestors of the Arawa Tribes. It is a tribal heirloom and as such had divinatory powers. The island is also called Te Motutapu a Tinirau, sacred island of Tinirau, which links it to the island of the same name in the otherworld, where the waters of life flow to give fertility to fish. Tinirau is the god of fish.*

A godstick representing Hukere. He was particularly concerned with things that belonged in the Earth Mother and therefore was the god who oversaw the return of the bodies of men to the earth. Hukere was one of a set of three dealing with the sea, cultivations and death. It is held in Auckland Museum.

appears when the senior member is to die. In the Urewera tribe Ngati Whare, a particular ancestress appears as a giant cormorant hovering over the village, a sign that the chief will die or, in the olden days, be attacked or lose a battle. The cries of birds heard on the left side or the right could be lucky or unlucky.

Other manifestations of the spirit world, which are sometimes but not always ancestral, are the *tipua kura* (strange objects) and the *taniwha* (mythical monsters). *Tipua kura* are named and their appearance *can* be good but is usually a warning. Many of them are natural objects which behave in unnatural ways: Papakauri, for example, is a log that floats in the Waihou River near Thames and moves up the river against the current, thus presaging the death of a chief.

SECOND SIGHT

The gift of *matakite*, or second sight, presaging death or calamity, is a fairly usual occurrence. Misfortune and death are often attributed to the breaking of the laws of *tapu* (sacredness), by which the ancestral remains and sacred treasures are protected. A divinatory dance, a *haka tutohu*, was sometimes done to determine the culprit. If the wrong was shown to be a transgression by another tribe, then war may have resulted. The death of the culprit was often the only way to redress the wrong. It was the *tohunga*, or divinatory expert, who divined the wrong and recommended the steps to be taken, a function that continues to this day.

THE WILL OF THE GODS

Communication with the gods living in the 10 or 12 heavens is a two-way process. Men acknowledge the *mana* or prestige of the gods. Tane is god of the forest and birds, Tangaroa is god of the sea, Tawhirimatea god of winds, Tumatauenga god of man and of war, and so on. Then there are the local gods who may be tribal or family. The task of men is to observe good manners towards these beings whose bounty, in the form of their children, is their everyday food. In return, the gods allow the harvest and make the land and sea fruitful – always provided that humans, who are also their descendants, employ all their skill in any task undertaken. The gods make their wishes known by celestial or natural phenomena. Lightning, thunder, wind and rain are all personified as children of the Sky Father and Earth Mother.

NATURAL PHENOMENA

Each tribe has sacred peaks where lightning is seen and portents read. Many sung poems heard on the *marae* start like this lament for Te Huhu.

Tera te uira e hiko i te rangi,
E whawhai rua ana na runga Tauwhare,
Kaore ianei, ko te tohu o te mate.

There is the lightning flashing in the sky,
Hunting the lightning pit on Tauwhare [mountain],
It is for today a sign of the death [of Te Huhu].

The way the lightning flashes, whether straight down, which is bad for the locals, away towards another tribe, which is bad for them and good for the locals, or as broad summer lightning without thunder which portends war, and the place where the lightning starts and finishes are all noted and interpreted.

A red glow in the sky in front of a party is very ominous. Similarly, a low rainbow in front of a person or party will cause them to turn back, as will fragments of rainbow. A high-arched rainbow almost forming a circle is the best sign there can be.

Old-time *tohunga* are said to have been able to send messages by natural signs such as a ring around the Moon or a ring around the Sun, and these are still good signs.

DIVINATORY RITES

Before embarking on an enterprise it was, and still is, wise and polite to invoke the blessing of the spiritual powers. However, good manners can be backed up by knowing that the task is likely to succeed. Various divinatory rites were used in the old days to ascertain the outcome of any new undertaking.

These rites were particularly concerned with war: whether the tribe would be victorious or suffer defeat, and who out of their chiefs would be killed. The *niu* and *raurau* rites were often used for this.

War divination was sometimes done by man-shaped kites (middle); omens were drawn by the way they flew over the battleground or village.

Casting lots in the niu *and* raurau *rites was done by the* tohunga *(top and bottom). In the* raurau *rite a small mound was made and named for the tribes, and green twigs of* karamu *were placed in each. In front of these, small sticks were placed on the ground. Invocations were said. The small sticks would then move towards the twigs, and leaves would drop off to show how many would be killed. The* niu *takes two or more forms. The* tohunga *spread a mat on the ground, then took fern stalks in his hand and named each one of them for the chiefs who were to go on the war party. Each stick was tied with a piece of flax. Another set – without the flax ties – was named for the chiefs of the opposing tribes. The enemy chief sticks were then stuck upright through the mat. The* tohunga *took up the sticks with the ties and threw one of them at a stick without a tie. If it dropped to the left of the upright stick, the chief would fall. If it dropped to the right he would survive. This was done for all the chiefs. Another* niu *rite involved placing sticks in the ground and balancing named sticks with flax ties on them on each. The* tohunga *then waited for these to fall to the left or right.*

FORMS OF THE GODS

Gods can communicate with men by sending their *aria*, or semblance, often as lizards. The green gecko is a sign of death, while illness was thought to be caused by a god in the form of a lizard gnawing at the body. *Tohunga* used to produce lizards from a sick person's body as proof that the illness was conquered by prayer, and then give medicine. *Aria* may also be in the shape of dogs, birds, insects (particularly the green mantis), trees, rocks, weapons, rainbows, comets and stars. All of these manifestations are regarded as portents.

OBJECTS OF *MANA*

Ancestral treasures, images of the gods, symbols of chieftanship and many other items had *mana*, or power, of their own and could be used (and some are still used) to ask the goodwill of the gods. For exactly the same reason they can be used in divinatory rites. Such an item may turn over, move sideways, or otherwise answer the questions asked by those who have the right to ask, the legitimate holders and descendants of the *mana* of the gods. Their task is to ensure the continuation of, and if necessary restore, the balance between the realms of existence.

Living in the world of today for Maori people involves embracing and looking back to the past. The Maori vision of time is of a group looking back to what has gone before and backing into the unknown future. The dead are thought of as going before, returning to the past yet at the same time preparing the future place for their relatives and descendants.

The continuation of this world-view is illustrated by the following story. As noted earlier, when a person or group goes onto the *marae* (ceremonial meeting place) of another tribal group they are never alone, for their dead are with them to protect them from harm. Both sides are very conscious of any omens or portents that may appear. Quite recently, when a small party was waiting to be called and welcomed onto a *marae*, the local elders looked out and decided they did not need to do very much as the group appeared to be of little importance and mainly European.

Just then there was a short, sharp shower which fell out of a clear sky only on the *marae* courtyard. The elders immediately called for their women and the other people around the *marae* to come and help welcome the visitors. These were *waewae tapu*, sacred footsteps, and the ancestral spirits were telling their descendants to welcome them properly lest evil befall.

A house lintel from Hauraki depicts the birth of
the gods from the Earth Mother. At the sides are manaia,
which represent the spirit world and are probably a
combination of bird and lizard.

WORLD-WIDE SYSTEMS

We have seen points of similarity between many of the divinatory systems. Some are almost globally disseminated, and for this reason they are discussed here separately.

Numerology, for example, can be seen to have arisen more or less spontaneously in Greece, Assyria, Egypt and the greater part of Europe. In most instances there seems to be a recurring pattern of discovery that numbers equate to the natural patterns observable in the universe. This, of course, gave them magical significance and provided those who possessed the wisdom to understand them with superior qualities. The importance of crystals throughout much of the world may also have played a part in the origin of the science of numbers, since crystalline forms themselves display a numerical quality and are seen as the foundation of much of created matter. The antiquity of the examples collected by Norman Shine to illustrate his chapter indicates that numerology is one of the oldest divinatory systems in the world.

Geomancy, which has spread throughout the world and underlies many of the divinatory systems we have discussed, itself relies heavily on numerical patterns, though it is perhaps more related to the profound understanding of the elements and natural cycles – a theme that we have encountered again and again in this study.

Geomancy is also related to the work of the classical augurs (Chapter Seven) and to the practitioners of Feng Shui, whose earth-orientated skills are part of the geomantic heritage. When we read the description of the basic methods used by geomancers to foretell future events or to decide upon the positioning of a building, we may well be reminded of the methods used by more than half the diviners we have followed throughout this collection.

Dowsing may perhaps be considered the 'odd man out' in this section, yet the ability to divine lost objects, and to discover the relationships of one thing to another, is very much part of the diviner's art. Like numerology and geomancy it is known to have flourished in many different areas of the world – as, indeed, it still does today. Dowsers operate in all kinds of ways, seeking things as diverse as the discovery of murder victims, the recovery of lost works of art or (traditionally) hidden springs of water.

The degree of interest in divination throughout the world continues unabated and has even, in the last few years, begun to expand. Hence in the appendix to this collection Eileen Campbell discusses a few of the many new or newly rediscovered systems which are arousing interest all over the world. Several of these have grown out of a consideration of the ancient systems we have examined above; they are restatements or fresh developments which have emerged from the old. Their existence makes it clear that we are as eager today as were our ancestors to know the answer to the question with which we began: What *does* the future hold in store?

COUNTING ON THE FUTURE

The Art and Science of Numerology

Norman Shine

Numerology, the science of numbers, has its origins early in the history of man. Among the Aryans and Greeks, the Assyrians and Egyptians, the Chinese and the early prehistoric Europeans, we find evidence of a symbolic system that was concerned with something more than mere enumeration.

Behind the Cosmos there is an intelligence which we see expressed in Nature. God appears to be mathematical, and in Nature we have the geometric expression of Divine intelligence. Crystallization takes place according to definite laws: water, for example, crystallizes at an angle of 60°. The universe can therefore be seen as the crystallized imagination of God, as a divine thought-form. By the study of numbers we can learn the laws of divine expression, from the constitution of the universe down to the most trivial occurrences.

One of the earliest attempts at a numerological representation of time and space is the arrangement of nine small, round cavities carved in the rock in the pre-historic Jean Anglier cave near Noisy-sur-Ecole in France, which is reminiscent of the early Chinese numerological 'maps'. The *I Ching*, the Book of Changes, is the earliest Chinese reference to a number system. The Chinese described the difference between odd and even numbers, allocating to the odd numbers heavenly qualities, and to the even numbers earthly qualities. The texts associated with the *I Ching* include a 'magic square' where the sum of the digits horizontally, vertically and diagonally always adds up to 15. These 'magic squares' are found at various times and in a number of different cultures. The Vedic Square is a table of multiplication numbers and, as the name implies, is associated with the early Sanskrit texts, the Vedas. The basis for the calculations of the Vedic Square is the multiplication table from one to nine, but instead of using the double numbers obtained by the multiplication of single numbers, they are reduced here to single numbers, e.g. $6 \times 6 = 36 = 9$ (see overleaf). Note that in the Vedic Square, with the exception of the numbers 3, 6 and 9, each number appears six times. Numbers 3 and 6 appear twelve times. Number 9 appears twenty-one times. By joining the mid-points of the squares where the number 1 repeats itself, the pattern for number 1 is formed. The designs obtained from the Vedic Square have been used as decorations in holy places by both Moslem and Hindu craftsmen throughout the ages.

The sixth-century BC Greek philosopher Pythagoras made a very considerable contribution to numerology. His work on mathematics was primarily orientated towards religion and philosophy, as witnessed by his statement in the *Sacred Discourses*: 'Number is the ruler of form and ideas and is the cause of gods and demons.' This statement echoes the Chinese observation from the beginning of the second millennium BC: 'The sum total of heavenly numbers and earthly numbers is 55. It is this ...which sets gods and demons in movement.' Pythagoras related the sequence of numbers to the sequence of letters in the Greek alphabet so that alpha = 1, beta = 2, gamma = 3, and so on. Pythagoras operated only with the number sequence 123456789; the

Hebrews, in the development of the Cabbala, operated with the number sequence 1 to 22. The 22 letters in the Hebrew alphabet served as the basis for a numerology which incorporated a very broad range of associated concepts.

NUMBERS AND PLANETS

A key to understanding numerology is found in the sequence of the days of the week. The global acceptance of the seven-day week suggests that there is a symbolic meaning to the number sequence 1234567. What we find is that the sequence of the days – whose names are derived from those of the planets – is the same as the sequence of the planets in early Hindu astrology.

1 Sun (Sunday)
2 Moon (Monday)
3 Mars (Tuesday)
4 Mercury (Wednesday)
5 Jupiter (Thursday)
6 Venus (Friday)
7 Saturn (Saturday)

The basis of numerology is this relationship of numbers to planets. The correlation between number and planet is far from arbitrary: the associations we form with the different numbers harmonize well with the attributions given astrologically to the planets. Keywords and examples of these associations are:

1 Unity. The personal resources of the individual. Divine presence. Ego. Synthesis. Sun.

2 Polarity. Duality. Good/bad; day/night; either/or. The mind. Emotions. Antithesis. Dilemma. Choice. Ambivalence. Moon.

3 Action. Personal creativity. The Divine triangle: Heaven, man, Earth. The Holy Trinities of God the Father, Son and Holy Ghost; Brahma, Vishnu and Shiva. Thought, word and action. Mars.

4 The number of the world. The concrete. Practice. The stable square. The four seasons. The four directions. The four elements. The lower intellect and instincts. The quantitative. Order and classification. The first arithmetic square (2x2). Mercury.

5 The five senses. Five toes. Five fingers. Learning through the senses. Expansion. Jupiter.

6 The double triangle. The Star of David. Higher intellectual creativity. The abstract. Perfection. The world created in six days. Beauty. Harmony. Sense of discrimination. Imagination. Venus (rules the sexual organs) and Uranus (rules the sexual glands).

7 The limit of matter. Time. Chronos, the Greek god of time. The colours of the rainbow. The seven tones of the musical scale. The seven days of the week. The seven cardinal virtues and deadly sins. The seven seals of the Book of Revelations. Stability and endurance. Duration of the material. Saturn.

To complete the correlation of numbers with astrological phenomena we can take two important symbols of Hindu astrology, the lunar nodes. We can correlate the number 8 with the north lunar node. The north node of the Moon is now commonly accepted as an indicator of the individual's fate in a specific lifetime. The number 9 can be correlated with the south lunar node. The south node of the Moon is acknowledged as an indicator of individual karma, the unresolved residue of earlier lives.

The number 8 has always been a mystic number, with its association with infinity (∞) and being beyond the force of time. The number 8 symbolizes the material, the temporary, whereas the number 9 symbolizes truth and love, the Divine, the eternal reality. Their other associations are:

8 The double square. The first arithmetic cube (2x2x2). The number of dissolution. The law of cyclic evolution. As a cubic number it adds the new dimension of timeless (beyond 7) space. In contrast to 2 (either/or), this number symbolizes the absolute reality of matter, which is bound by time. Thus, it symbolizes good *and* bad, right *and* wrong, night *and* day. All these are bound by time. Because of its shape it is also associated with

the caduceus (staff) carried by Mercury. It illustrates the balance between opposing forces, or the equilibrium between the spiritual powers and the powers of nature. It is associated with Pluto as well as with the north node of the Moon. It represents the breakdown of the barrier between the material and the spiritual, in order to complete transformation.

9 The triple three (3x3). A complete picture of the three worlds: the physical (1, 2, 3), the intellectual (4, 5, 6), and the spiritual (7, 8, 9). The last of the symbols in the numerical sequence before it returns to unity, raised to a higher level (10). For the Hebrews 9 is the symbol of truth, for the Hindus it is the number of Brahman. It is associated with the planet Neptune (Neptune is the ruler of the last of the astrological signs, Pisces, symbolizing the relinquishing of the ego) as well as with the south node of the Moon.

For the numerologist there are, then, only nine numbers from which all calculations concerning the material world are made. By a simple method of addition all numbers beyond 9 can be reduced

NUMEROLOGY AROUND THE WORLD

Numerology is truly a world-wide phenomenon and lies behind many other systems of divination. The mystical possibilities inherent in numbers have fascinated people throughout the ages, although the precise forms of numerological science depend on the cultures in which they originate, as the examples on the map indicate.

This detail from the prehistoric Jean Anglier cave near Noisy-sur-Ecole in France appears to illustrate an attempt at ordering time and space.

1	2	3	4	5	6	7	8	9
2	4	6	8	10	12	14	16	18
3	6	9	12	15	18	21	24	27
4	8	12	16	20	24	28	32	36
5	10	15	20	25	30	35	40	45
6	12	18	24	30	36	42	48	54
7	14	21	28	35	42	49	56	63
8	16	24	32	40	48	56	64	72
9	18	27	36	45	54	63	72	81

5. The Cabbala's complex correlation system is based on the Hebrew alphabet. Today it is mostly used in conjunction with the Tarot.

Hebrew Letter	English Letter	Number	Planetary or Zodiacal Ru...
Aleph	A	1	Mercury
Beth	B	2	Virgo
Gimel	G	3	Libra
Daleth	D	4	Scorpio
He	E	5	Jupiter
Vau	V U W	6	Venus
Zain	Z	7	Sagittarius
Cheth	H	8	Capricorn
Teth	Th	9	Aquarius
Jod	I J Y	10	Uranus
Caph	C K	11	Neptune
Lamed	L	12	Pisces
Mem	M	13	Aries
Nun	N	14	Taurus
Sameck	X	15	Saturn
Ayin	O	16	Mars
Pe	F P	17	Gemini
Tzaddi	Ts Tz	18	Cancer
Quoph	Q	19	Leo
Resh	R	20	Moon
Shin	S	21	Sun
Tau	T	22	Earth

1. The Vedic Square is a table of multiplication numbers: the table on the left is used as a base for calculating the Vedic Square on the right. The double numbers of the multiplication table (left) are reduced to single numbers, e.g. $6 \times 6 = 36 = 3 + 6 = 9$.

1	2	3	4	5	6	7	8	9
2	4	6	8	1	3	5	7	9
3	6	9	3	6	9	3	6	9
4	8	3	7	2	6	1	5	9
5	1	6	2	7	3	8	4	9
6	3	9	6	3	9	6	3	9
7	5	3	1	8	6	4	2	9
8	7	6	5	4	3	2	1	9
9	9	9	9	9	9	9	9	9

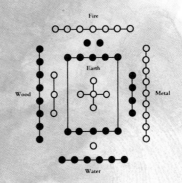

2. This diagram, known as *Ho T'u*, the Yellow River Map, dating from the second millennium BC, shows the development out of odd and even numbers of the 'five stages of change' (usually incorrectly called elements).

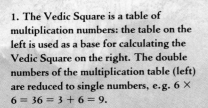

```
4   9   2

3   5   7

8   1   6
```

4. This diagram shows an important 'magic square', where the sum of the digits horizontally, vertically and diagonally is 15 in each case. This square is found throughout Europe during the Middle Ages.

3. This arrangement, also found in texts associated with the *I Ching*, is known as the *Lo Shu*, the Writing from the River Lo. It is here stated that 'the sum total of heavenly numbers and earthly numbers is 55. It is this that . . . sets demons and gods in movement.'

to single whole numbers. The number 10 is not a single whole number, it is actually only a 1 with a zero.

Zero is not a number and thus has no numerological value. The Western world has not recognized zero as long as the Eastern world: both the Indian and the Chinese cultures used the zero during the Stone Age period of the Western world. Beginners are advised to be careful when interpreting the role of zero numerologically, as it has certain negative attributes when found in dates.

NUMEROLOGY IN PRACTICE

The application of the numerological correlates in the Cabbala is complex, so those who are new to numerology are advised to apply Pythagoras' system. Pythagoras employed a pragmatic and logical approach:

1	2	3	4	5	6	7	8	9
A	B	C	D	E	F	G	H	I
J	K	L	M	N	O	P	Q	R
S	T	U	V	W	X	Y	Z	

Thus AJS = 1, BKT = 2, and so on.

The principle is that one sequence (numbers) is correlated with the other sequence (here, the alphabet). This principle can also be employed should we wish to relate colours to numbers. Here, however, we must decide whether we should employ the seven colours of the rainbow, in which case the association of colour with number follows the sequence 1234567. According to the modern colour therapist Marie Louise Lacy, a key to the colours and their numerological vibrations is:

1 Red	4 Green	7 Violet
2 Orange	5 Blue	8 Silver
3 Yellow	6 Indigo	9 Gold

If we bear in mind that there are over 20 different house systems in astrology, we should not be surprised that there are many different systems within numerology. The systems must not, however, be mixed. If we use a system in one way, then it must be followed consistently at all times with the same name or date.

NUMEROLOGY WITH DATES

The birth date, time and place are equally valid for divining purposes in numerology. The example here shows the numerological analysis of the birth date 28 August 1954.

The *day of birth* is symbolic of the way the individual sees him or herself. This *psychic number* is obtained by making a single whole number of the day of the month, here $28 = 2 + 8 = 10 = 1 + 0 = 1$.

The *destiny* or *fate number* is where the individual can see what he or she has deserved. It is the single whole number obtained from the addition of the day, month and year of birth: 28 August 1954 $= 2+8+8+1+9+5+4 = 37 = 3+7 = 10 = 1+0 = 1$.

NUMEROLOGICAL ANALYSIS OF NAMES

The *name number* is a synthesis of both psychic and destiny numbers and illustrates how the individual will react to specific situations. The name number may be seen as a whole (personal name(s) plus family or surname) or may be treated specifically as personal name (symbolizing the individual's personal relationship to others and society in general).

The name number is illustrated as a single whole number obtained by the addition of the number equivalents of the letters of the name. For example, Birgitte Shine $=2+9+9+7+9+2+2+5+1+8+9+5+5 = 73 = 7+3 = 10 = 1$.

Once the numerologist has the psychic, destiny and name numbers it is possible to assess the way in which these numbers work together. In the above example we can see that all three numbers are 1. Quite clearly this is an illustration of great intensity of energy in one particular area: a narrow front with great depth. Where all three numbers are different (for example: psychic number 6, fate number 7 and name number 8) we find a broad energy front that is more shallow. Interpretation may vary, but it must rest on the classical understanding of number symbolism.

Most numerological systems simply add all the digits to arrive at a name number, as in the example above. An interpretation here is simple: the name is 'read' numerologically as a '1'. The analysis will be as limited as an astrological analysis of the Sun-sign: born on 8 October I am seen as being born under the sign of Libra, and all other relevant astrological data are ignored. An interpretation of the basic characteristics of number 1s is that they are resourceful and talented. They have a clear sense of their own identity, are self-sufficient and have stable values. They also have leadership abilities. The negative traits are that they are wilful, inconsiderate and tend to complacency.

Obviously, the sum of the digits description just given is too simple. When we look at the name diagram shown below, we can see that in fact there is very little 1 in the name Birgitte Shine. It is found only once. In the diagram this is illustrated by one circle around the number 1. On the other hand, number 2 and number 5 are both found three times, 9 is found four times, and 7 and 8 are each found once. A fuller analysis of the name should thus take into account these other features of the personality.

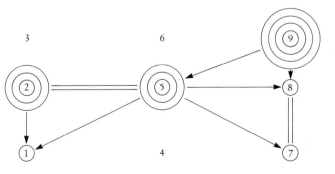

Birgitte Shine: 2,9,9,7,9,2,2,5,1,8,9,5,5

An analysis of the name could include the following observations:

Number	Characteristic	Frequency	Manifestation (personal)
1	Awareness of personal resources	1	Relatively low self-confidence. Needs to build this up by meeting new challenges with open mind and use of instincts.
2	Awareness of feelings and emotions	3	High emotionality. Feminine emotional responses.
3	Awareness of personal creativity	0	Low awareness. No conscious controls. Impetuosity. Rashness. Ruled by emotions (high 2 and low 1).
4	Awareness of concrete, logical and intellectual processes	0	Neither practical nor logical. Non-intellectual but highly instinctive and intelligent (note high emotionality – 2).
5	Awareness of senses	3	Relatively high. Sensuality linked closely to emotions (2 and 5 have same frequency).
6	Awareness of abstract, imaginative, intellectual processes	0	Low imagination awareness. High intuitive abilities.
7	Awareness of material limitations (time and space)	1	Well developed. Matches awareness of own resources. Risk of sense of inadequacy. Limits of action (low awareness of activity ability).
8	Awareness of eternity (materiality/ spirituality)	1	Well developed but subject to emotions (high) and compulsive unconscious urges and reaction patterns (see 9 below).
9	Awareness of inborn talents and compulsive urges	4	A main motive force in the personality working through feelings (intense) and with spiritual awareness and the setting of limits. Dominated by unconscious mechanisms.

The lines and arrows in the diagram show the direction and intensity of the energy flow. Where the number 2 is high and the number 1 is low it shows that the individual's emotions are stronger than her awareness of her resources. Emotions are used to develop resources.

Where there is a low frequency of a number (fewer circles) and, most of all, where a number is not represented in a name, that number attracts most energy from the surrounding numbers, and much energy is used in attempting to exploit the hidden resources in the number(s) lacking. We tend to be controlled by those energies we are not conscious of. In the energy pattern of Birgitte Shine, the absence of a number 3 means that emotional self-control is necessary for her to become aware of her strong (but concealed) ability to act and think creatively. If she uses her massive awareness of her inborn subconscious and unconscious powers (high frequency number 9) to her own advantage, she can cease to respond automatically to emotional situations by compulsive action and near-compulsive setting of limits. (Low frequency 7 and no 3s attract too much 9 energy.)

As we can see, the name number (by addition) is 1, which is identical with her psychic number (based on birthdate) and her fate number (based on total birth data). Her true psychic picture of herself is of a resourceful person. Her life is exciting and full of challenges. But when we see her name analysis in detail we see that she is inhibited by lacking a functional awareness of her powers. This is mainly as a result of (a) compulsive behaviour and (b) over-emotionality.

APPLICATIONS OF NUMEROLOGY

Numerology is useful in rapid analysis of personal qualities and behavioural patterns. By combining and comparing names the numerologist is able to describe compatibility potential. Such analyses are used in marriage counselling, personnel and staff management (who will work best with whom) and parent counselling (in ascertaining why some parents have great difficulties with their children).

Numerology is also useful for a rapid investigation of the change in an individual's energy pattern in the case of name change (by marriage, adoption, etc.). The numerologist is of great assistance in helping those who, in an identity crisis, are able to find solutions to their problems by finding a new name to reflect a new development in their life.

There is, as has been indicated, a certain overlapping between numerology and astrology. The knowledge of the planetary cycles (in both Western and Hindu astrology) is invaluable in determining prognoses for future events. For this reason, a good numerologist should also have knowledge of astrology, psychology, palmistry and graphology. Where a client wishes to change his or her name, the numerologist is, by an investigation of a birth chart (horoscope), able to confirm to the client the wiseness of his or her choice. The choice of names, however, is best left to the client.

LUCKY NUMBERS?

Almost everyone has his or her 'lucky' number or numbers. And it is a fact that individuals respond especially strongly to certain numbers. Some numbers we can call friendly numbers, others we can call neutral numbers, and finally there are numbers we might just as well call enemy numbers. 'Lucky' or friendly numbers are useful in finding what house number to live in, which lottery ticket to buy, which numbers to play on in roulette and racing. In his practice the numerologist can give advice on such matters on the basis of birthdays and names. Certain dates are also luckier for an individual than others.

The means of calculating such numbers are relatively complex and lie outside the scope of this article. The value of such advice is far from being frivolous: although the numerologist cannot bring luck where no luck is merited, he can reduce the risk of the client bringing bad luck on himself by not maximizing his awareness of the potential of a given situation. The 'lucky' person is one who listens to an inner voice, the instincts and intuition. Those who are not too good at this can always find a numerologist.

ANCIENT SECRETS OF THE EARTH

The Oracle of Geomancy

Nigel Pennick

Geomancy is one of the systems of divination that use aspects of the four elements. The other three elemental systems are aeromancy, using the air; pyromancy, using fire; and hydromancy, using water. Correspondingly, geomancy gives its messages by or through the earth. The word geomancy comes from the Greek words *Ge*, Gaia, Mother Earth, and *manteia*, divination; or, alternatively, the second part of the word may come from *magos*, knowledge. It is thus knowledge of earthly things, for, according to traditional belief, geomancy works through the agency of the Earth Goddess or through the elemental spirits of the Earth.

Today, the word geomancy refers to two distinct yet related forms of divination. They are oracular geomancy, which deals with prediction, and locational geomancy, the esoteric science of placement, which looks for good and bad places in the landscape. In the East, locational geomancy has several related forms. The most important are Vastuvidya (India), Yattara (Burma) and Feng Shui (China) (see Chapter Seventeen). In the West, locational geomancy includes the practices of Greek, Etruscan and Roman augurs, and the work of the 'locators' of medieval and baroque Europe, men who founded cities, cathedrals and churches.

Throughout history, geomantic patterns have been made by almost any available method. Among the most common methods are: scattering handfuls of earth on the ground; throwing seeds, nuts or sea-shells onto a special tray; pricking marks on paper with a pin, or making dots with a pen. A larger version of the pin or pen marks can be made using a tray of sand or on the earth with a rod, a technique closely related to *rhabdomancy*, which is a form of dowsing. Special dice or divination chains are also used occasionally. What these techniques have in common is that, from marks made unconsciously, patterns are created which can be interpreted by the experienced geomant.

THE HISTORY AND SPREAD OF GEOMANCY

Because of its wide-ranging techniques, the origin of geomancy is uncertain. Although ancient Greek and Latin writings refer to geomancy, they do not give comprehensive descriptions, which makes it difficult to reconstruct precise details of techniques. It is known that during the siege of Syracuse the geometer Archimedes (278–212 BC) drew figures in the sand to predict the outcome of the battle; but precisely what he was doing is unknown.

The most coherent and developed system of geomancy arose among the Arabs in North Africa. Arab geomancy is known as Raml, from *'ilm al-raml* (the science of sand), and is the type of geomancy used today all over the world. It seems to have been formalized into the present system around the eighth century AD. It may have been devised in Alexandria, derived from ancient Greek or Egyptian methods, but this is not historically proven.

As with many other divination systems (for example the Ogams and the *I Ching* – see Chapters Three and Sixteen), the discovery of geomancy is attributed to a single inspired man. The Arab tradition ascribes it to the prophet Idris (the Islamic name for the Egyptian sage Hermes Trismegistus, founder of alchemy), who was taught the art by the angel Gabriel. Alternative 'originators' of geomancy are said to have been the Jewish prophet Daniel and the Indian Tum-Tum el-Hindi.

As a means of foretelling the future, Raml fits in well with Islamic belief in predestination, and the initial spread of geomancy from North Africa reflects Islamic conquests and influence. There are two distinct areas of geomantic practice in sub-Saharan Africa – eastern and western. To the east is Madagascar, where Arab colonies existed in the ninth century. They were

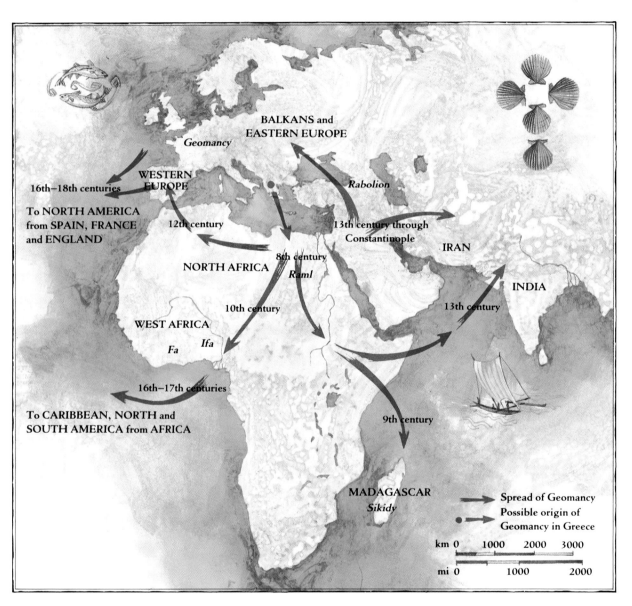

THE SPREAD OF GEOMANCY

The Oracle of Geomancy may have been used in ancient Greece but its present form almost certainly originated after the Arab conquest of Egypt. As Islam expanded further into Africa during the ninth century, geomancy followed. In West Africa, it became Fa and Ifa, while in Madagascar it became Sikidy. The Arabs also took it to Islamic Spain, whence it came into Christian Western Europe. At the other end of the Mediterranean Sea, it entered Eastern Europe through Constantinople, where it became Rabolion. In the thirteenth century, geomancy reached India by land through Iran and by sea from Arabia and East Africa. After Columbus, geomancy was taken to the New World from Africa by slaves and from Western Europe by the conquerors.

the means by which Raml entered Malagasy culture and became Sikidy. Later, it was synthesized with the Malay magico-religious tradition of Bintana and Chinese ideas about Feng Shui to make a distinctly Malagasy system, Vintana.

The second area of sub-Saharan geomancy is in West Africa, which Raml reached overland via the Sahara. In the countries around the Gulf of Guinea, it became Fa and Ifa (see Chapter Twelve). It is likely that these contacts occurred around the tenth century.

Geomancy also spread north of the Mediterranean by two distinct routes. First, it came into Western Europe from Islamic Spain and spread through Christian scholarly writings. The first Latin texts, *Ars Geomantiae* and *Geomantia Nova*, were written in Aragon around 1140, with information from Arabic sources. The author of these works was Hugh of Santalla, who was the first writer to describe Raml as *Geomantia*, giving it its modern name. Some time later, Arab geomancy entered Christian Europe by a second route, through the Eastern Roman Empire. There, the Byzantine Greeks called it Rabolion.

In medieval Europe, geomancy was a popular form of divination. Following Hugh of Santalla, other intellectuals wrote about geomantic divination, adding their own interpretations to a growing European literature on the subject; most notable were Gerard of Cremona (1114–87); Plato of Tivoli (*c.* 1140), Michael Scot (*c.* 1175–*c.* 1235) and Albertus Magnus (1193–1280). Geomancy was also part of the medieval Jewish tradition in Europe, where it was known as Goral Ha-hol (the lot by sand), or Hokhmah Ha-nekuddot (the science of points).

Sometimes, along with astrology, astronomy and alchemy, geomancy was condemned by the Church as heretical. In his *Parson's Tale* (1386), Geoffrey Chaucer notes:

What do we say of those who believe in divinations, as by the flight or sounds of birds, of beasts, of sortilege, by geomancy, by dreams, by creaking of doors, or cracking of houses, by gnawing of rats, and such manner of wretchedness? Certainly, all this is forbidden by God and all the Holy Church. (Author modernization)

But at other times, churchmen have been avid followers of geomancy, and it has flourished. Perhaps its high point was the sixteenth century, in both the Arab world and Europe. Heinrich Cornelius Agrippa (1468–1535), Europe's most famous Renaissance magus, connected geomancy with astrology. In the English edition of his *Fourth Book of Occult Philosophy* (London, 1655), Agrippa gives the following definition:

Geomancy is an art of divination ... [which] consisteth especially in certain points whereof certain figures are deducted according to the reason or rule of equality or inequality, likeness or unlikeness; which figures are also reduced to the celestial figures, assuming their natures and properties, according to the course and forms of the signs and planets.

Connecting the geomantic figures with corresponding astrological signs subsequently became an important subsidiary of geomancy, with parallels in the Sikidy of Madagascar, where geomancy is an integral part of astrology and geolocation. Writing in 1558, the Italian geomant Christopher Cattan was explicit in the connection:

Geomancy is a science and art which consisteth of points, pricks and lines, made instead of the four elements, and of the stars and planets of heaven, called the Science of the Earth ...every prick [point] signifieth a star, and every line an element, and every figure, the four quarters of the world.... Wherefore it is easy to know that geomancy is none other thing but astrology....

Geomancy is also mentioned in an astrological context by Dante in his *Purgatorio*: 'In the hours when the day's heat ...can no longer temper the cold of the Moon, when the geomancers see their Fortuna Major rise in the east before dawn....' (Canto XIX).

During the Renaissance period, geomancy was taken to the colonies in the Americas, first by Spanish conquistadors, later by English and French magicians. The African version, Ifa, was also taken to the New World by people transported there to work as slaves. Today it remains part of their descendants' culture in the United States, Haiti, Cuba and Brazil.

In nineteenth-century Europe, a version of geomancy using a book called *Napoleon's Book of Fate* gained popularity. It is a kind of Western *I Ching* (see Chapter Sixteen). Figures consisting of five lines rather than four are created by geomantic methods, and each figure corresponds to a reading from the book. Despite the fact that Napoleon never used it, and it has been called a fake, it still works.

During the twentieth century, geomancy continues to flourish in traditional societies as well as modern ones. It was an important part of the magical tradition of the Hermetic Order of the Golden Dawn, the most influential order of modern magic, and from this school have come several important publications on geomancy (see Further Reading).

HOW IT WORKS

As an oracle, geomancy gives its messages by forming certain distinct patterns. There are 16 possible geomantic figures (tetragrams), each composed of dots (or alternatively stars, points or lines). Each geomantic figure has a name and a corresponding meaning, and may be interpreted either alone or in combination with the other figures.

The Dogon geomant (left), of Mali, West Africa, creates his geomantic figures directly on the ground. He uses sand in a specially prepared sacred enclosure. Ground nuts, magically linked with the element of earth, are used to make the actual geomantic figures.

Dogon geomants (right) interpret animal tracks across a geomantic pattern left overnight. The type of animal making the track, as well as its position on the geomantic grid, is significant. Animal tracks can be used as an oracle by themselves, or may give useful additional information to a divination performed on the previous day.

The principles used in creating the tetragrams of geomancy are the same as those for making the hexagrams of the *I Ching* with yarrow stalks. Technically, these oracles work on the mathematical principle known as 'sensitive dependence on initial conditions', where the final result depends significantly on the first move. Both geomancy and the *I Ching* use binary mathematics. Geomancy has 16 (2^4) figures, whilst the *I Ching* has 64 (2^6). Both start with a series of alternative choices that narrow down the options, step by step, until only one of the possibilities remains.

Each culture has its own names for the geomantic figures, but, wherever they are used, the meaning of each figure is the same. In Europe, it is customary to use the Latin names for the geomantic figures. They are arranged in their complementary or opposite pairs (see overleaf).

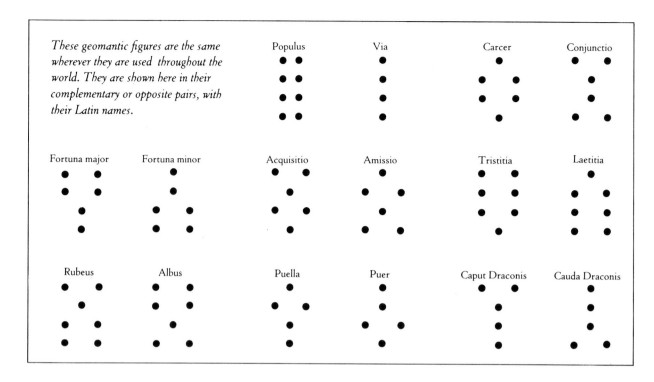

These geomantic figures are the same wherever they are used throughout the world. They are shown here in their complementary or opposite pairs, with their Latin names.

Populus Via Carcer Conjunctio

Fortuna major Fortuna minor Acquisitio Amissio Tristitia Laetitia

Rubeus Albus Puella Puer Caput Draconis Cauda Draconis

THE UNIVERSAL MEANING OF THE GEOMANTIC FIGURES

POPULUS (THE PEOPLE): an assembly, union, society, crowd, gang, congregation. This figure has a changeable character. Sometimes it can be good and sometimes bad, relative to the other figures in the reading.

VIA (THE WAY): path, street, highway, journey, direction, ways and means, the way of (the questioner's) life. *Via* has an unfavourable effect on other good figures, but it is beneficial when the question is about travel.

CONJUNCTIO (UNION): connection, recovery of lost things, gathering together, reunion, collection, contracts. *Conjunctio* is on the positive side of neutral.

CARCER (PRISON): a prison, cell, confinement, servitude, binding, delay.

FORTUNA MAJOR (THE GREATER FORTUNE): good luck, fortune, success, victory, safe property, a good position in society,

entry into good things. An extremely good figure.

FORTUNA MINOR (THE LESSER FORTUNE): assistance from others, protection from harm. A beneficial figure, but not so good as *Fortuna Major*.

ACQUISITIO (GAIN): profitable business, extension of existing property, success, gains from a request or investigation, great benefit.

AMISSIO (LOSS): things taken away, possibly loss through illness, or through theft of property or financial problems.

TRISTITIA (SADNESS): sadness, misery, melancholy, humiliation, dwindling resources, poverty, a change for the worse.

LAETITIA (JOY): delight, gladness, beauty, grace, sanity, balance, good health, matters of the head. This is a very good geomantic figure.

RUBEUS (RED): passion, vice,

temper, destructive fire, a stop sign. A warning to stop now.

ALBUS (WHITE): dazzling beauty, illumination, wisdom, sagaciousness, profitability. Good results in business and all actions of entry.

PUELLA (GIRL): a girl, daughter, young wife, nurse, a pleasant character, purity, cleanliness. This may appear to be a good figure, but it can be deceptive, as fine external appearances may hide unpleasantness.

PUER (BOY): a boy, son, servant, employee, rashness, inconsiderateness, combativeness. A negative figure, except in combat or love.

CAPUT DRACONIS (DRAGON'S HEAD): a place of entry, a doorway to the heavenly Upperworld.

CAUDA DRACONIS (DRAGON'S TAIL): a way out, the Underworld, possible problems.

USING THE ORACLE

Before starting, think seriously about the question you are asking. Write it down. Then, bearing the question in mind, make a line of dots at random. Repeat this until you have 16 lines of dots. Then count the number of dots in each line and write the numbers down. An odd number gives a single point in the geomantic figure, and an even number gives two points. The 16 lines give four geomantic figures, the Mothers, in all.

Next, four further figures, the Daughters, are made from the four Mothers. The first Daughter is made from the top lines of the four Mothers. The second Daughter is made up from the second line of the four Mother figures in the same way. The third Daughter is made from the third line, and the final Daughter is composed of the bottom line of the four Mother Figures.

Then, four Nephews are made. The first Nephew figure is made by adding together the corresponding points of the first two Mothers. If the sum of points is odd, then that line of the Nephew has one point. If it is even, then there are two points in that line. The second Nephew figure is made by adding together the other two Mothers. The third Nephew is made by adding the first two Daughters, and the fourth Nephew by adding the third and fourth Daughters. There are now 12 geomantic figures in all – four Mothers, four Daughters and four Nephews. The next step is to make two more figures, the Witnesses. The first is created by adding the first and second Nephew figures together. The second comes from adding the third and fourth Nephews. Finally, add together the two Witnesses to make the Judge. The process of geomantic divination means that the Judge will be one of eight figures. These are *Acquisitio*, *Amissio*, *Carcer*, *Conjunctio*, *Fortuna Major*, *Fortuna Minor*, *Populus* and *Via*. None of the other figures can ever be the Judge. The resulting geomantic figures are interpreted in the light of the original question.

In the example shown opposite, the question was whether a new business venture should be started. The lines of dots made at random combine to make the final geomantic figure, or Judge, which in this case is *Via*. This is not a particularly favourable outcome, but is also not negative enough to abandon the enterprise.

CHAPTER TWENTY-FOUR

DOWSING THE WAY

Divining with Pendulum and Rod

Sig Lonegren

Dowsing is the ability to find objects, or the answers to questions, through the use of both the rational and the intuitive aspects of our being. Also called raedesthesia or, perhaps more significantly, divining, dowsing uses a tool that indicates 'yes' or 'no', or the direction to, or specific location of, a target. There are four basic types of dowsing tools: Y-rods, the pendulum, L-rods and the bobber.

Perhaps the best-known dowsing device is the Y-rod, or forked stick. Primarily used by water dowsers, traditionally a Y-rod is cut from an apple or willow tree, although many competent diviners today use plastic because it doesn't break under the constant twisting of the downward pull of the rod. This forked stick is held in both hands, thumbs outwards, with the tip of the 'Y' pointing upwards. This is called the search position. The tip of the rod then goes down sharply when the dowser is over the target.

A pendulum, also known as a plumb bob, can be any well-balanced weight on the end of a thread or light chain. Each dowser sets up his own code to interpret the movements of the pendulum. For some, back and forth means 'yes' (like nodding one's head in affirmation) and an oscillation from side to side means 'no'. For others, a clockwise rotation is 'yes' and counterclockwise means 'no'. As there are other possibilities and combinations of pendulum movement, each dowser has to find his own signals for 'yes' and 'no'. Pendulums are used by many different kinds of dowsers, from those who look for water to those who use divining to help resolve personal problems.

L-rods are bent coat-hangers or lengths of welding rod held in the hands like six-guns in the old cowboy movies. When you get over your target, the rods swing either out or in depending what you have programmed them to do. L-rods are used by water dowsers and by those interested in the Earth Energies found at sacred sites. L-rods are also used by healers, as they are very effective at locating disease in the body.

The fourth dowsing tool is the bobber. Imagine that you are holding a fishing pole at the wrong end. It will bob up and down to tell you 'yes' and go from side to side to tell you 'no'. The bobber is used primarily by oil dowsers who call themselves 'doodlebugs'.

THE HISTORY OF DOWSING

No one knows for certain where dowsing first originated. In the Tassili-n-Ajjer caves, on a plateau in the Sahara desert in south-eastern Algeria near the Libyan border, there are pictoglyphs that could be up to 8,000 years old of a group of people watching someone holding what appears to be a forked stick (Y-rod). This could be the oldest depiction of dowsing.

Various mythological figures are credited with inventing dowsing tools, or at least bringing them to humans. For example, both the Egyptian god Thoth and the Greek inventor Daedalus,

Cornish dowser Hamish Miller, a blacksmith by trade, made these L-rods at his forge to use while tracking the Earth Energies of the famous Michael Line in England, a geomantic corridor that runs from St Michael's Mount in Land's End north-eastward, passing through several churches of St Michael, Glastonbury Tor, Avebury and other ancient holy sites.

who built the Cretan labyrinth, are credited with inventing the plumb bob (i.e. pendulum).

In the latter part of the third millennium BC, a Chinese adventurer by the name of Yü apparently travelled to the United States, went down the Grand Canyon and ended up on the west coast of Mexico before returning to China where he became the emperor. Emperor Yü is the earliest recorded dowser in history whom we know by name. In the Freer Gallery in Washington, DC, there is a Han Dynasty bas-relief that shows Emperor Yü with the following inscription, 'Yü of the Hsia Dynasty was a master of the science of the earth and in those matters concerning water veins and springs; he was well acquainted with the Yin principle and, when required, built dams.'

Although the Bible in more than one place severely censures dowsers and diviners, we are also told two stories where Moses finds water with the use of his rod – the magical one he used to create the plagues in Egypt that convinced Pharaoh to let his people go. One divining story occurs in Exodus (17:1–6) in the Wilderness of Sin in western Sinai at the beginning of the Hebrews' 40 years in the wilderness; the other happens just before they reached the Promised Land. At this second time (in Numbers 20:1–12), the people of Israel were in the Wilderness of Zin in what is now called the Negev Desert. They were tired of their two generations of wandering, and they had once again run out of water. They came to Moses and his brother Aaron and complained bitterly and seemed ready to rebel against Moses' leadership.

Then Moses and Aaron went from the presence of the assembly to the door of the tent of the meeting, and fell on their faces. And the glory of the Lord appeared to them, and the Lord said to Moses, 'Take the rod, and assemble the congregation, you and Aaron your brother, and tell the rock before their eyes to yield its water....' And Moses took the rod from before the Lord, as he commanded him.

And Moses and Aaron gathered the assembly together before the rock, and he said to them,

'Hear now, you rebels; shall we bring forth water for you out of this rock?' And Moses lifted up his hand and struck the rock twice, and water came forth abundantly, and the congregation drank, and their cattle (drank also).

Dowsing has always been a threat to established religions because the layperson can tune in directly to the spiritual realms without going through the priesthood as intermediaries. While this is empowering to the individual, it disempowers the priestly hierarchy. This was one of the reasons that the Christian Church suppressed many forms of dowsing during the Inquisition. Fortunately, several kinds of dowsing were not able to be exterminated. Dowsing can be used for all kinds of targets, but 'water witching', or the ability to find water, is

There are many connections that linguistically tie dowsing with spiritual realms. The French word is 'le sourcier'. In the United States, some call it 'water witching'. Dowsing puts us in touch with things that we can otherwise not see.

Some dowsers believe that the material their tools are made of is important. These L-rods are copper. The Y-rod is not the old, forked apple-stick of yore, but a modern one of metal that provides the same pull (reaction) every time.

indispensable, so it was one dowsing skill that made it through that time of persecution.

Another kind of dowsing that was not suppressed by the Church was written about by the sixteenth-century magician Georgius Agricola. In 1556, in *De Re Metallica* (On Metals), Agricola described how miners in Germany were using dowsing to find underground veins of metal. The German miners later brought their dowsing skills to Britain to help British miners locate tin in Devon and Cornwall.

DOWSING FOR ENVIRONMENTAL HEALTH

In the twentieth century dowsing has flourished once again. Science and rationalism had led Western man to the conclusion that dowsing was just superstition, and therefore not a threat. In the 1920s in Germany, however, it was noticed that people in certain houses – generation after generation – got cancer, while people in neighbouring houses did not. This was true even if different families moved into these 'krebs' (cancer) houses. Medical doctors were mystified by this phenomenon, until dowsers were called in and reported significant numbers of underground veins of water crossing under the *krebs* houses but not under adjoining homes. It has since been found by many dowsers around the world that spending time over crossing veins of water may induce various kinds of degenerative diseases like cancer and arthritis, as well as colic in babies and sleeplessness.

Erich Schuck, watched by a farmer, dowses on Mindanao Island, Philippines, in search of the hiding place of Second World War Matsushita gold. Schuck was working with psychic archaeologist Umberto di Grazia.

Before they go out onto the site, many dowsers first employ map dowsing. Here a dowser looks for a suitable site to drill a well. He uses the pin in his left hand as a pointer and watches the responses in his pendulum.

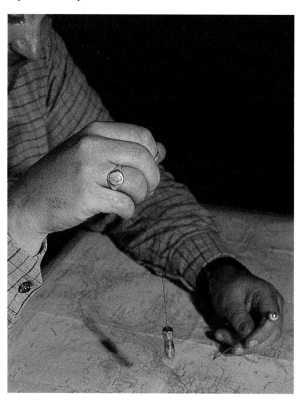

Today there is a great deal of interest in environmental healing, and various remedial techniques have been developed, from putting loops of wire around the frame of the bed where the veins of water cross underneath (the Lakhovsky loop), through putting blue tape on the floor over the veins, to actually driving metal rods into the heart of the veins of water as they enter and exit the house. This last is a form of Earth acupuncture and needs to be done with a great deal of care, preferably under the supervision of an expert dowser. It is my belief that all of these techniques work on a magical level to neutralize the negative effects of the veins.

DIVINING THE EARTH'S SPIRITUAL ENERGY

Reginald Allender Smith was the Keeper of the Egyptian and British Antiquities for the British Museum. After he retired from his job in the 1930s, this respected archaeologist shocked his academic colleagues when articles written by him began to appear in the *Journal of the British Society of Dowsers* saying that he was also a dowser, and that he was finding underground veins of water at sacred sites in Britain.

In 1969, a book by British dowser Guy Underwood, *The Pattern of the Past*, was published posthumously by the executors of his estate. It was the first book devoted to what one dowser found at sacred sites. Underwood dowsed all kinds of curving patterns that in one way or another conformed to the site itself. He had various names for these lines: aquastats, track lines and water lines, to name but a few. While this book has been widely read by dowsers studying what has come to be known as the Earth Energies, not many have pursued Underwood's findings; however, many have found that Allender Smith's veins of water are integrally connected with sacred space.

Underground water is only one of the things that dowsers find at sacred sites. Another type of energy that is found by many dowsers is based on the work of another Englishman, Alfred Watkins. During the early decades of this century he discovered that ancient sacred sites

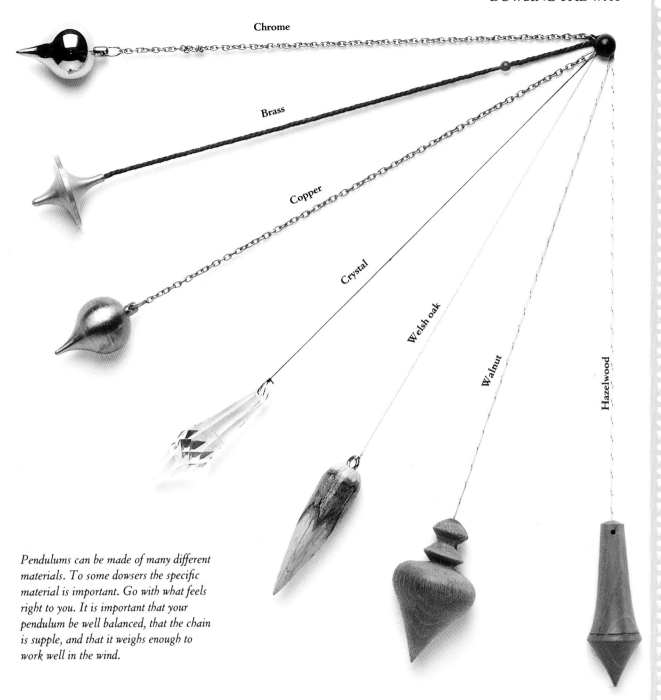

Chrome

Brass

Copper

Crystal

Welsh oak

Walnut

Hazelwood

Pendulums can be made of many different materials. To some dowsers the specific material is important. Go with what feels right to you. It is important that your pendulum be well balanced, that the chain is supple, and that it weighs enough to work well in the wind.

are connected along straight lines in the land. He called these alignments 'leys' and wrote about them in his book, *The Old Straight Track*. While Watkins himself was not a dowser, many people have found energy associated with these leys. In the 1930s, for example, Glastonbury psychic Dion Fortune wrote about straight lines of energy that she perceived, and in the late 1960s American dowser Terry Ross brought the notion of dowseable leys to the United States.

These straight lines of energy, six to eight feet wide, are now called energy leys to differentiate them from Watkins' alignments of holy sites; while energy leys often run concurrently with Watkins' leys, sometimes they do not. Energy leys are described as having yang (masculine) energy, while underground water has yin (feminine) energy.

British dowser Tom Graves has dowsed for energy patterns at a number of sacred sites in recent years. He has found 'overgrounds' that seem to resemble energy leys, and inside stone circles he has found concentric rings of energy which he initially called haloes. He has since come to feel that, instead of rings, what he was actually finding was a spiral of energy going round and round, in towards the centre. Cornish dowser Hamish Miller also finds spirals at sacred sites.

Other dowsers have found different patterns of energy at sacred sites, including Maltese crosses, clusters of circles similar to a bunch of grapes, grids of straight lines.

DOWSING TODAY

So, given all these different experiences, what exactly is it that dowsers find at sacred sites? I have been dowsing for over 30 years now, and have been using this skill at sacred sites for about 20 years. I consistently find Reginald Allender Smith's undergound veins of water and Terry Ross's energy leys crossing at the centre of sacred spaces as far apart as Machu Picchu in Peru, the circular underground kivas of the Anasazi in the American south-west, the underground stone chambers of New England, the stone circles and long barrows of Britain, the high altar of Chartres Cathedral in France, and the stone labyrinths of Sweden. While I am consistent in my findings, it would be less than candid of me if I did not also say that very few other Earth Energy dowsers find what I do. Divination by dowsing is an extremely individual

thing. Each dowser seems to find something different. As a result, I have come to the conclusion that, unless they were trained by the same teacher, no two dowsers will find the same thing in sacred space.

This, I believe, is the challenge that dowsing faces in the 1990s. We all 'see' the energies differently. We all bring to the sacred our own individual level of consciousness. We also all come with our own expectations and, as a result, we each see different parts of the whole. This is anathema to modern science where repeatability is the key. A scientist would say, 'I ought to be able to find exactly the same thing that you do at a given sacred site.' But this just is not the case.

It's the same with any form of divination. No two people would read the tea-leaves in the bottom of a cup in exactly the same way (unless, perhaps, they too were trained by the same teacher). No two readers of Tarot cards would read a given spread in exactly the same way. Divination is an art, not a science, and divining in sacred space leads the dowser to exactly what he or she needs.

Sacred spaces are places on this Earth where the location itself enhances the possibility of spiritual growth. If I were new to dowsing and I came to a sacred space like one of the places mentioned in this chapter, I would take out my dowsing tool of choice and say, 'Point to the spot on this site where it would benefit me the most to be right now.' Then I'd go there and see what happens.

MODERN RESTATEMENTS

An Overview of Contemporary Systems

Eileen Campbell

As the modern world has become ever more complex, we have as human beings become less in touch with the rhythms of life and our inner selves. While much of our technology provides us with the illusion of being in control of our lives, we know that unexpected change and upheaval are constants that cannot be controlled. Divination tools, however, can be rather like the weather forecast for the sailor. They can help us navigate our lives, increasing our awareness about favourable and unfavourable times – past, present and future. Divination helps us to use our intuition so that we can harmonize our actions and face what may befall us or indeed deal with what has already happened. At one level fortune-telling (human beings naturally tend to want to know what might happen to them), at its highest level divination is about what is best for psychological and spiritual growth. Even when times are difficult, there is always positive action which can be taken.

In recent years many completely newly devised systems, based on old lore, have been made available. Ironically, it is we in the West who have been busily devising new systems, while in some parts of the world the ancient systems continue to be used.

Almost every method of divination is a philosophy about the world presented in a series of symbols. Ancient cultures provide the basis for many of the new systems of divination, and I will review some examples of these in this chapter (derived from the Germanic tribes of pre-Christian Europe, the Celts, the Greeks, the Tibetans and the Native Americans).

Some new divination methods are intentionally more popular in appeal, though often grounded in an older philosophy or esoteric art. So I look at *The Astrology Kit, Know Yourself Through Colour, The Crystal Oracle, The Phoenix Cards, The Pendulum Kit* and *The Russian Gypsy Fortune-Telling Cards*.

Finally, since Tarot has proved one of the most popular divination systems of all, and since there has been a proliferation of Tarot decks in recent years, this chapter gives a flavour of some of the most exciting decks now available.

SYSTEMS BASED ON ANCIENT CULTURES

RUNES

Runes were the magical alphabet used by the Germanic tribes of pre-Christian Europe to ward off enemies and diseases, or to promote good health or fertility. Today in their revived form they are helpful in all kinds of problem solving.

Two rune sets have been developed in recent years, the first and probably the most successful being *The Book of Runes* by Ralph Blum and the more recent one being *Rune Stones* by D. Jason Cooper. Each consists of 25 rune stones (24 lettered and one blank) and both include accompanying books which give detailed descriptions of the history of runes and the various methods of using them. Several spreads are given in D. Jason Cooper's book, including the Celtic Spread invented by A.E. Waite for the Tarot. Ralph Blum also gives a number of spreads, such as the Three Rune Spread, the Runic Cross, and Rune Poker. D. Jason Cooper's accompanying book gives instructions for the making of magical talismans and practical exercises for ritual magic using runes. Both give details of how to make a personal rune set.

There are two main methods of using the rune stones. Either put them in a bag or container and shake them, focusing on the question, and then pull out however many are required for a particular spread. Or stand in a circle marked on the ground, focus on the question and toss the rune stones, and see where they land. The closer they are to you, the more significant they are in answering your question. They are interpreted according to where they fall in relation to the inquirer and to other rune stones.

CELTIC ORACLES

To the Celts all trees were sacred. Every tree was an image of the Cosmic Tree, which was itself a symbol of the universe with its three worlds, representing the underlying basis of Celtic spirituality. The qualities and virtues of the major sacred trees were incorporated into an alphabet of twenty letters, the Ogams (see Chapter Three, By Stick and Stone).

The Ogam alphabet is one of the oldest systems of writing still in existence. It was almost certainly used by the Druids as long ago as the sixth century BC, although they probably inherited it from an even older tradition. At some stage the letters of the alphabet were given names, taken from trees or plants.

There is evidence to suggest that Ogam was used in divination, and working from this Colin and Liz Murray created *The Celtic Tree Oracle*, an excellent modern system of divination using a variety of meanings for each of the letters. These are presented as a set of 25 cards, painted by Vanessa Card and showing the tree or plant in question together with its Ogam letter. These are shuffled and laid out in a square. Cards are then turned over at random to produce a reading which

is entered on a record sheet ready for detailed interpretation. According to the positions of the cards on a spread-sheet, various meanings are set forth and internal patterns of relationship drawn up.

Another modern interpretation of Ogam divination is *The Celtic Oracle* by Nigel Jackson and Nigel Pennick, again containing 25 cards: twenty cards represent the tree-letters of the Ogam alphabet; one card – the White Roebuck – represents a Celtic tree, and stands for the mistletoe, the holiest plant of the Druids; four other cards are the Four Holy Treasures of the gods of Celtic tradition, corresponding to the four elements, and are like the four Tarot suits.

The Ogam letters are ordered magically – B L N F S H D T C Q M G NG St R A O U E I – and the meaning of one letter leads on to the next. Each letter has a name, which is the traditional Irish name of a tree. It also has a number of correspondences, for example the first Ogam letter is Beth, the letter B, which represents the birch tree. Its deities are the White Goddess, Belin; its bird is the pheasant; its animal the white cow; its herb is the Fly Agaric mushroom; its colour is white; its uses are for cradles, broomsticks and yule logs.

The book accompanying the deck in *The Celtic Oracle* gives a description of all 25 cards, with correspondences and meanings, upright and reversed, and provides the necessary information on interpretation. A number of spreads are given, from the simple Three Weavers Spread through to more complicated spreads like the Thirteen Treasures Spread.

OLYMPUS: SELF-DISCOVERY AND THE GREEK ARCHETYPES

This is a do-it-yourself psychoanalysis system which anyone can use. Devised by Murry Hope, it

makes the ancient Greek wisdom available to everyone who would like to know themselves better.

Within Greek mythology is embedded a profound understanding of human psychology. In *Olympus* Murry Hope breaks down the psychological meaning of the various myths and characters and translates them into modern terms, providing a system to help us discover the real truth about ourselves, our friends and our associates.

Olympus was the home of the gods, but it represents a state of mind that can be achieved when we have overcome the imbalances which are naturally associated with the human condition. The gods had a right to reside on Olympus because of the deeds and labours which enabled them to achieve immortality, immortality here meaning a state of mental equilibrium or self-mastery.

Olympus contains 36 cards illustrated by Anthea Toorchen, together with a guide book. The 36 cards comprise:

> *The Twelve Olympians – who represent the major gods of Olympus (Zeus, Hera, etc.), exemplifying archetypal principles.*
> *The Three Tutors – who represent the lessons we need to assimilate in life and the instructions that might prove of benefit to us (in classical mythology, both mortals and immortals were tutored by non-humans who often assumed the form of fabulous beasts like Chiron the centaur, Silenus the satyr or the goat-footed Pan).*
> *The Four Heroes – who represent the four humours: sanguine, choleric, phlegmatic and melancholic. Although most of us are a mixture of all four types, one may be more appropriate than the others.*
> *The Seventeen Indicators – who represent a variety of mythological characters such as Gorgons, Sirens, Fates, etc. These will help highlight some hopes and fears.*

There are two methods of consulting *Olympus*: The Greek Key – used for a mini self-analysis or to gain insight into a problem or question; The Maze, or Labyrinth – used for an in-depth analysis or to ascertain future trends.

THE CELTIC BOOK OF THE DEAD

The Celtic stories of the Voyage to the Otherworld, known as the '*immrama*' (mystical voyages), are comparable to the better known Egyptian and Tibetan books of the dead. These stories, with their guardians and entities who sit at the boundaries between life and death and guard, guide and challenge, can teach us about death, and ease the transition between the states of living and dying. They also teach us better ways of living, and can now be used as a divination tool by those facing problems or decisions in life.

Caitlín Matthews has used the Voyage of Maelduin to devise *The Celtic Book of the Dead*. Maelduin travels across the water to the West, in keeping with Celtic tradition, to discover his destiny. Like Homer's *Odyssey*, this is a voyage of self-discovery. The 42 cards of the Immram deck, exquisitely executed by Danuta Mayer, depict the experiences of the voyage of the soul and the otherworldly islands, and so we have images both magnificent and terrifying, e.g. the Islands of Singing Birds and Plenteous Salmon and the Islands of Cannibal Horses and Fiery Pigs. These cards are laid out on the reading cloth, according to the spread used.

In the accompanying book there is a full translation of the Voyage of Maelduin, plus a shortened prose retelling and commentary. Each card is reproduced in the book and the Celtic background and the divinatory meaning are provided together with a challenge for the querent to address. There are 33 otherworldly destinations and two guide cards which represent the soul friends of the voyager who show us the otherworldly wonders. In addition there are seven gift cards, each of which represents an empowering aspect of the Otherworld. There are two ways of consulting *The Celtic Book of the Dead*: choose the Outward Passage (Immram One), which has nine positions arranged as a journey, when seeking an answer to a problem or situation; and choose the Homeward Passage (Immram Two), which reverses the course of Immram One, when you have a good idea of the circumstances surrounding the situation, but feel uncertain how to proceed.

The Celtic Book of the Dead is intended as a guide to be consulted in times of crisis and explores the inner quest for meaning. However, it can also be used in two further ways: for shamanic journeying, to find empowerment and assistance, to seek information and to help bring healing from the Otherworld into this; and for soul-leading, to conduct the dying person from this world to the other so that fear of the unknown is lessened.

MO: TIBETAN DIVINATION SYSTEM

The Tibetans have consulted oracles of various kinds throughout their history and the teachings of the Buddha are part and parcel of the life of the Tibetans. MO, which is one of the ways an answer to a predicament or an insight into a problem can be gained, should not be seen as separate from the teachings of the Buddha.

The system of MO is compiled from the sacred scriptures by the great saint and scholar, Jamgon Mipham. It comprises a divination manual, translated from the Tibetan by Jay L. Goldberg and Lobsang Dakpa, together with 36 MO cards (beautifully illustrated by Doya Nardin), and one Tibetan dice. The method calls for you first to visualize the form of Manjushri, the Bodhisattva of Wisdom, in the sky in front of you and to invoke his blessing so that you can receive a clear answer to your enquiry. Having recited his mantra (sacred sound) and another mantra, provided in the divination manual, you throw the dice twice, and thus obtain one of the possible 36 answers.

MEDICINE CARDS AND SACRED PATH CARDS

Realizing that most human beings in the modern world are out of touch with Nature, Jamie Sams and David Carson decided to create a set of cards with pictures on them that would key the seeker back into the traditional wisdom that comes from contact with the natural world. They therefore devised the first system of Native American divination based on the teachings of the animals. The *Medicine Cards* are beautifully illustrated with 44 animals that have been used by Native Americans as guides and teachers. The primary strength or characteristic of each animal is described in the accompanying book.

A Medicine Card can be drawn as a lesson for the day, or for a longer period of time (for example at the start of a new year). The questioner can also pick several cards to lay out as a spread. Each animal's lesson sheds new understanding on any given situation, and will assist the seeker in coming to decisions or choosing how to grow.

The *Sacred Path Cards*, created by Jamie Sams, cover the initiation steps that every human being has to learn on the path to wholeness. The 44 cards in this pack have Native American symbols that each hold a special Medicine. There is a history of each one so that the reader can understand how the Medicine of each symbol came into being. The Counting Coup card, for example, is an old tradition in which victory over an enemy was celebrated. In modern times our victories are different, and might include breaking a habit or developing our intuition.

These two packs can be used in conjunction with each other to create double meanings that give a deeper level of understanding. For example, the Raven Medicine Card (which teaches that magic is a shift in consciousness) combined with the Counting Coup Sacred Path Card shows that the seeker has been victorious in shifting an old way of looking at things and perhaps reclaimed the magic of being alive due to this new attitude.

A VOICE FROM THE EARTH: THE CARDS OF WINDS AND CHANGES

This is a new divination system created by Judith Pintar, a story-teller and musician, who served a four-year apprenticeship with an Ojibwe medicine woman.

Drawing on ideas and images from the Native American peoples of the Great Lakes and Canada, whose traditions demonstrate an awareness of the unique spiritual wisdom of the Earth and the importance of its preservation, Judith Pintar has designed the 49-card deck to be used as a tool to regain balance in our lives.

The deck comprises seven suits, or Winds, representing the seven directions: East, South, West, North, Earth, Great Spirit, and Here and Now. There are seven cards, or Changes, in each suit. They also represent the seven directions, but are named for the spiritual energy of that direction: Vision, Incarnation, Transformation, Transcendence, Gaia, All That Is, Stillness.

There are seven primary cards in the deck. A primary card occurs when both the Wind and Change of a card represent the same direction, so the primary card of Vision is the East/Vision card, and so on.

The deck is accompanied by a book which has a detailed guide to the Cards of Winds and Changes with instructions on how to interpret, and also contains stories, advice and songs. The questioner can use a spread of seven cards, or pick a card at random.

POPULAR DIVINATION SYSTEMS

THE ASTROLOGY KIT

We all know what our Sun-sign is and will probably read what a particular columnist in a newspaper or magazine predicts for the week, but this is a far cry from astrology proper, which is both a science and an art. Yet not all of us are in a position to visit an astrologer and have our chart drawn up and interpreted. However, with *The Astrology Kit*, based on the work of Grant Lewi (a very successful astrologer in his day), everyone can cast their own horoscope in about 15 minutes, without having to have any astrological knowledge.

The Astrology Kit consists of: an introductory book, 'How to Cast a Horoscope', which contains the Table of Years (or Ephemeris, as it is known in astrological circles) covering the years 1900–1999, with a page for each year, showing the aspects between the Sun, Moon and planets for each day; a printed Personal Notepad, on which to write down details about the positions of the Sun and Moon in the chart and the basic conjunctions and aspects, so that it can then be looked up in the Book of Readings; a Zodiac Wheel, a colourful circular device divided into the 12 signs with 36 numbered divisions, with a moving inner circle containing squares and triangles, accompanied by a special marker pen for writing in the position of the planets; A Book of Readings – the horoscope interpretations.

The kit is fun and easy to use both for oneself and for friends. All you need to know is your birthdate.

KNOW YOURSELF THROUGH COLOUR

We are all affected by colour far more than we realize, and there are many ways in which colour can be used to benefit ourselves and others. The Ancient Egyptians knew all about the healing power of colour and the virtues of the seven rays:

Red Ray	The Spirit of Life
Orange Ray	The Spirit of Health and Purity
Yellow Ray	The Spirit of Knowledge and Wisdom
Green Ray	The Spirit of Evolution
Blue Ray	The Spirit of Truth
Indigo Ray	The Spirit of Power with Knowledge
Violet Ray	The Spirit of Sacrifice and High Ideals

Marie Louise Lacy, an experienced colour therapist, devised this divination tool of 28 Colour Keys, through which we can learn more about ourselves. The Colour Keys are 28 coloured cards, seven of which are one colour, five of which have a clear top and a colour below, and 16 of which show dual colours. The cards can be used for divinatory readings, through which we can discover where our attributes lie and can remedy deficiencies occurring in any of the four realms – physical, emotional, mental and spiritual.

Accompanying the 28 colour cards is a full-colour chart and a book. The book describes methods of bringing colour into our lives, the ways of using colour for healing, the deeper meaning of numbers when linked to the colours, how decor and design can help transform negative energy, and the influence of different colours throughout the day. Methods of reading and instructions for interpretation are provided.

THE CRYSTAL ORACLE

Throughout history crystals have been endowed with powers both to heal and protect. Worn in jewellery and armour, adorning crowns and sceptres, many myths and legends are associated with crystals.

Devised by Leroy Montana, Linda Waldron and Kathleen Jonah, *The Crystal Oracle* can be used to answer questions, seek guidance or provide a message for the day ahead. It comprises five semi-precious stones, to which various qualities are attributed:

amethyst   spirituality, justice, creativity
aquamarine   happiness, clarity
carnelian   self, current conditions
rose quartz health, prosperity
tourmaline   power, activity

The Crystal Oracle contains a velvet casting cloth divided into 15 sections and a book giving full instructions on how to use and interpret it.

Crystals are unique in that they have a geometrically perfect atomic structure, and they also have electrical properties, something which modern technology has capitalized on. This electric potential is tapped in the Crystal Oracle, each of the five crystals having a complementary function:

amethyst   receiver
aquamarine   tuner
carnelian   earth
rose quartz transmitter
tourmaline   amplifier

Leroy Montana has described the Crystal Oracle as a New Age radio set! When the crystals are held in the hand, they receive electrical impulses from the brain, and then conduct that energy to the casting cloth. Whether this is the case or not, the Crystal Oracle is certainly great fun to use. It is consulted by holding the crystals in one hand, palm down, a few inches above the cloth. The question is asked of the crystals, which are then allowed to drop on to the cloth. Each one will fall on or near 15 points of reference or the centre. According to where the crystals land (there are rules for where and how they fall), there is a message or reading. There are 140 possible readings contained in the accompanying book.

THE PHOENIX CARDS

This is the first method of divination created specifically for exploring past-life influences. We all experience particular affinities for different places, times and cultures, and it may be that this has been carried over from some previous existence. Unexplained fears may be based on karmic memories, puzzling aspects of our personalities may be a hangover from something unresolved in an earlier incarnation. In all kinds of ways we are influenced by our past lives.

The Phoenix Cards were created by psychic and artist Susan Sheppard and illustrated by Toni Taylor. The 28 cards draw on ancient monuments and symbols of many cultures, and each represents a spiritual symbol. They are designed to trigger memories and feelings from previous lifetimes, and thus help unravel past-life experiences. They are consulted by choosing seven cards to which you feel drawn, and then meditating on them.

THE PENDULUM KIT

Dowsing is a way of balancing our rational and intuitive selves. Also called divining, dowsing generally employs a swinging pendulum to find answers to questions.

This divination kit contains a brass pendulum and a cord. It also contains an instruction book by Sig Lonegren, complete with charts, maps and exercises. Finding underground water, recovering a lost object, forecasting the weather, discovering which foods are best for your health or which particular healing remedy to use – all these are possible using *The Pendulum Kit*.

RUSSIAN GYPSY FORTUNE-TELLING CARDS

This is one of the most beautiful of recent divination packages. Based on the authentic Gypsy teachings of nineteenth-century Russia, the 25 large-format cards are illustrated in the Russian 'Palekh' style by Kathleen M. Skelly and Svetlana Alexandrovna Touchkoff.

The cards divide diagonally into four quarters, and when they are laid out in five rows and swivelled, they can form a picture card from two quarters. There are 50 complete pictures, and the meaning of each picture is contained in the elegant hardback book packaged together with the cards.

Svetlana Alexandrovna Touchkoff acquired the cards from her mother (her grandmother had also used such cards). They originated from the south-western part of Russia and are a blend of Gypsy wisdom and Russian folklore, using simple and universal symbols:

animals e.g. fox, bear, dog
natural landscape e.g. mountains, forest, moon
Christian images (though not exclusively so) e.g. lily, bread, angel

The person asking the question lays out five rows of five cards each, turning the cards in any direction to see if they form pictures with the adjacent cards. Particular attention is paid to the last card, which consolidates the meaning of the reading. The accompanying book provides an interpretation for the picture itself and for each of the four positions in which the picture lies.

TAROT DECKS

Often used to foretell the future, like all divination methods Tarot is also a powerful tool for exploring the subconscious. Prior to the 1970s there were really only two main Tarot decks in general use – the Tarot de Marseilles and the Rider-Waite deck, named after the publisher and A.E. Waite. In the past 20 years an enormous range of Tarot decks have been developed and are widely available. Tarot has proved to be very adaptable because it consists of images rather than text.

ESOTERIC TAROTS

From the end of the eighteenth century when Antoine Court de Gebelin claimed that the Tarot formed an ancient Egyptian book of wisdom, the Book of Thoth, there has been a steady stream of claims linking Tarot with various esoteric systems – with Cabbala, Rosicrucianism and with Masonic and Theosophical ideas. Members of the Order of the Golden Dawn had to create their own decks using MacGregor Mather's original deck (painted by Moira Mathers). The Thoth Tarot of Aleister Crowley and Lady Frieda Harris was published as a deck in 1969, although the paintings existed long before that.

The Magical Tarot, designed by Anthony Clark, is based primarily on Aleister Crowley, but also on John Dee's ideas, as well as being influenced by a quite different divination system, the *I Ching*. Anthony Clark has also collaborated on a more recent deck for the Servants of the Light, one of the leading schools of magical practice. The deck was begun by Jo Gill, who painted the Major Arcana. Under Dolores Ashcroft-Nowicki's direction (Dolores being the current head of the Servants of the Light), Anthony Clark completed the deck, combining magical and Cabbalistic insights.

The Enochian Tarot was created by Gerald and Betty Schueler and painted by Sallie Ann Glassman.

Based upon the principles of Enochian magic (a special branch of magic begun by John Dee and Edward Kelly), this deck actually has 86 cards rather than the usual 78. There are 30 regions or Aethyrs for the Major Arcana (instead of 22) and four suits for the Minor Arcana.

CULTURAL TAROTS

A recent development has been the devising of cultural Tarots, including cultures which had no previous connection with Tarot. Tarot is very much a Western system of divination, so it is fascinating that it can be taken and adapted to the symbols of quite different cultural traditions.

One of the first cultural Tarots to appear was Peter Balin's *Xultun Maya Tarot* in 1976. The cards are designed in the vivid and elaborate style of Mayan art, and something quite unique about this deck is the fact that the cards of the Major Arcana join together to make a single picture.

Another recent pack is *The Australian Contemporary Dreamtime Tarot*, devised by Keith and Daicon Courtney-Peto. This is based on the imagery and symbolism of the Australian Aborigines. The number of cards remains unchanged, and the division into Major and Minor Arcana and four suits is traditional, but the cards have acquired new names, drawn from the mythology of the Dreamtime. Thus the Fool is now called Karadji, the Lovers become Wejas and Strength is Thalera. The suits have become Muggils (Swords), Kundas (Staves), Coolamons (Cups) and Wariats (Pentacles). Full divinatory meanings are given in the accompanying booklet; for the Major Arcana this is extended to include gems, animals, plants or herbs, elements, musical notes, etc.

Since 1976 all kinds of cultural Tarots have appeared, from Egyptian, to Norse, to Tibetan (*The*

Secret Dakini Oracle) to Japanese (*Ukiyoe Tarot*). In *The Native American Tarot*, designed by Magda and J.A. Gonzalez, we have the lore of many of the native tribes of North America gathered in one deck: Apache, Arapaho, Cherokee, Cheyenne, Chippiwa, Comanche, Hopi, Huron, Inuit, Iroquois, Kiowa, Navaho, Pagamo, Pima, Pueblo, Shawnee, Sioux and Yaqui – and this is a partial listing!

MYTH AND STORY-TELLING TAROTS

Some recent decks are based on myth and story. *The Celtic Tarot*, designed by Courtney Davis, draws on Celtic myth and legend. The popular *Merlin Tarot*, designed by Bob Stewart and illustrated by Miranda Gray, again uses Celtic imagery and myth in showing the esoteric myths of the British tradition, but is also very much designed as a story-telling Tarot.

Another myth-orientated Tarot is *The Mythic Tarot*, devised by Juliet Sharman-Burke and Liz Greene and illustrated by Tricia Newell. This takes its inspiration entirely from Greek myths. It consists of the usual 78 cards, divided into Major and Minor Arcana, each of which retains its normal title. However, the designs show deities and heroes/heroines from classical tradition, so that the Fool becomes the god Dionysus, Justice is Athena with her owl, and the Heirophant is the wise centaur Chiron.

The Jungian Tarot is an unusual deck, devised by the distinguished Tarot expert Robert Wang. It derives from the system of psychological archetypes discovered by the great Swiss psychologist C.G. Jung (1875–1961). These correspond to certain basic patterns seen as present within every individual, regardless of culture or background. The cards retain their traditional names and order, but are interpreted in Jungian terms. Thus the Empress and Emperor are designated the Father and Mother, while Death becomes 'Mother as Gateway' and the Star is the Virgin Daughter. The four suits represent different stages on the Jungian path to individuation, which we might understand as enlightenment. The Five of Cups is thus designated as Troubles, and the Seven of Swords as Love. The marriage of these two important systems provides a set of visual glyphs of the modern psychological movement, as well as showing once again how varied and deep-rooted the Tarot symbolism is. The accompanying handbook includes a 34-week course in personal study, aimed at opening up an inner awareness of individual archetypes.

Undoubtedly the best example of a myth and story-telling Tarot is *The Arthurian Tarot*. Designed by Western tradition experts John and Caitlín Matthews, and again illustrated by Miranda Gray (although this time in a more mature style), *The Arthurian Tarot* is based on the legends, history and tradition of Arthurian Britain. The Arthurian stories are not just literary inventions but arise from the mythic and oral traditions of Britain. The Greater Powers (the Major Arcana) feature such characters as the Lady of the Lake, the Wounded King, the Green Knight, whilst the Lesser Powers (the Minor Arcana), the Suits of Swords, Spear, Grail and Stone, are the empowering objects of the Quest.

WOMEN'S TAROTS

Again the fact that the Tarot works through images rather than text has enabled it to be taken up and designed by women for women. Concerned with feminine values, these Tarots describe the experiences of women and hark back to an earlier, pre-patriarchal period of history.

Vicki Noble's *Motherpeace* deck is perhaps the best known, its very roundness symbolizing a different approach to life. It is full of images, drawn by Karen Vogel, of ancient goddesses, and seeks a woman-centred spirituality. The *Barbara Walker Tarot* comes from the illustrations she created for her book *Secrets of the Tarot*. Again, goddesses and ancient rituals feature, as well as figures from the Grail stories. An exciting new Tarot is *The Shining Woman Tarot*, devised and designed by Rachel Pollack, based on the world-wide traditions of shamanism.

PUBLICATION DETAILS OF THE SYSTEMS DESCRIBED

Ashcroft-Nowicki, Dolores, *The Servants of the Light Tarot*, London, Aquarian, 1991.

Balin, Peter, *The Xultún Tarot: The Maya Tarot Deck*, Wilmot, Wisconsin, Arcana Publishing, 1976.

Blum, Ralph, *The New Book of Runes*, London, Headline, 1990.

Clark, Anthony, *The Magical Tarot*, London, Aquarian, 1992.

Cooper, D. Jason, *Rune Stones: A Comprehensive Introduction to the Art of Runecraft*, London, Aquarian, 1990.

Courtney-Peto, Keith and Daicon, *The Australian Contemporary Dreamtime Tarot*, Queensland, Goldrope, 1991.

Davis, Courtney, *The Celtic Tarot*, London, Aquarian, 1990.

Goldberg, Jay L. and Dakpa, Lobsang, MO: *Tibetan Divination System*, Ithaca, New York, Snow Lion, 1990.

Hope, Murry, *Olympus: Self-Discovery and the Greek Archetypes*, London, Aquarian, 1991.

Jackson, Nigel and Pennick, Nigel, *The Celtic Oracle*, London, Aquarian, 1992.

Lacey, Marie Louise, *Know Yourself Through Colour*, London, Aquarian, 1989.

Lonegren, Sig, *The Pendulum Kit*, New York, Simon & Schuster, 1990; London, Virgin, 1992.

Matthews, Caitlín, *The Celtic Book of the Dead*, New York, St Martins Press, 1992; London, Aquarian, 1992.

Matthews, John and Caitlín, *The Arthurian Tarot*, London, Aquarian, 1990.

Montana, Leroy, Waldron, Linda and Jonah, Kathleen, *The Crystal Oracle*, London, Aquarian, 1989.

Murray, Liz and Colin, *The Celtic Tree Oracle*, London, Rider, 1988.

Noble, Vicki, *The Motherpeace Tarot*, New York, US Games, 1981.

Pintar, Judith, *A Voice from the Earth: The Cards of Winds and Changes*, London, Unwin Hyman, 1990; New York, Stirling, 1990.

Pollack, Rachel, *The Shining Woman Tarot*, London, Aquarian, 1992.

Sams, Jamie, *Sacred Path Cards: The Discovery of Self Through Native Teachings*, San Francisco, HarperCollins, 1990.

Sams, Jamie and Carson, David, *Medicine Cards: The Discovery of Power Through the Ways of Animals*, Santa Fe, Bear and Co., 1988.

Schuel, Gerald and Betty, *The Enochian Tarot*, St Paul, Minnesota, Llewellyn, 1989.

Sharman-Burke, Juliet and Greene, Liz, *The Mythic Tarot*, London, Rider, 1986.

Sheppard, Susan, *The Phoenix Cards: Reading and Interpreting Past-Life Influences with the Phoenix Deck*, Rochester, Vermont, Destiny, 1990.

Skelly, Kathleen M. and Touchkoff, Svetlana Alexandrovna, *Russian Gypsy Fortune-Telling Cards*, San Francisco, HarperCollins, 1990.

Stewart, R.J., *The Merlin Tarot*, London, Aquarian, 1988.

Walker, Barbara, *The Barbara Walker Tarot*, New York, US Games, 1986.

Wang, Robert, *Jungian Tarot Set*, Neuhausen, Urania Verlag, 1988.

THE CONTRIBUTORS

Eileen Campbell read history at the University of Reading in the 1960s. Since that time she has travelled extensively and studied all kinds of traditions and philosophies. A leading New Age publisher, she has been responsible for the publication of many important books and has published many of the modern divination systems. She has written and broadcast on the New Age and has compiled a series of successful inspirational anthologies, which include *A Dancing Star* (1991) and *A Lively Flame* (1992).

James G. Cowan is a distinguished author and poet. He has spent much of his life exploring the world of traditional peoples such as the Berbers, the Tuareg, the Torres Strait Islanders, the Iban of Borneo, the Rajputs of the Sind and the Monks of Mount Athos. For the past ten years he has documented the spiritual life of the Australian Aborigines. In books such as *Mysteries of the Dreaming, Sacred Places, Letters from a Wild State* and *The Elements of Aboriginal Tradition* he unveiled their rich metaphysical perspective. He has lectured in England, the USA and India on similar themes. Other recent books include *The Painted Shore* and a translation of Rumi's odes to Shems of Tabriz, *Where Two Oceans Meet*.

Nevill Drury is a specialist in occult mythology, magical philosophy and shamanism. He has contributed numerous articles to periodicals and journals and is the author of over 20 books on esoteric thought, many of them published internationally. His books include *Don Juan, Mescalito and Modern Magic, Inner Visions, The Shaman and the Magician, The Elements of Shamanism* and, most recently, *The Visionary Human*. He holds a Master of Arts degree in anthropology.

Cherry Gilchrist is concerned with bringing back ancient knowledge into the light of day. Her books on alchemy, astrology, divination and feminine symbolism all reflect this. Cherry is both an author and a singer, directing the professional early music ensemble, Arcadia. She was the first to write about the connection between alchemy and the birth of baroque music, and her latest book investigates the nature of performance itself. Cherry holds a degree in English and anthropology from Cambridge University.

Judith Gleason received her PhD in comparative literature from Columbia University in 1963. Her thesis on African novels in English and French was subsequently published by Northwestern University. Combining field work with scholarly investigation, she has published several books on West African as well as Caribbean religion and oral traditions, most recently *Oya: In Praise of an African Goddess*. She lives and practises a Jungian-oriented psychotherapy in New York City.

Jay L. Goldberg is a Buddhist scholar and practitioner who has spent 17 years living in Asia, where he trained in Buddhist thought and the Tibetan language. He received his Masters degree in Indian philosophy at Banaras Hindu University and studied at the Sakya College where he engaged in translations of Tibetan texts. His recent books include *MO: Tibetan Divination System* and *The Beautiful Ornament of the Three Visions*, and he has previously had other books and texts of Tibetan translations published. He has translated for many Tibetan lamas during their lecture tours of Asia and North America, so his knowledge of Tibetan culture, customs and beliefs is extensive.

Marian Green is a leading exponent of the Western magical arts. She has edited *Quest*, a quarterly magazine on magical traditions, since 1970, and is the author of many books, including *Magic for the Aquarian Age, The Elements of Natural Magic, The Elements of Ritual Magic* and *A Witch Alone*. She runs training courses in the UK, USA and Europe on magic, divination, Celtic mythology, the Grail and Arthurian legends and witchcraft. She has broadcast on radio and television.

Alan Haymes' study of medieval history at university generated a deep interest in the underlying cultures of Northern Eurasia and initiated his research into the mythologies and shamanic traditions of the Indo-European, Uralic, Altaic and Paleo-Siberian speaking peoples. The importance of the wisdom of the ancestors and the links with the distant past has led him to appreciate the teachings of the 'perennial philosophy' and in particular the writings of the French thinker, René Guénon.

Prudence Jones has lectured widely on astrology and its history, and has conducted original research into ancient astronomy and calendars. She has contributed to books on astrology and has edited her own collection, *Creative Astrology: Experiential Understanding of the Birth Chart*. She is a practising psychotherapist, a Pagan priestess and a theologian. She edited, with Caitlín Matthews, *Voices from the Circle: The Heritage of Western Paganism* and is writing a history of Pagan Europe with Nigel Pennick.

Kunderke Kevlin (previously Kooijman) studied social anthropology at the Universities of Durban and Johannesburg, South Africa, and cultural anthropology at the University of Leiden. She did 18 months fieldwork among a Tswana tribe in Botswana, focusing on social-economic change. At Leiden University she changed her subject to the world-view, symbolism and religion of the Southern African tribes, particularly their divination systems.

Sig Lonegren was taught by his mother to dowse in 1960. He has been a student of sacred enclosures since the early 1970s, and has a Masters degree in Sacred Space, the study of pre-Protestant Reformation spiritual centres. He is the author of the *Earth Mysteries Handbook: Wholistic Non-Intrusive Data Gathering Techniques*, which discusses sacred geometry, archaeoastronomy and dowsing, *Spiritual Dowsing, The Pendulum Kit* and *Labyrinths: Ancient Myths and Modern Uses*.

John Matthews was born in the north of England in 1948. He has been a full-time writer for 12 years and has made the Arthurian field his own territory, exploring the grail mysteries, Arthurian legends and esoteric wisdom in his numerous books. His most recent publications include *Ladies of the Lake: A Study of the Feminine Archetypes in the Arthurian Tradition, Taliesin: Shamanism and the Bardic Mysteries in Britain and Ireland* and *Choirs of the God: Revisioning Masculinity.* He is an established lecturer and gives many talks in Europe and America.

Nigel Pennick is a writer and lecturer on ancient and modern mysteries, an authority on northern European geomancy, runemaster, practising geomant and traditional symbolic craftsman. A founder and co-ordinator of the Institute for Geomantic Research, he organized five Cambridge geomantic symposia and has co-ordinated an international conference on labyrinths. He has written many books, including *Secret Lore of Runes and Other Ancient Alphabets* and *The Celtic Oracle.*

Rachel Pollack was born in Brooklyn, New York. She has studied the Tarot for 20 years and has taught classes and workshops in England, USA and Europe. She is the author of several books, including *78 Degrees of Wisdom, The Open Labyrinth* and *The New Tarot.* She has also devised her own pack, *The Shining Woman Tarot.*

Valerie J. Roebuck read oriental studies at the University of Cambridge and is a specialist in the art and religion of India. She teaches Sanskrit and Comparative Religion, and has a keen interest in astrology, astronomy, myth and language. Her publications include *The Circle of Stars: An Introduction to Indian Astrology* and entries for *Who's Who of World Religion.*

Jamie Sams is a Native American medicine teacher and a member of the Wolf Clan teaching lodge of the Seneca Nation. She is of Iroquois and Choctaw descent, and has been trained in Seneca, Mayan, Aztec and Choctaw medicine. She has taught in England, France, Egypt, Kenya, Mexico, Peru and Guatemala, as well as in the United States. Her books include *Midnight Song: Quest for the Vanished Ones, Medicine Cards: The Discovery of Power Through the Ways of Animals* (with David Carson), *Sacred Path Cards: The Discovery of Self Through Native Teachings, Other Council Fires Were Here Before Ours* (with Twylah Nitsch) and *The Thirteen Original Clan Mothers: The Story of the Sisterhood and the Legacy of Woman.*

Bruce Scofield has earned a living as an astrological consultant since 1980. He maintains a private practice in Massachusetts, working with his clients by telephone and mail. He is the author of several books on astrology, including two on Mesoamerican astrology.

Norman Shine was born in London and has lived in Copenhagen since 1963. After graduating in history and psychology he became a civil service interpreter. He was subsequently associate professor of literature at the University of Cophenhagen and associate professor of intepreting and applied linguistics at the Copenhagen School of Economics. He is now a consultant numerologist and writer.

David Simmons was born in 1930 in New Zealand. He attended university in Auckland, Wellington, Paris and Rennes, obtaining a Master of Arts degree in anthropology and a Diploma in Celtic Studies. On his return to New Zealand he taught in secondary schools before taking up a post as Keeper in Anthropology at Otago Museum, Dunedin. He moved to Auckland Museum to become Ethnologist and later Assistant Director of Auckland Institute and Museum until 1986. He was co-curator of the Te Maori Exhibition which toured the USA, and he has been associated with many Maori projects. He has published books on Maori history and culture.

Peter Taylor is an exponent of the practical aspects of the perennial Magic Tradition, having a particular interest in the current resurgence of the Starry Wisdom – which, he believes, provides us with the means to return scientific endeavour to a proper basis in spiritual reality. He works with various magical symbol systems, including the Runes. The raw material for much of his writing comes from experimental magical work carried out in small groups.

Robert Temple is the author of seven books, which have been translated into a total of 43 languages. His first book, *The Sirius Mystery,* was a best-seller and dealt with mysterious aspects of the ancient world. *Conversations with Eternity* contained the first popular account of the techniques of extispicy (divination by the entrails). Temple's extensive studies in the subjects of trance and hypnosis appeared in his book *Open to Suggestion.* His latest book, *He Who Saw Everything,* is a modern translation of the Epic of Gilgamesh, with notes and commentary. Temple is also a television producer with his own independent production company.

John Turpin is a minister of Ifa, a Babaláwo, in the tradition of the Yoruba of southwest Nigeria. He was ordained in Ijabu Remo, Nigeria, in 1980. This ordination was the culmination of a six-year period of study and training in the United States, Europe and Africa, and began the period of his active ministry in the United States. In 1991 he founded the Temple Orunmila and the Center for Ifa Studies in Oakland, California.

Derek Walters was born in Manchester in 1936, and lives in Manchester and London. In later life, after many years of fringe interest in Chinese culture, he has devoted his entire time to the study of Chinese astrology and philosophy. He is the author of several books, and has travelled widely throughout Southeast Asia. He is regarded as one of the Western world's foremost authorities on traditional Chinese divination, and has been admitted to the Hong Kong fraternity of diviners.

Jennifer Westwood has made a lifelong study of myth, legend, folktale and folklore. She graduated from Oxford and Cambridge universities in Anglo-Saxon and medieval Icelandic literature, and has since gone on to write several books on myth, folklore and legend. Her most recent publications include *Albion: A Guide to Legendary Britain* and *The Atlas of Legendary Places.* She gives frequent lectures and has appeared several times on radio and television.

FURTHER READING

CHAPTER ONE
SEERS AND HEALERS
(Shamanism)

Doore, G. (ed.), *Shaman's Path*, Boston, Shambhala, 1988.

Drury, N., *The Elements of Shamanism*, Shaftesbury, Element Books, 1989.

Eliade, M., *Shamanism*, New Jersey, Princeton University Press, 1972.

Furst, P.T. (ed.), *Flesh of the Gods*, London, Allen & Unwin, 1972.

Halifax, J. (ed.), *Shamanic Voices*, New York, Dutton, 1979.

Halifax, J., *Shaman: the Wounded Healer*, New York, Crossroad, 1982.

Harner, M. (ed.), *Hallucinogens and Shamanism*, New York, Oxford University Press, 1973.

Harner, M., *The Way of the Shaman*, San Francisco, Harper & Row, 1980.

Kalweit, H., *Dreamtime and Inner Space*, Boston, Shambhala, 1988.

Nicholson, S. (ed.), *Shamanism*, Illinois, Quest Books, 1987.

Wasson, R.G., *The Wondrous Mushroom*, New York, McGraw Hill, 1980.

CHAPTER TWO
THE FROZEN NORTH
(Arctic systems)

Bäckman, Louise and **Hultkrantz, Åke**, *Studies in Lapp Shamanism*, Stockholm, Stockholm Studies in Comparative Religion no.16, 1978.

Diszegi, Vilmos and **Hoppál, Mihály** (eds), *Shamanism in Siberia*, Budapest, Akademiai Kiado, 1978.

Hajdú, Petér (ed.), *Ancient Cultures of the Uralian Peoples*, Budapest, Corvina Press, 1976.

Hoppál, Mihály (ed.), *Shamanism in Eurasia*, Göttingen, Herodot, 1984.

Michael, Henry N. (ed.), *Studies in Siberian Shamanism*, Toronto, University of Toronto Press, 1963.

Oinas, Felix J., *Studies in Finnic Folklore*, Helsinki, Finnish Literature Society, 1985.

Pentikäinen, Juha, *Kalevala Mythology*, Indiana, Indiana University Press, 1989.

CHAPTER THREE
BY STICK AND STONE
(Celtic methods)

Calder, G., *Auraicept Na N-Eces (The Scholar's Primer)*, Edinburgh, John Grant, 1917.

Davidson, H.E. (ed.), *The Seer in Celtic and Other Traditions*, Edinburgh, John Donald, 1990.

Matthews, J., *The Celtic Shaman*, Shaftesbury, Element Books, 1991.

Matthews, J., *Taliesin: Shamanism and the Bardic Mysteries in Britain and Ireland*, London, Aquarian, 1991.

Matthews, J. 'Incubatory Sleep and Precognitive Dreaming in the Celtic World', *Psychology and the Spiritual Traditions*, ed. R.J. Stewart, Shaftesbury, Element Books, 1991.

Pennick, N., *The Secret Lore of Runes and Other Ancient Alphabets*, London, Rider, 1991.

Sutherland, E., *Ravens and Black Rain: the Story of Highland Second Sight*, London, Constable, 1985.

CHAPTER FOUR
THE MESSAGE OF THE RUNES
(Runes)

Byock, Jesse L., *The Saga of the Volsungs* (Introduction and Translation), Berkeley, University of California Press, 1990.

Elliott, R.W.V., *Runes*, Manchester, Manchester University Press, 1980.

Faulkes, Anthony (translator), *Edda*, Snorri Sturlson, London, Everyman Classics, J.M. Dent & Sons, 1987.

Hollander, Lee M., (translator), *The Poetic Edda*, Austin, University of Texas Press, 1990.

Pennick, Nigel, *Practical Magic in the Northern Tradition*, London, Aquarian, 1989.

Turville-Petre, E.O.G., *Myth and Religion in the North*, London, Weidenfeld & Nicolson, 1964.

CHAPTER FIVE
THE KEYS OF TAROT
(Tarot)

Fairfield, Gail, *Choice-Centered Tarot*, North Hollywood, California, Newcastle, 1985.

Foster Case, Paul, *The Tarot*, New York, Macoy, 1947.

Greer, Mary K., *Tarot For Yourself*, North Hollywood, California, Newcastle, 1984; UK edition: *Tarot Transformations*, London, Aquarian, 1987.

Kaplan, Stuart J., *Encyclopedia of Tarot*, Vols I-III, New York, US Games Systems Inc., vol. I 1978, vol. II 1985, vol. III 1986.

Knight, Gareth, *The Treasure House of Images*, London, Aquarian, 1986.

Pollack, Rachel, *Seventy-eight Degrees of Wisdom*, Parts 1 and 2, London, Aquarian, 1980 and 1983.

Pollack, Rachel, *The New Tarot*, London, Aquarian, 1989.

CHAPTER SIX
PATTERNS OF WESTERN ASTROLOGY
(Western astrology)

Baigent, M., **Campion, N.** and **Harvey, C.**, *Mundane Astrology*, London, Aquarian, 1991.

Barclay, Olivia, *Horary Astrology Rediscovered*, Pennsylvania, Whitford Press, 1990.

Campion, Nicholas, *An Introduction to the History of Astrology*, London, ISCWA, 1982.

Cozzi, Steve, *Planets in Locality*, St Paul, Minnesota, Llewellyn, 1988.

Doane, Doris Chase, *Profit by Electional Astrology*, Tempe, Arizona, American Federation of Astrologers, 1990.

Huntley, Janice, *The Elements of Astrology*, Shaftesbury, Element Books, 1991.

Parker, Derek and **Julia**, *The New Compleat Astrologer*, London, Mitchell Beazley, 1990.

Ridder-Patrick, Jane, *A Handbook of Medical Astrology*, London, Arkana, 1990.

CHAPTER SEVEN
CONSULTING THE ORACLES
(Classic systems)

Artemidorus, *The Interpretation of Dreams (Oneirocritica)*, trans. Robert J. White, New Jersey, Noyes Press, 1975.

Cicero, *On Divination (De Divinatione)*, trans. in vol. 154 of the Loeb Classical Library series, London, Heinemann, 1923.

Fontenrose, Joseph, *The Delphic Oracle*, Berkeley, University of California Press, 1978.

Meer, L.B. van der, *The Bronze Liver of Piacenza*, Amsterdam, J.C. Gieben, 1987.

Parke, H.W. and **Wormell, D.E.W.**, *The Delphic Oracle*, Oxford, Blackwell, 1939; new edition 1956.

Plutarch, *The E at Delphi, Oracles at Delphi No Longer Given in Verse* and *Obsolescence of Oracles*, trans. in vol. 306 of the Loeb Classical Library series, London, Heinemann, 1936.

Temple, Robert K.G., *Conversations With Eternity*, London, Rider, 1984.

Vitruvius, *On Architecture*, trans. in vols 251 and 280 of the Loeb Classical Library series, London, Heinemann, 1931 and 1934.

Weinstock, Stefan, 'Martianus Capella and the Cosmic System of the Etruscans', *Journal of Roman Studies*, London, Society for the Promotion of Roman Studies, vol. XXXVI, 1930, p. 122.

CHAPTER EIGHT
THE TREE OF LIFE
(Galgal)

Gilchrist, Cherry, *Divination: The Search for Meaning*, London, Dryad Press, 1987.

Halevi, Z'ev ben Shimon, *Kabbalah: Tradition of Hidden Knowledge*, London, Thames & Hudson, 1979.

Kaplan, Aryeh, *Meditation and Kabbalah*, York Beach, Maine, Samuel Weiser, 1982.

Knight, Gareth, *A Practical Guide to Qabalistic Symbolism*, Watford, Herts, Helios Books, 1965.

Parfitt, Will, *The Living Qabalah*, Shaftesbury, Element Books, 1988.

Scholem, Gerschom, *Major Trends in Jewish Mysticism*, New York, Schocken Books, 1971.

CHAPTER NINE
WISE WOMEN COUNSELLORS
(Popular methods)

Glass, Justine, *The Story of Fulfilled Prophecy*, London, Cassell, 1969.

Green, Marian, *A Calendar of Festivals*, Shaftesbury, Element Books, 1992.

Green, Marian, *A Witch Alone*, London, Aquarian, 1990.

Harding, M. Ester, *Women's Mysteries*, London, Rider, 1971; New York, Putnam, 1972.

Tindall, Gillian, *A Handbook on Witches*, London, Panther Books, 1967.

Valiente, Doreen, *Natural Magic*, London, Hale, 1975.

CHAPTER TEN
THE SEASONAL ROUND
(Folklore)

Aubrey, John, *Three Prose Works*, ed. John Buchanan-Brown, Fontwell, Centaur Press, 1972.

Hole, Christina, *English Folklore*, 2nd edition, revised, London, B.T. Batsford, 1944–5.

Leach, Maria and **Fried, Jerome** (eds), *Funk and Wagnall's Standard Dictionary of Folklore, Mythology and Legend*, New York, Harper & Row, 1984.

Opie, Iona and **Peter**, *The Lore and Language of Schoolchildren*, Oxford, Clarendon Press, 1959.

Radford, E. and **M.A.**, *Encyclopaedia of Superstitions*, edited and revised by Christina Hole, London, Hutchinson, 1961.

Thomas, Keith, *Religion and the Decline of Magic*, Harmondsworth, Peregrine Books, 1978.

CHAPTER ELEVEN
ORACLES IN BONE
(Southern Africa)

Dornan, Rev. S.S., 'Divination and Divining Bones', *South African Journal of Science*, vol. XX, pp.504–11, 1923–4.

Hunt, N.A., 'Some Notes on the Witchdoctor's Bones', *Nada*, XXVII, pp.40–46, 1950; XXXI, pp.16–23, 1954; XXXIX, pp.14–16, 1962.

Junod, H.A., 'La Divination au moyen de Tablettes d'Ivoire chez les Pedis', *Bull. Soc. Neuchat. Geogr.*, 34, pp.38–56, 1925.

Krige, E.J. and **Krige, J.D.**, *The Realm of the Rain Queen*, London, International African Institute, 1943.

Peek, M., (ed.), *African Divination Systems: Ways of Knowing*, Indiana, Indiana University Press, 1991.

Roberts, N., 'Bantu Methods of Divination: a Comparative Study', *South African Journal of Science*, vol. XIII, pp.397–408, 1917.

Tracey, H., 'The Hakata of Southern Rhodesia', *Nada*, XL, pp.105–7, 1963.

CHAPTER TWELVE
IFA
(A Yoruba system of oracular worship)

Abimbola, Wande, *Ifa Divination Poetry*, New York, Nok Publishers, 1977.

Bascom, William, *Ifa Divination*, Bloomington, Indiana University Press, 1969.

Fahd, Toufic, *La Divination Arab*, Leiden, Brill, 1966.

Idowu, E. Bolaji, *Olodumare: God in Yoruba Belief*, New York, Praeger, 1963.

Maupoil, Bernard, 'La Géomancie à l'Ancienne Côte des Esclaves', *Travaux et Mémoires de l'Institut d'Ethnologie*, XLII, Paris, 1943.

CHAPTER THIRTEEN
SACRED MEDICINE
(Native American systems)

Lake, Bobby Grislybear, *Native Healer*, Wheaton, Illinois, Theosophical Publishing House, 1991.

McGaa, Ed (Eagleman), *Mother Earth Spirituality*, San Francisco, HarperCollins, 1990.

Medicine Eagle, Brooke, *Buffalo Woman Came Singing*, New York, Ballantine, 1991.

Sams, Jamie, *Sacred Path Cards: The Discovery of Self Through Native Teachings*, San Francisco, HarperCollins, 1990.

Sams, Jamie and **Nitsch, Twylah**, *Other Council Fires Were Here Before Ours*, San Francisco, HarperCollins, 1991.

Sams, Jamie and **Carson, David**, *Medicine Cards: The Discovery of Power Through the Ways of Animals*, Santa Fe, Bear & Co., 1988.

A comprehensive list of books about Native Americans can be obtained from the University of Oklahoma Press, Norman, Oklahoma 73019, USA.

CHAPTER FOURTEEN
SUN, TIME AND SYMBOLISM
(Mesoamerican astrology)

Arguelles, Jose A., *The Mayan Factor*, Sante Fe, New Mexico, Bear & Co., 1987.

Aveni, Anthony F., *Skywatchers of Ancient Mexico*, Austin, University of Texas Press, 1980.

Aveni, Anthony F., *Empires of Time*, New York, Basic Books, 1989.

Burland, C.A., *The Gods of Mexico*, New York, Putnam, 1967.

Edmonson, Monro S., *The Book of the Year: Middle American Calendrical Systems*, Salt Lake City, University of Utah Press, 1988.

Sahagun, Fray Bernardino de, *Florentine Codex: A General History of the Things of New Spain, Books 4 and 5*, trans. C.E. Dibble and A.J.O. Anderson, Ogden, University of Utah Press, 1957.

Schele, Linda and **Freidel, David**, *A Forest of Kings: The Untold Story of the Ancient Maya*, New York, William Morrow, 1990.

Scofield, Bruce and **Cordova, Angela**, *The Aztec Circle of Destiny*, St Paul, Minnesota, Llewellyn, 1988.

Scofield, Bruce, *Day Signs: Native American Astrology from Ancient Mexico*, Amherst, Massachusetts, One Reed Publications, 1991.

Tedlock, Barbara, *Time and the Highland Maya*, Albuquerque, University of New Mexico Press, 1982.

Thompson, J. Eric S., *Maya Hieroglyphic Writing: An Introduction*, Norman, University of Oklahoma Press, 1960.

Two programs on Aztec astrology, including one that prints reports, are available from Astrolabe Software, Box 1750-R, Brewster, MA 02631, USA.

CHAPTER FIFTEEN
THE WAY OF THE EMPEROR
(Mah Jongg)

Loewe, Michael, *Ways to Paradise*, London, Allen & Unwin, 1979.

Millington, A.D., *The Complete Book of Mah Jongg*, London, Barker, 1977.

Walters, Derek, *Your Future Revealed by Mah Jongg*, London, Aquarian, 1982.

CHAPTER SIXTEEN
THE CHINESE BOOK OF CHANGES
(I Ching)

Blofeld, John, *I Ching*, London, George Allen & Unwin, 1965.

Legge, James, *The I Ching*, New York, Dover, 1963.

Loewe, Michael and **Blacker, Carmen** (eds), *Divination and Oracles*, London, George Allen & Unwin, 1979.

Moore, Stephen, *The Trigrams of Han: Inner Structures of the I Ching*: London, Aquarian, 1989.

Temple, Robert, *Conversations with Eternity: Ancient Man's Attempts to Know the Future*, London, Rider, 1984.

Wilhelm, Richard, *The I Ching or Book of Changes*, London, Penguin/Arkana, first edition 1951.

CHAPTER SEVENTEEN
DRAGON LINES IN THE LAND
(Feng Shui)

Eitel, E.J., *Feng Shui*, Trubner, 1873; reprinted Bristol, Pentacle Books, 1979.

Feuchtwang, Stephan, *An Anthropological Analysis of Chinese Geomancy*, Vientiane, Laos, Editions Vithagna, 1974.

Pirazzoli-T'Serstevens, Michele, *Living Architecture: Chinese*, London, Macdonald, 1972.

Walters, Derek, *Chinese Geomancy*, Shaftesbury, Element Books, 1991.

Walters, Derek, *The Feng Shui Handbook*, London, Aquarian, 1991.

CHAPTER EIGHTEEN
STAR LORE IN THE EAST
(Sidereal astrology)

Bhat, M. Ramakrishna, *Fundamentals of Astrology*, New Delhi, Motilal Banarsidass, 1967.

Filbey J. and **Filbey P.**, *The Astrologer's Companion*, London, Aquarian, 1986.

Oken, Alan, *Astrology; Evolution and Revolution; A Path to Higher Consciousness through Astrology*, New York, Toronto and London, Bantam, 1976.

Marinelli, Luciana, *Astrologia Indiana: Teoria e Pratica*, Rome, Edizione Mediterranee, 1983.

Pingree, David, *Jyotihśāstra: Astral and Mathematical Literature*, Otto Harrassowitz, in Jan Gonda, *A History of Indian Literature*, vol. VI, fasc. 4, Wiesbaden, 1981.

Quaritch Wales, H.G., *Divination in Thailand: the Hopes and Fears of a Southeast Asian People*, London, Curzon Press, 1983.

Robson, Vivian E., *The Fixed Stars and Constellations in Astrology*, London, Aquarian, 1969.

Roebuck, Valerie J., *The Circle of Stars: an Introduction to Indian Astrology*, Shaftesbury, Element Books, 1992.

CHAPTER NINETEEN
MIRRORS IN THE SKY
(Tibetan divination)

Avedon, John F., *In Exile From The Land Of Snows*, New York, Alfred A. Knopf, 1984.

De Nebesky-Wojkowitz, Rene, *Oracles and Demons of Tibet*, The Hague, Mouton & Co., Publ., 1956.

Goldberg, Jay L. and **Lobsang, Dakpa**, *MO: Tibetan Divination System*, Ithaca, NY, Snow Lion Publications, 1990.

Snellgrove, David and **Richardson, Hugh**, *A Cultural History of Tibet*, Boulder, CO, Prajna Press, 1980.

Stein, R.A., *Tibetan Civilization*, Stanford, Stanford University Press, CA, 1972.

Waddell, Austine L., *Tibetan Buddhism*, New York, Dover Publications, 1972.

CHAPTER TWENTY
WILD STONES
(Aboriginal divination)

Berndt, R.M. and **C.H.**, *The World of the First Australians*, Sydney, Ure Smith, 1976.

Cowan, James, *Mysteries of the Dreaming*, Bridport, Prism Press, 1988.

Cowan, James, *Letters from a Wild State*, Shaftesbury,

Element Books, 1990; New York, Bell Tower, 1992.

Cowan, James, *Sacred Places in Australia*, Sydney, Simon & Schuster, 1991.

Cowan, James, *The Elements of Aboriginal Tradition*, Shaftesbury, Element Books, 1992.

Elkin, A.P., *Aboriginal Men of High Degree*, Brisbane, University of Queensland Press, 1974.

CHAPTER TWENTY-ONE
ANCESTORS, GODS AND MEN
(Maori methods)

Oppenheim, Roger *Maori Death Customs*, Wellington, A.H. & A.W. Reed, 1973.

Servant, Catherin, *Customs and Habits of the New Zealanders 1838–1842* (ed. D.R. Simmons), Wellington, A.H. & A.W. Reed, 1973.

Simmons, David, 'Iconography of New Zealand Maori Religion', *Iconography of Religions II.I*, Leiden, E.J. Brill, 1986.

Stafford, Donald, *Te Arawa*, Auckland, Reed Books, 1991.

Te Rangi Hiroa (Sir Peter Buck), *The Coming of the Maori*, Wellington, Maori Purposes Fund Board, 1977.

CHAPTER TWENTY-TWO
COUNTING THE FUTURE
(Numerology)

Cheiro, Count Louis Hamon, *Cheiro's Book of Numbers: The Complete Science of Numerology*, New York, Prentice Hall Press, 1988.

Drayer, Ruth, *Numerology: The Language of Life*, El Paso, Texas, Skidmore-Roth Publishing, 1990.

Javane, Faith and **Bunker, Dusty**, *Numerology and the Divine Triangle*, West Chester, Penn., Whitford Press, 1979.

Johari, Harish, *Numerology with Tantra, Ayurveda, and Astrology: A Key to Human Behaviour*, Rochester, Vermont, Destiny Books, 1990.

Konraad, Sandor, *Numerology: Key to the Tarot*, Rochester, Vermont, Destiny Books, 1990.

CHAPTER TWENTY-THREE
ANCIENT SECRETS OF THE EARTH
(Geomancy)

Crowley, Aleister, *Magick in Theory and Practice*, Paris, Lecram, 1929.

Pennick, Nigel, *Madagascar Divination*, Cambridge, Fenris-Wolf, 1975.

Pennick, Nigel, *Secret Games of the Gods*, York Beach, Maine, Samuel Weiser, 1992.

Regardie, Francis Israel, *A Practical Guide to Geomantic Divination*, London, Aquarian, 1972.

Skinner, Stephen, *Terrestrial Astrology: Divination by Geomancy*, London, Routledge & Kegan Paul, 1980.

CHAPTER TWENTY-FOUR
DOWSING THE WAY
(Dowsing)

Agricola, Georgius, *De Re Metallica (On Metals)*, New York, Dover Publications, 1950; translated by Herbert Clark Hoover and Lou Henry Hoover.

Bird, Christopher, *The Divining Hand*, New York, E.P. Dutton, 1979.

Graves, Tom, *Needles of Stone Revisited*, Glastonbury, Gothic Image, 1986.

Graves, Tom (ed.), *Dowsing and Archaeology*, Wellingborough, Turnstone Press, 1908; a selection of articles from the *Journal of the British Society of Dowsers*.

Lonegren, Sig, *The Pendulum Kit*, New York, Simon & Schuster, 1990; Melbourne, Lothian, 1990; London, Virgin, 1992.

Lonegren, Sig, *Spiritual Dowsing*, Glastonbury, Gothic Image, 1986.

Ross, Edward T. and **Wright, Richard D.**, *The Divining Mind*, Rochester, Vermont, Destiny Books, 1990.

Underwood, Guy, *The Pattern of the Past*, New York, Abelard-Schuman, 1973.

Watkins, Alfred, *The Old Straight Track*, London, Abacus, 1974.

INDEX

ACKNOWLEDGEMENTS

Photographers

t = top   b = below   c = centre   l = left   r = right

2 Derek Jones; 4–5 Werner Forman Archive/Statens Historiska Museum, Stockholm; 9 Werner Forman Archive/National Museum of Man, Ottowa; 10–11t Robert Estall; 11tr Nevill Drury; 11b The Hutchison Library; 12 Werner Forman Archive; 13t Werner Forman Archive/The Danish National Museum; 13b Werner Forman Archive/The Anchorage Museum of the History of Art; 15t The Hutchison Library; 15b Nevill Drury; 16 Dr Elmar R. Gruber/The Fortean Picture Library; 26b Werner Forman Archive; 28 Derek Jones; 30 Monica Sjöo; 33, 37 C.M. Dixon; 38–39 Derek Jones; 41 British Museum; 44t Ancient Art and Architecture Collection; 44b C.M. Dixon; 46, 48–49, 50–51, 52 Derek Jones; 55 British Museum; 62 Dr A. Perkins, RGO Archives, University Library; 64 Matrix/ASTRO *CARTO* GRAPHY is a registered trademark of Jim Lewis; 65, 66 C.M. Dixon; 68l Robert Temple; 68–69 Camerapix Hutchison Library; 70–71 C.M. Dixon; 71b, 73t, 73c Ancient Art and Architecture Collection; 73bl, 73br C.M. Dixon; 75 Cherry Gilchrist; 78 C.M. Dixon; 80 Liz Eddison; 82 Derek Jones; 83t Werner Forman Archive/British Museum; 83b Liz Eddison; 84, 86 Derek Jones; 87t Edward Parker/The Hutchison Library; 87b Liz Eddison; 96–97, 100 The Hutchison Library; 101 Barry D. Maurer; 102 Judith Gleason; 104 Falette Collection; 105 J.F. Hammer, Hammer Collection; 106 Judith Gleason; 107 Fred Holly; 112, 113, 114t, 114b, 115t, 115b, 118 Jamie Sams; 121 The Hutchison Library; 122t C.M. Dixon; 122b Ancient Art and Architecture Collection; 123, 126t, 126b Bruce Scofield; 128–129 Melanie Friend/The Hutchison Library; 132t Derek Walters; 132b Eye Ubiquitous/Trip; 133 British Museum; 134–135 Derek Jones; 136 Ancient Art and Architecture Collection; 137 C.M. Dixon; 139 Jean-Loup Charmet; 140 Werner Forman Archive/British Library; 145, 146, 148, 149, 150 Derek Walters; 154–155 Alistair Shearer; 155tl Ancient Art and Architecture Collection; 157t Helene Rogers/Trip; 157b Bob Turner/Trip; 159t, 159b C.M. Dixon; 160 Helene Rogers/Trip; 164–165, 167 Alistair Shearer; 170 Ancient Art and Architecture Collection; 173 C. Beard; 175 Baldwin Spencer; 176 C. Beard; 177t D. Lambert; 177b Baldwin Spencer; 179 C. Beard; 180 By permission of the Ariki; 183l, 183r David Simmons; 185t James MacDonald/National Museum of New Zealand; 185c Josiah Martin/Auckland Museum Library; 185b James MacDonald/National Museum of New Zealand; 186 David Simmons; 190 M. König; 198 M. Csaky/The Hutchison Library; 199 The Hutchison Library; 203 Paul Broadhurst/The Fortean Picture Library; 204 Jean-Loup Charmet; 205 Derek Jones; 206t Dr Elmar/The Fortean Picture Library; 206b The Fortean Picture Library; 207 Derek Jones.

Note: The publishers have made every effort to trace copyright holders for illustrations which appear in this book and wish to offer their apologies for any unintentional errors or omissions.

Thank you to Mysteries, 9–11 Monmouth Street, London, England for the loan of divinatory equipment to photograph.

The extract on page 56 is from R.W. Holden, *The Elements of House Division*, Romford, Fowler, 1977.

Editorial Director Ian Jackson
Project Editor Marion Russell
Editorial Assistance Gillian Haslam and Graham Smith
Proof-reader Sam Merrell
Indexer Mike Allaby
Creative Director Nick Eddison
Map and Decorative Designer Sarah Howerd
Designer Hilary Krag
Map Artist Andy Farmer
Line Artwork Anthony Duke
Picture Researcher Liz Eddison
Production Hazel Kirkman and Charles James

Eddison Sadd would like to record its thanks to Marion Russell and John Matthews for their contributions to this book.

Phototypeset in Cloister Roman by
Bookworm Typesetting, Manchester, England
Origination by Columbia Offset, Singapore
Printed and bound by Dai Nippon, Hong Kong